Arctic Breakthrough

Franklin's Expeditions, 1819-1847

Sir John Franklin R.N.

With an introduction by Dr. Trevor Lloyd, former chairman
of the Arctic Institute of North America

PAUL NANTON

Arctic *Franklin's Expeditions*
1819-1847
Breakthrough

WILLIAM KIMBER · LONDON

Acknowledgements

For permission to reproduce the quoted material which appears between pages
246 and 253 of the appendix grateful acknowledgement is made to Ernest Benn
Limited for the excerpt from *Franklin, Happy Voyager* by G. F. Lamb; Longmans
Canada Limited for the excerpt from *In Quest of the North West Passage* by
L. H. Neatby; and McIntosh and Otis, Inc. for the excerpt from *Unsolved
Mysteries of the Arctic* by Vilhjalmur Stefansson.

Copies of the photographs which appear between pages 154 and 155 were made
available by the Metropolitan Toronto Library Board. The original sketches
were made by one of Franklin's officers, George Back, during the first
two expeditions. The sketch on which the cover drawing is based, showing
H.M.S. *Terror* thrown up by arctic ice, was made by Back in 1837 when he
himself was in command of the ship.

The front endpaper shows a portion of J. Arrowsmith's map of America
drawn in 1804. The back endpaper—a portion of his map of British North
America drawn in 1859—shows the extent to which the northern coastline
of North America had been filled in by that time. Photographs of both
maps are from the Public Archives of Canada.

SBN 7183 0132 3

First published in Great Britain 1971 by
WILLIAM KIMBER & CO. LIMITED
Godolphin House, 22a Queen Anne's Gate, London S.W.1

Printed in Great Britain by
Unwin Brothers Ltd., Old Woking

Contents

*To the young men who are now committing
themselves to the development of the far north.
They will add a new dimension to Canada.*

Introduction

Three centuries have passed since the founding of the Hudson's Bay Company in London on May 2, 1670. The presence in Canada today of the Company of Adventurers of England is a reminder that the fur trade was one of the few direct benefits derived from the search for a sea route between western Europe and eastern Asia by way of North America. (It is interesting to recall that a similar trading venture, the Muscovy Company, was established in London more than a century before by some of those who sought a passage to the Pacific by way of northern Asia.)

The map of North America suggests why the search for a route through the continent was so baffling. The east coast of the United States and Canada is replete with inlets great and small, any one of which might have proved to be the key to a westward crossing. Even the Hudson River was tried, as was the Gulf of St. Lawrence (a fact we are reminded of by the name Lachine given to what is now a suburb of Montreal). Farther north (passing over the fjords of Labrador) are Hudson Strait, Frobisher Bay, Cumberland Sound, Pond Inlet, Lancaster Sound, Jones Sound and Smith Sound. All were searched in the hope that they led to the Pacific.

By contrast, the Northeast Passage is relatively straightforward. Once the North Cape of Norway was rounded (and this was achieved well over 1000 years ago) there were few land barriers to prevent a passage eastward. Ice, shallow water and sheer distance provided the problems, then as now. One hazard not of significance in the Canadian Arctic was the effective opposition put up by northern peoples—particularly the Chukchi of northeast Siberia—against the exploring free-booters. Although no single vessel had completed the through passage until Nordenskjold's *Vega* negotiated it in 1879, the route's existence had been known from Peter the Great's Siberian expedition in the early 1700's, that vast and complex undertaking which led to Russian discovery of Alaska.

The Northwest Passage was quite a different matter. It was recognized late in the seventeenth century that, if only because of the high latitude, any route which might be found would be of minor commercial usefulness. This presumably accounts for the lessened interest in searching operations. These were not renewed until, with the end of the Napoleonic Wars, skilled mariners and stout ships became available, and boredom called for something new in the way of naval training. For the next half century the Royal Navy was schooled in the Arctic.

In 1815 there were only three known geographical points in a possible northwest passage. William Baffin had provided the first in 1616 when he followed the route of John Davis up the west coast of Greenland and pushed on into unknown seas to north and west. Two westward-running passages—Jones Sound and Lancaster Sound—he named after supporters in the City of London. (Not until 1853 was his northernmost point in Smith Sound surpassed.) The eastern entrance to the Northwest Passage was therefore charted in the early seventeenth century. Fourteen hundred miles to the west of it, there was, by 1815, another known link in the passage—placed there by Captain James Cook, who in 1778 had sought a way home from the Pacific by a northerly route. He was turned back at a point on the north coast of Alaska which he named Icy Cape. The third place—the mouth of the Coppermine River—was less accurately located. It had been reached by Samuel Hearne after travelling overland from Fort Prince of Wales (now Churchill) in 1771. If we add to these three, the delta of the Mackenzie River, reached by Alexander Mackenzie in 1789, we have the very brief gazetteer of geographical knowledge of the Canadian Arctic coast 150 years ago.

The almost total absence of landmarks on the charts was perhaps the least of the problems facing the new generation of explorers who put to sea after 1815. Their vessels had to cross the Atlantic from Britain in late spring, struggle against heavy ice in Davis Strait, cut across the southward-flowing ice stream—including heavy pack ice and icebergs —so as to enter Lancaster Sound. Somehow, the explorers had to find a way westward and plot it precisely on the chart. In the early days they used sailing vessels which were difficult to manoeuvre in ice-filled seas. Always they faced a severe climate, the uncertainty of their magnetic compasses, the absence of stars to steer by, and only about two months of useful work if they were to escape to clear water before winter.

In 1818 the British Admiralty sent an expedition to explore and chart the area first seen by William Baffin and to search for a possible route westward. In command was John Ross, with W. E. Parry as his deputy. The expedition reported, erroneously, that Lancaster Sound was blocked to the west by a range of mountains, a feature that it took an additional expedition to remove from the charts. Meanwhile, it was logical to search for the Arctic seacoast overland, using the rivers and lakes known to the Canadian fur trade, and Hudson Bay itself, since it gave easy access to the heart of the country. This meant following up the explorations of Hearne and Mackenzie, with the important addition of charting the coastline to east and west, in the hope that eventually Lancaster Sound and Icy Cape might be linked.

It was this overland search which first brought John Franklin, a thirty-three-year-old Royal Navy officer, to the Canadian Arctic, with which his name is today so intimately linked. The two journeys he made to the shore of the polar sea are described in this book on the basis of his own records. His third and final expedition to Arctic Canada—and his best known—was, on the face of it, a failure, since the expedition and all its members vanished. Yet a quarter-century afterwards the elaborate and sustained search for the lost expedition had completed the basic mapping of the Arctic coast of Canada and delineated the long-sought Northwest Passage.

In 1970 the Passage is again attracting widespread attention. There is renewed interest in a sea route which can link the Atlantic Ocean and the north coast of Alaska. Although more than a century has passed since the Franklin search ended, the passage charted with such determination, skill and courage, and at such a high price in human suffering, has in fact proved of negligible commercial significance. Captain Roald Amundsen was the first to take a vessel through it from the Atlantic to the Pacific (a little Norwegian boat, *Gjoa*) in a voyage lasting from 1903 to 1906. The Royal Canadian Mounted Police patrol ship *St. Roch* made the passage in both directions during the Second World War. In the 1930's the Hudson's Bay Company made use of much of the route for its normal supply needs, although no single vessel went the whole way through. During the period of defence construction in the Arctic in the late 1940's and in the 1950's, when many supply ships were in Arctic waters, several ice-breakers—United States and Canadian—made their way through the Passage. But in contrast to the Soviet northern sea route, which is the twentieth century Northeast Passage, the seaway through northern Canada has been of no commercial significance.

All this may be changing. The discovery of large oil fields in northern Alaska, and the likelihood that similar finds will take place in Arctic Canada, have raised the possibility of using the Passage as a route for oil tankers or possibly tanker submarines, since the most profitable markets for the oil lie in the North Atlantic area. Contemporary interest in the Passage is therefore less because of its use as a short sea route between Atlantic and Pacific than as a means for exporting natural resources found in the Arctic itself.

Modern exploration and charting has removed most of the uncertainty about where the coastlines and the islands lie. But the ice remains. To combat it, very powerful and expensive vessels are required, assisted by aerial reconnaissance, the best of modern aids to navigation, weather and ice forecasts, and skilled and experienced mariners. The need today—and it is an urgent one—is for a new generation of men of the calibre of Bylot, Baffin, Davis, Parry, Franklin and the rest, trained in the use of the sophisticated ships and instruments that are available today. The Soviet Union has, through foresight and the need to operate the northern sea route, been training such men for a generation or more. Canada has scarcely begun to do so.

Canadians, particularly young Canadians, are realizing that north of the narrow populated belt that parallels the United States border from coast to coast, lies another Canada, the development of which may give scope for different and perhaps greater capacities than has the south. Canada has never been inclined to honour its pioneers; all too often it has accepted substitute heroes at second-hand from the south. Yet as the North becomes settled and communities take root, the local population shows interest in those who passed that way long ago: The school children at *Gjoa Haven* on King William Island wish to hear about Amundsen, who wintered there. Sir Martin Frobisher, who visited Baffin Island in the reign of Elizabeth I, is now regarded as a sort of founding father of the town that bears his name. And the fine vocational high school at Yellowknife is named after Sir John Franklin, whose portrait hangs in the foyer.

Publication of *Arctic Breakthrough* will, I hope, encourage this interest in the early exploration of northern Canada and lead Canadians, especially young Canadians, to turn back to the early records of northern travel and exploration. They will find that there were giants in those days. And John Franklin was one of them.

TREVOR LLOYD

McGill University
Montreal

Author's Preface

The exploits of the men of the Royal Navy have been world-wide. *Arctic Breakthrough* tells the story of one of these that has not received the recognition it deserves. John Franklin's Arctic expeditions of 1819 and 1825 are less well known than the drama of his disappearance after 1845, although in these he and his men "put a roof" on the North American continent, accurately mapping over 1700 miles of Arctic coastline.

The purpose of this book is to bring together the career and achievements of Franklin, as well as to discover something of the man himself. I have drawn on his massive and detailed Journals recording the first two expeditions, quoting sections verbatim where the original presentation is particularly interesting and important and omitting a considerable amount of unnecessary detail. The records of the final expedition were, of course, lost and I have turned to the accounts of the men who participated in the searches to complete the picture.

The Arrowsmith maps, drawn in 1804 and 1859 and reproduced at the front and back of the book, show dramatically the change brought about during the Franklin era. Canadians, for whom the Arctic has now become vitally important, owe a lasting debt of gratitude to the courage and persistence of those seamen from Britain who made known the outlines of that frozen world.

PAUL NANTON

Toronto
January, 1971

Arctic Breakthrough

Franklin's Expeditions, 1819-1847

John Franklin was born in 1786, the youngest of a family of twelve. His father had decided that he should enter the Church and Franklin was satisfied with this plan—until the day he was taken to the seaside. For hours that day he sat watching the waves, and decided as he did so that he would spend his life at sea. His father tried to discourage him but he was so persistent that two years later the elder Franklin gave in and shipped his son aboard a small merchant ship bound for Lisbon. The ship's course would take her through the Bay of Biscay and Franklin's father hoped that the rough weather would cure him of his fascination with the sea. But when the boy returned more determined than ever his father had the wisdom to end his opposition and began to help.

John's career in the Royal Navy began in 1800 at the age of fourteen. The next year he saw action in the Battle of Copenhagen. Though the engagement was one of Nelson's great victories, the casualties ran into the thousands. It was a bloody battle for a boy of fifteen to experience. Two months later Midshipman Franklin sailed for Australia aboard HMS *Investigator*, which was commanded by his cousin Matthew Flinders. Flinders was probably the leading cartographer of his day and Franklin received invaluable training from him in the science of navigation and signals.

Back in England, Franklin was appointed, in August 1804, to HMS *Bellerophon* as signals midshipman. The next year, in the Battle of Trafalgar, the *Bellerophon* was in the thick of the action. The poop deck, where Franklin was stationed, was the most exposed area of the ship and most of the men on duty there, including the Captain, were killed. The acting captain wrote later that Midshipman Franklin had performed his duties "with very considerable zeal and ability."

When the war finally ended in 1815, Franklin, by then a lieutenant, continued in peacetime naval service. Three years later he had his first taste of Arctic exploration. In that year he was appointed second in command under David Buchan of an expedition sent "to discover a northern passage by sea from the Atlantic to the Pacific ocean." The party set out in two ships—HMS *Dorothea* and HMS *Trent*—in May of 1818 but did not get much farther than Spitzbergen. It returned in October of the same year, the *Dorothea* in a sinking condition.

The following year the Admiralty sent two expeditions to the Arctic. The first was headed by Lieutenant Edward Parry, with the ships *Hecla* and *Griper* under his command. He was instructed to proceed through Lancaster Sound and westward as far as possible.* The second expedition, under the leadership of Franklin, was "to amend the very defective geography of the northern part of North America. . . ." The Admiralty's instructions were to determine "the latitudes and longitudes of the northern coast of North America, and the trending of that coast from the mouth of the Coppermine River to the eastern extremity of that Continent." It was hoped that the two expeditions would make contact at some point.

Franklin was given freedom to decide which route to follow, whether by ship north of Hudson Bay and then westward along the Arctic shore to the Coppermine, or overland to the west, proceeding down the Coppermine River to its mouth and then travelling along the Arctic coast in an easterly direction. Franklin noted, ". . . in the adoption of either of these plans, I was to be guided by the advice and information which I should receive from the wintering servants of the Hudson's Bay Company, who would be instructed by their employers to co-operate cordially in the prosecution of the objects of the Expedition, and who would provide me with the necessary escort of Indians to act as guides, interpreters, game-killers, etc.; and also with such articles of clothing, ammunition, snow-shoes, presents, etc., as should be deemed expedient for me to take."

Franklin was told to keep careful records of the latitude and longitude of all bays, rivers, headlands and possible harbours encountered along the coastline. He was to erect conspicuous markers at points where ships might enter, depositing information and charts at places where they might be found by Lieutenant Parry. He was to record the temperature at least three times a day, the state of the wind and weather and any other meteorological phenomena. The dip and varia-

---

*As it turned out, Parry advanced much farther west than anyone had previously. He wintered his ships at "Winter Harbour" on an island which he named in honour of Viscount Melville, First Lord of the Admiralty.

tion of the magnetic needle and the intensity of magnetic force were to be recorded, as well as any effect that the Aurora Borealis seemed to have on the magnetic needle, and everything that could be discovered about this phenomenon. Franklin was instructed also to look for any traces of copper near the mouth of the Coppermine River and to estimate whether it had commercial value. For some years Indians had been bringing samples of native copper from this area to the trading posts and the Admiralty was curious.

The officers appointed to accompany Franklin were Dr. John Richardson, surgeon in the Royal Navy, and two midshipmen, George Back and Robert Hood. Richardson was to be the naturalist of the party as well as its physician. Back and Hood were to keep the scientific records and to make drawings of the country, its natives and everything of special interest in the field of natural history.

John Richardson, at twenty-nine, was well equipped for the task that had been assigned to him. He had received his medical degree at seventeen and thereafter had spent twelve years either serving with the navy in different parts of the world or taking training in anatomy, botany and minerology. He was to become Franklin's closest associate, accompanying him again in 1825 on his second overland expedition to the Arctic coast.

The two midshipmen were also well qualified for the work they were to do. Both were excellent artists. George Back, in particular, has left some superb drawings of the country covered by the expedition. Moreover, he was no stranger to adventure, having been captured by the French a year after he joined the Royal Navy at the age of twelve. He and other prisoners had been taken across the Pyrenees to the fortress of Verdun; Back was so small that they had carried him in a basket slung across a mule. While in prison he had studied mathematics, French and drawing, and when he had obtained his freedom he had walked across France and made his way back to England. At twenty-two he had served under Buchan and Franklin on their short-lived Arctic expedition.

John Hepburn, an able seaman, was to accompany Franklin as general factotum. (Things would probably have gone better if there had been several more men like him.) In the course of their travels he and Franklin developed a great respect and friendship for each other and their association continued for many years. In the foreword to his journal Franklin paid tribute to the work of his fellow officers and to "the fidelity, exertion and uniform good conduct in the most trying situations, of John Hepburn, an English seaman, and our only attendant, to whom in the latter part of our journey we owe, under Divine Providence, the preservation of the lives of some of the party."

As soon as his appointment was announced, Franklin plunged into the round of activity that preceded departure. He knew nothing of the country to which he was going but received much-needed information from the Governor of the Hudson's Bay Company, Joseph Berens, and from Simon McGillivray of the North West Company. He valued especially his talks with the famous explorer Sir Alexander Mackenzie, one of the two white men who had already been to the region which he was about to explore.

On May 28, 1819 Franklin and his party sailed from London aboard the Hudson's Bay Company ship *Prince of Wales*, bound for York Factory on Hudson Bay. They had as fellow passengers some company trading officers and a group of Selkirk Settlers—Scottish crofters and their families headed for the tiny and precarious settlement that the Earl of Selkirk was fighting to establish. Two smaller company ships, the *Wear* and the *Eddystone*, accompanied them.

Three years were to pass before Franklin returned to England. During that time Robert Hood was murdered and the rest of the party suffered the most extreme privations. Out of those three years only thirty-seven days were spent doing what the expedition was sent to do—explore and map the Arctic coast of the American continent. But in that time Franklin and his men, sailing in two birch-bark canoes, accurately mapped 550 miles of the coastline.

When the ships were a week out of London they had advanced only as far as the Isle of the Wight, off the south coast of England. Here strong contrary winds forced them into harbour at Yarmouth Roads. Franklin took immediate advantage of the stop to test the accuracy of his instruments, comparing the longitude of the Yarmouth church on the Ordnance Map with that indicated by his chronometers. Several other officers and passengers went ashore as well.

Suddenly the wind shifted to a favourable direction and the ship's captain fired his guns to signal immediate departure. In the scramble back to ship everyone made it except Midshipman George Back, who was three miles from town visiting friends. The captain refused to delay departure and risk missing the wind, so all Franklin could do was leave a note telling Back to travel overland to Stromness in the Orkney Isles, where the ships were to put in for additional supplies before heading across the Atlantic.

Favourable winds carried the ships to Stromness in four days, and there they remained for nearly two weeks. Franklin was given the use of a house, where he continued to test his instruments. His other concern was to recruit boatmen who could transport his party to the northwest once they had reached York Factory. Though the Admiralty had instructed him to hire such men at York Factory, the trading officers aboard ship told him that none would be available there. He accordingly wrote the Admiralty asking permission to hire men at Stromness instead. No reply came but he went ahead anyway. In Stromness, the recognized equivalent of a want ad was a notice tacked to the church door. Franklin put up his notice, and after some days four men approached him and eventually agreed to join the expedition. They showed such caution that Franklin, in his journal, compared them very unfavourably with the average English seaman, who as likely as not would sign up for a voyage without knowing where he was going or why. Franklin had hoped to secure ten men but he had to settle for the four.

Meantime George Back had acted with characteristic energy. The moment he had heard the guns of the *Prince of Wales* at Yarmouth Roads he was out of his friend's house and on his way. The ship was passing quite close to shore when he reached the beach at Caistor. In reply to his urgent request a group of boatmen said they could get the officer out to the ship but it would be a long haul, and since it was an emergency they figured it should be worth his while to pay double the usual rate. They were wrong. The officer was against missing the ship but dead against being swindled! All the boatmen got was a blast from the irate Back, who continued on his way.

The distance from Yarmouth Roads to Stromness is about 600 miles as the crow flies, but there was no direct route. Journeying by stage-coach where there were passable roads, and on horseback the rest of the way, Back travelled almost non-stop, allowing himself only brief hours of sleep, and made it to Stromness in nine days. It was dusk as he approached the small town and he was dog tired, but when he heard that a party had just begun he forgot his weariness and joined in the fun until dawn.

After numerous delays due to contrary winds the three ships sailed from Stromness on June 16. It was an arduous crossing, with periods of buffeting northwest winds and high seas. The ships took fifty-three days to reach Resolution Island at the eastern entrance to Hudson Strait and here the party ran into serious trouble. A dense fog blanketed the ships, strong currents were running between the masses of ice that now surrounded them, and the ships became quite unmanageable.

As the fog briefly lifted, the crew of the *Prince of Wales* saw, immediately ahead of them, a barren coast towering higher than the masts. Moments later the ship struck a reef and her rudder was displaced. Then the swell lifted her off the reef and the current carried her along the shore. Again she was caught in the swell and put aground but, amazingly, the blow shifted the rudder back into a working position. She was lifted off once more, once more beached and refloated, and this time a light breeze carried her away from shore.

Now the current slammed the ship violently against an iceberg. The force of the blow might well have snapped the masts but miraculously they held, and the ship drifted away from the berg. The fog now lifted a second time and the captain was dismayed to find that the *Wear* had disappeared. The *Eddystone*, however, was close at hand, her three small boats vigorously engaged in towing her away from the rocks.

Water was flooding into the hold of the *Prince of Wales* and she was in danger of sinking. Seeing this, the captain of the *Eddystone* hurriedly sent across his carpenter and as many of his crew as he could spare to help in an all-out operation with the pumps. He then took the *Prince of Wales* in tow in order to free everyone aboard her for other duties.

The stricken ship was holding her own until a gale forced her to separate from the *Eddystone*. Heavy ice surrounded her and the force of the wind split her sails. Still worse, the exhausted men and women at the pumps could no longer keep up the pace, and the water rose until there was five feet in the hold. At this point the captain decided to remove the older women and the children to the *Eddystone*. Fortunately, the seas became calm enough to enable him to carry out this operation. The younger women stayed with the ship and showed such determination at the pumps that they challenged the men to redouble their efforts. The carpenters worked desperately below decks and at last discovered and repaired the weakened timbers that had let in most of the water. A sail covered with grease was hauled under the hull and in a few hours the pumps had won the battle.

On August 11 the two ships entered Hudson Strait. Next day the passengers encountered their first Eskimos. About forty men, each in his own kayak, surrounded the ships. The women and children followed in their larger canoes (umiaks) until there must have been 150 natives assembled. Franklin described the scene in his journal:

The Eskimos immmediately evinced their desire to barter and displayed no small cunning in making their bargains, taking care not to exhibit too many articles at first. Their principal commodities were oil, sea-horse teeth (walrus tusks), whalebone, seal-skin dresses, caps, and boots, deer-skins and horns, and models of their canoes; and they received in exchange small saws, knives, nails, tin-kettles and needles. It was pleasing to behold the exultation, and to hear the shouts of the whole party, when an acquisition was made by any one; and not a little ludicrous to behold the eagerness with which the fortunate person licked each article with his tongue, on receiving it, as a finish to the bargain and an act of appropriation. They in no instance omitted this strange practice, however small the article; the needles even passed individually through the cere-mony. The women brought imitations of men, women, animals and birds, carved with labour and ingenuity out of sea-horse teeth. The dresses and figures of the animals were not badly executed, but there was no attempt at the delineation of the countenances and most of the figures were without eyes, ears and fingers, the execu-tion of which would perhaps have required more delicate instru-ments than they possess. The men set most value on saws; kuttee-swa-bak, the name by which they distinguish them, was a constant cry. Knives were held next in estimation. An old sword was bartered from the Eddystone and I shall long remember the universal burst of joy on the happy man's receiving it. It was delightful to witness the general interest excited by individual acquisitions. There was no desire shown by anyone to over-reach his neighbour or to press towards any part of the ship where a bargain was making, until the person in possession of the place had completed his exchange and removed; and if any article happened to be demanded from other canoes, the men nearest assisted willingly in passing the thing across. . . .

Their faces were broad and flat, the eyes small. The men were in general stout. Some of the younger women and the children had rather pleasing countenances, but the difference between these and the more aged of that sex bore strong testimony to the effects which a few years produce in this ungenial climate. . . . We thought their manner very lively and agreeable. They were fond of mimicking our speech and gestures; but nothing afforded them greater amuse-ment than when we attempted to retaliate by pronouncing any of their words.

The canoes were of seal-skin and similar in every respect to those used by the Eskimos in Greenland; they were generally new and very complete in their appointments. Those appropriated to the *women were of ruder construction and only calculated for fine weather; they were however useful vessels, being capable of containing twenty persons with their luggage. An elderly man officiates as steersman and the women paddle, but they have also a mast which carries a sail made of dressed whale-gut.**

(It was no novelty for these Eskimos to meet white men, for the ships of the Hudson's Bay Company sailed through Hudson Strait every summer. The reaction of Eskimos who met ships in Davis Strait the year before was very different. It was their first encounter with white men and the commander described the occasion: "They first pointed to the ships and eagerly asked what great creatures were they, and had the strangers come from the sun or the moon? The interpreter told them that he was a man and had a mother and father like themselves. Pointing to the south he said that he came from a distant country in that direction. They answered that this could not be, for there was nothing but ice there. Pointing to the ships they asked again: 'What creatures are these?' When told that they were houses they did not believe it and said: 'No, they are alive. We have seen them move their wings.' "†)

The passage through Hudson Strait was uneventful. Passing Digges Island, at the entrance to Hudson Bay, the passengers and crew of the *Prince of Wales* regretfully saluted the *Eddystone* as she left them to sail for Moose Factory in James Bay. At last on August 30, fourteen weeks after setting sail from London, the *Prince of Wales* anchored off York Factory. Everyone was relieved to have arrived safely, but what roused each one to cheers was the sight of the long-lost *Wear*, awaiting them at anchor. The Governor of the Hudson's Bay posts, Mr. Williams, lost no time in coming aboard. He was accompanied by the commander of the *Wear* and a joyful reunion ensued, for everyone aboard the *Prince of Wales* had believed that captain and crew had perished. Their escape had been due to a large mass of ice that had providentially drifted between the ship and some rocks that it was about to strike. They had been able to secure the ship to the ice until a favourable breeze enabled them to continue on their way.

Governor Williams had already received word from the Committee of the Hudson's Bay Company in London instructing him to give all

---

*Except for occasional changes to update spelling and punctuation, the excerpts from Franklin's journals are unchanged from the original text.
†*A Voyage of Discovery for the purpose of Exploring Baffin's Bay*, Captain Sir John Ross. R.N. (London, John Murray, 1819)

possible assistance to Franklin. The honour of a salute was given the members of the expedition as they entered the company buildings and they received their first taste of traditional northern hospitality. Franklin spent the next few days carefully questioning the Governor and his officers regarding the best route to follow westward. On the strength of their information he decided to strike across country to Great Slave Lake and then proceed down the Coppermine River to the Arctic sea. The company men gave tangible expression of their good-will by supplying him with one of their largest river boats, first giving it a thorough refit.

Before leaving London Franklin had been warned not to get mixed up in the bitter conflict between the Hudson's Bay and North West companies. Both companies had promised every assistance and it was essential that no one on the expedition take sides. At York Factory Franklin discovered that several North West Company partners were actually being held under lock and key. He was allowed to see them and "received from them the most friendly and full assurance of the cordial endeavours of the wintering partners of their company to promote the interests of the expedition." As is turned out, these and similar promises made by both companies, though sincerely meant by the officials in London, were frequently not kept by their men on the ground, a fact of the most serious consequence for the expedition. Competition between the two companies had reached the stage of undeclared civil war and the traders on both sides had little time for anything else. A rough brand of justice was being handed out, with both sides capturing and imprisoning men who got in their way. Occasionally there were cases of actual murder.

In this kind of rivalry it was Indians who suffered most. The two companies competed for their furs, and rum was the great persuader. McGillivray and his North West partners went to greater lengths in its use, but the Hudson's Bay Company was in the business too. In 1800, just before competition reached its height, 10,000 gallons of rum were distributed to the Indians in return for furs, and 648 packs of prime furs were delivered to the posts in fifteen canoes. By 1803 the handout of rum increased to 21,000 gallons, but by that time the natives had so deteriorated that they produced only 182 packs of furs.

On the 9th of September, 1819 our boat being completed, arrangements were made for our departure as soon as the tide should serve. But, when the stores were brought down to the beach, it was found that the boat would not contain them all. The whole, therefore, of the bacon, and part of the flour, rice, tobacco, and ammunition, were returned to the store. The bacon was too bulky an article to be forwarded under any circumstances; but the Governor undertook to forward the rest next season. In making the selection of articles to carry with us, I was guided by the judgement of Governor Williams, who assured me that tobacco, ammunition and spirits could be procured in the interior, otherwise I should have been very unwilling to have left these essential articles behind. We embarked at noon, and were honoured with a salute of eight guns and three cheers from the Governor and all the inmates of the fort, who had assembled to witness our departure. We gratefully returned their cheers, and then made sail, much delighted at having now commenced our voyage into the interior of America.

Within six miles of the fort the current of the Hayes River became too rapid to use oars and the men had to start tracking, walking along the bank towing the boat by a long line. The shoreline was soft and slippery and often blocked by fallen trees, and the best the crew could do was two miles an hour. The men took turns on the line, half of them replacing the other half every ninety minutes. At sunset they halted and pitched their tent for the night, having advanced twelve miles. A large fire was kindled, supper quickly prepared and eaten and everyone lay down with his buffalo robe for the first night's sleep.

As the party travelled up the Hayes, Back and Hood worked on the river survey by taking bearings at every curve of the river with a pocket compass, estimating the distance between each point and drawing a

connected sketch of the whole. Each evening Hood protracted the route
on a ruled map, and when weather permitted, observations were made
for longitude and latitude.

Franklin described in his journal the autumn colours along the Steel
River:

> The light yellow of the fading poplars formed a fine contrast to the
> dark evergreen of the spruce, while the willows of an intermediate
> hue, served to shade the two principal masses of colour into each
> other. The scene was occasionally enlivened by the bright purple
> tints of the dogwood, blended with the browner shades of the dwarf
> birch, and frequently intermixed with the gay yellow flowers of the
> scrubby cinquefoil. With all these charms, the scene appeared deso-
> late from the want of human species. The stillness was so great, that
> even the twittering of the whiskey-johneesh, [whiskey-jack] caused
> us to start.

Five days out of York Factory they reached the head of the Steel
River. Mr. McDonald,* on his way to Red River in a small canoe manned
by two Indians, overtook the party at that place. Three other company
canoes caught up with them later that day and they proceeded together
up Hill River. At this point the River became very shallow, with one
rapid succeeding the other, and the men had to jump into the water
constantly to haul the boat over large boulders. Franklin's boat was
heavily loaded, and in spite of their best efforts his crew could not keep
up with the lighter company boats. But when Franklin asked the company men to relieve him of part of his cargo they refused, choosing to
disregard Governor Williams' circular, which gave strict instructions
to all company servants to give the expedition every assistance. The
other boats soon disappeared from sight leaving Franklin and his in-
experienced steersman and crew to blunder ahead as best they could.
Since they often took the wrong channel, progress was both frustrating
and slow. Some relief was afforded when the man in charge of one of
the company boats decided to wait for them at the most difficult places,
to help them over.

With this assistance they made better time and on September 17
arrived at Rock House, a company depot. Franklin noted:

> Here we were informed that the rapids in the upper parts of Hill
> River were much worse and more numerous than those we had

*A Hudson's Bay Company trader

passed, particularly in the present season, owing to the unusual lowness of the water. This intelligence was very mortifying, especially as the gentlemen in charge of the Company's boats declared that they were unable to carry any part of our stores beyond this place; and the traders, guides, and most experienced of the boatmen, were of the opinion, that unless our boat was still further lightened, the winter would put a stop to our progress before we could reach Cumberland House, or any eligible post. Sixteen pieces were therefore necessarily left with Mr. Bunn, the gentleman in charge of the post, to be forwarded by the Athabasca canoes next season. . . .

The rugged magnificence of their surroundings awed Franklin and his men. Hood took advantage of every spare moment to draw sketches, while Dr. Richardson scrambled after specimens of plants and rocks. They passed one hill from which it was said that thirty-six lakes could be seen. But the going was too difficult and winter too obviously approaching to allow much time or energy for the contemplation of the beauties of nature. As the difficulties of travel increased, Franklin was given reason to have second thoughts about the courage of his men from Stromness:

It is not easy for any but an eye-witness to form an adequate idea of the exertions of the Orkney boatmen in the navigation of this river. The necessity they are under of frequently jumping into the water to lift the boat over the rocks compels them to remain the whole day in wet clothes, at a season when the temperature is far below the freezing-point. The immense loads, too, which they carry over the portages is not more a matter of surprise than the alacrity with which they perform these laborious duties.

One day they progressed only one and a quarter miles, a quarter mile of which involved carrying the cargo through a deep swamp.

The whole of the 2nd of October was spent in carrying the cargoes over a portage of thirteen hundred yards in length, and in launching the empty boats over three several [sic] ridges of rock which obstruct the channel and produce as many cascades. I shall long remember the rude and characteristic wildness of the scenery which surrounded these falls; rocks piled on rocks hung in rude and shapeless masses over the agitated torrents which swept their bases, while the bright and variegated tints of the mosses and lichens that covered the face

*of the cliffs, contrasting with the dark green of the pines that crowned
their summits, added both beauty and grandeur to the . . . scene. . . .*

*In the afternoon, while on my way to superintend the operations
of the men, a stratum of loose moss gave way under my feet, and I
had the misfortune to slip from the summit of a rock into the river
betwixt two of the falls. My attempts to regain the bank were, for a
time, ineffectual owing to the rocks within my reach having been
worn smooth by the action of the water; but after I had been carried
a considerable distance down the stream, I caught hold of a willow
by which I held until two gentlemen of the Hudson's Bay Company
came in a boat to my assistance. The only bad consequence of this
accident was an injury sustained by a very valuable chronometer. . . .*

That night there was a severe frost and at sunrise the thermometer
stood at twenty-five degrees. During the day the party was overtaken
by Governor Williams. Travelling light in an Indian canoe, he had
covered the distance from York Factory in thirteen days, compared
with the twenty-four days that it had taken Franklin. Governor
Williams expressed regret that Franklin had been forced to leave part of
his stores at the Rock depot, adding that he would have brought them
along if he had been able to obtain a boat of sufficient size.

The Echemamis River, which they now entered, was a small stream
that in the dry season became little more than a muddy ditch. To make
navigation possible, travellers often built dams to accumulate water.
Since beavers were also effective in this work, an effort had been made
to encourage them to breed in the area, though the Indians generally
killed the animals whenever they discovered them. Fortunately for
Franklin, there was ample water for the crew's passage because the
beaver had been doing their work farther down the river. The only
difficulty was the narrowness of the channel, which allowed the willows
on each bank to meet over their heads and made it almost impossible to
use the oars. When the men reached the beaver dam they opened it
sufficiently to get through and were told that the industrious animals
would have the breach closed again that very night.

On October 6 the party reached the Hudson's Bay post of Norway
House on Lake Winnipeg.

*The waters of Lake Winipeg and of the rivers that run into it, the
Saskatchewan in particular, are rendered turbid by the suspension of
a large quantity of white clay. Play Green Lake and Nelson River,
being the discharges of the Winipeg, are equally opaque, a circum-*

stance that renders the sunken rocks, so frequent in these waters,
very dangerous to boats in a fresh breeze. Owing to this, one of the
boats that accompanied us, sailing at the rate of seven miles an hour,
struck upon one of these rocks. Its mast was carried away by the
shock, but fortunately no other damage sustained. The Indians
ascribe the muddiness of these lakes to an adventure of one of their
deities, a mischievous fellow, a sort of Robin Puck, whom they hold
in very little esteem. The deity, who is named Weesakootchaht,
possesses considerable power, but makes a capricious use of it, and
delights in tormenting the poor Indians. He is not, however, invin-
cible, and was foiled in one of his attempts by the artifice of an old
woman, who succeeded in taking him captive. She called in all the
women of the tribe to aid in his punishment, and he escaped from
their hands in a condition so filthy that it required all the waters of
the Great Lake to wash him clean; and ever since that period it has
been entitled to the appellation of Winipeg, or Muddy water.

At Norway House Franklin and his men were greeted as long-lost
friends by the group of Selkirk Settlers who had crossed the Atlantic
with them and had started out from York Factory a day before them.
After stopping a day at the Post they sailed across Lake Winnipeg to
the mouth of the Saskatchewan River. Here they took a whole day
getting the boats to the foot of the Grand Rapids, a distance of two
miles. "At the grand rapid the Saskatchewan forms a sudden bend from
south to east, and works its way through a narrow channel deeply worn
into the limestone strata. The stream, rushing with impetuous force
over a rocky and uneven bottom, presents a sheet of foam, and seems
to bear with impatience the straitened confinement of its lofty banks."

After advancing up the Saskatchewan for several days the members
of the expedition landed at the site of an Indian tent. Two large families,
thirty persons in all, were crammed into it. All seemed to have
whooping cough or measles and were in a miserable state. Some of the
men were preparing a sweating house, which, along with singing and
drumming, was considered the best remedy for any disease.

As the season advanced, the weather became steadily colder, with
frost through the day except when the sun was especially bright. On
October 21 there was a heavy fall of snow and it became increasingly
difficult to advance. The spray froze to the oars as it fell and they
became so loaded with ice as to be almost unmanageable. On the
twenty-third—forty-four days and 690 miles from York Factory—the
men broke through heavy shore ice to land at Cumberland House, a

Hudson's Bay post established by Samuel Hearne. Governor Williams, who had been travelling with Franklin, invited him to winter at the post with his men, and Franklin was glad to accept.

A regular routine was immediately instituted. Extra housing was needed and the men went to work with a will to complete a building that was already half constructed. On November 6, when the ice was thick enough to carry sledges, dog teams were sent to bring in a supply of fish that had been caught in the Swampy River. Both men and dogs were excited to have this first outing of the winter and set off at a fast pace. Franklin and the other officers had lost no time in setting themselves a daily round of duties, making meteorological observations and studying the intensity of magnetic force, noting all changes in the weather and describing the Aurora Borealis in detail every time it was seen.

From time to time parties of Indians arrived at the post in a starving condition because sickness had kept them from hunting. One old man was so weak when he was brought in that food and warmth could not save him.

Two days before his death [Franklin wrote] I was surprised to observe him sitting for nearly three hours, in a piercingly sharp day, in the saw-pit, employed in gathering the dust and throwing it by handfuls over his body, which was naked to the waist. As the man was in possession of his mental faculties, I conceived he was performing some devotional act preparatory to his departure, which he felt to be approaching. Induced by the novelty of the incident I went twice to observe him more closely; but when he perceived that he was noticed he immediately ceased his operation, hung down his head, and by his demeanour intimated that he considered my appearance an intrusion.

Here, too, Franklin had his first contact with the Indians' custom of expressing their grief for the loss of relatives by stopping all work:

It is much to be regretted that these poor men, during their long intercourse with Europeans, have not been taught how pernicious is the grief that produces total inactivity, and that they have not been furnished with any of the consolations which the Christian religion never fails to afford. This, however, could hardly have been expected from persons who have permitted their own offspring, the half-castes, to remain in lamentable ignorance on a subject of such vital impor-

tance. It is probable, however, that an improvement will soon take place among the latter class, as Governor Williams proposes to make the children attend a Sunday school, and has already begun to have divine service performed at his post.

Franklin had been on excellent terms with Governor Williams from the time he first met him at York Factory. Now he also became very friendly with Mr. Connolly, the resident partner at the North West post near Cumberland House. Talks with these men convinced him that he should not wait until spring to push northward into the Athabasca country. The traders there would know much more about the character and resources of the area north of Great Slave Lake and it would be there that guides, hunters and interpreters could be engaged for the voyage down the Coppermine River to the Arctic sea. Franklin therefore decided to set out in January with Back and Hepburn and asked Governor Williams and Mr. Connolly to supply him with the necessary means of conveyance. Richardson and Hood were to remain at Cumberland House until spring, when they would join Franklin at Fort Chipewyan, bringing the supplies with them.

The new year [1820] was ushered in by repeated discharges of musketry; a ceremony which has been observed by the men of both trading Companies for many years. Our party dined with Mr. Connolly and were treated with a beaver, which we found extremely delicate. In the evening his Canadians [voyageurs]* were entertained with a dance, in which they exhibited some grace and much agility; and they contrived to infuse some portion of their activity and spirits into the steps of their female companions. The half-breed women are passionately fond of this amusement, but a stranger would imagine the contrary on witnessing their apparent want of animation. On such occasions they affect a sobriety which I understand to be very opposite to their general character.

Before leaving Cumberland House Franklin presented written requests to Governor Williams and Mr. Connolly asking them to supply Dr. Richardson and Mr. Hood with two canoes and adequate crews and provisions to transport them to Fort Chipewyan as soon as navigation opened. Both men agreed to do so. The four boatmen engaged at Stromness had now completed their contract and Franklin thanked

*Franklin used the word "Canadian" instead of "voyageur." For the sake of clarity I have hereafter substituted "voyageur" in such cases.—Ed.

them for their excellent work. One of the men wished to continue with
the expedition but arrangements were made for the other three to travel
to York Factory in the spring and take ship home from there. Franklin,
Richardson and Hood discussed all these and other matters and packed
up the drawings, natural history specimens and the map of their
route from York Factory to Cumberland House, which Hood had just
completed. These would be sent to England in the spring.

Dr. Richardson was to use the months at Cumberland House to learn
the language of the Cree Indians and to become acquainted with their
life and customs. He wrote a full report which Franklin incorporated
in his journal at this point in the narrative:

*The winter of our residence at Cumberland House proved ex-
tremely severe to the Indians. The whooping-cough made its appearance among them in the autumn and was followed by the
measles, which in the course of the winter spread through the tribe.
Many died, and most of the survivors were so enfeebled as to be
unable to pursue the necessary avocations of hunting and fishing.
Even those who experienced only a slight attack, or escaped the
sickness altogether, dispirited by the scenes of misery which en-
vironed them, were rendered incapable of affording relief to their
distressed relations, and spent their time in conjuring and drumming
to avert the pestilence. Those who were able came to the fort and
received relief, but many who had retired with their families to
distant corners to pursue their winter hunts, experienced all the
horrors of famine. One evening, early in the month of January, a
poor Indian entered the North West Company's House, carrying his
only child in his arms, and followed by his starving wife. They had
been hunting apart from the other bands, had been unsuccessful, and
while in want were seized with the epidemical disease. An Indian is
accustomed to starve and it is not easy to elicit from him an account
of his sufferings. This poor man's story was very brief; as soon as the
fever abated, he set out with his wife for Cumberland House, [Ed.:
Richardson probably meant to refer here to the nearby North West
Company House] having previously been reduced to feed on the bits
of skin and offal which remained about their encampment. Even this
miserable fare was exhausted, and they walked several days without
eating, yet exerting themselves far beyond their strength that they
might save the life of the infant. It died almost within sight of the
house. Mr. Connolly, who was then in charge of the post, received
them with the utmost humanity and instantly placed food before*

*them; but no language can describe the manner in which the miser-
able father dashed the morsel from his lips and deplored the loss of
his child.*

·   ·   ·   ·   ·

*The original character of the Crees must have been much modified
by their long intercourse with Europeans; hence it is to be understood, that we confine ourselves in the following sketch to their
present condition, and more particularly to the Crees of Cumberland
House. The moral character of a hunter is acted upon by the nature
of the land he inhabits, the abundance or scarcity of food, and we
may add, in the present case, his means of access to spirituous liquors.
In a country so various in these respects as that inhabited by the
Crees, the causes alluded to must operate strongly in producing a
considerable difference of character among the various hordes. It may
be proper to bear in mind also, that we are about to draw the
character of a people whose only rule of conduct is public opinion,
and to try them by a morality founded on divine revelation, the only
standard that can be referred to by those who have been educated in
a land to which the blessings of the Gospel have extended.*

*Bearing these considerations in mind then, we may state the Crees
to be a vain, fickle, improvident and indolent race, and not very strict
in their adherence to truth, being great boasters; but on the other
hand, they strictly regard the rights of property, are susceptible of
the kinder affections, capable of friendship, very hospitable, tolerably
kind to their women, and withal inclined to peace.*

·   ·   ·   ·   ·

*Every Cree fears the medical or conjuring powers of his neighbour;
but at the same time exalts his own attainments to the skies. "I am
God-like" is a common expression among them, and they prove their
divinity-ship by eating live coals and by various tricks of a similar
nature. A medicine bag is an indispensable part of a hunter's equipment. It is generally furnished with a little bit of indigo, blue vitriol,
vermilion or some other showy article; and is, when in the hands of
a noted conjuror, such an object of terror to the rest of the tribe that
its possessor is enabled to fatten at his ease upon the labours of his
deluded countrymen.*

*A fellow of this description came to Cumberland House in the
winter of 1819. Notwithstanding the then miserable state of the
Indians, the rapacity of this wretch had been preying upon their*

necessities, and a poor hunter was actually at the moment pining away under the influence of his threats. The mighty conjuror, immediately on his arrival at the House, began to trumpet forth his powers, boasting, among other things, that although his hands and feet were tied as securely as possible, yet when placed in a conjuring-house, he would speedily disengage himself by the aid of two or three familiar spirits, who were attendant on his call. He was instantly taken at his word, and that his exertions might not be without an aim, a capot or great coat was promised as the reward of his success. A conjuring-house having been erected in the usual form, that is by sticking four willows in the ground and tying their tops to a hoop at the height of six or eight feet, he was fettered completely by winding several fathoms of rope round his body and extremities, and placed in its narrow apartment, not exceeding two feet in diameter. A moose skin being thrown over the frame, secluded him from our view. He forthwith began to chant a kind of hymn in a very monotonous tone. The rest of the Indians, who seemed in some doubt respecting the powers of a devil when put in competition with those of a white man, ranged themselves around and watched the result with anxiety. Nothing remarkable occurred for a long time. The conjuror continued his song at intervals, and it was occasionally taken up by those without. In this manner an hour and a half elapsed; but at length our attention, which had begun to flag, was roused by the violent shaking of the conjuring-house. It was instantly whispered round the circle that at least one devil had crept under the moose-skin. But it proved to be only the "God-like man" trembling with cold. He had entered the lists stript to the skin, and the thermometer stood very low that evening. His attempts were continued however with considerable resolution for half an hour longer, when he reluctantly gave in. He had found no difficulty in slipping through the noose when it was formed by his countrymen; but in the present instance the knot was tied by Governor Williams, who is an expert sailor. After this unsuccessful exhibition his credit sank amazingly, and he took the earliest opportunity of sneaking away from the fort.

> · · · · ·

. . . such a lamentable want of morality has been displayed by the white traders in their contests for the interests of their respective companies, that it would require a long series of good conduct to efface from the minds of the native population the ideas they have formed of the white character. Notwithstanding the frequent viola-

tions of the rights of property they have witnessed, and but too often experienced in their own persons, these savages, as they are termed, remain strictly honest. During their visits to a post they are suffered to enter every apartment in the house without the least restraint, and although articles of value to them are scattered about, nothing is ever missed. They scrupulously avoid moving anything from its place, although they are often prompted by curiosity to examine it. In some cases, indeed, they carry this principle to a degree of self-denial which would hardly be expected. It often happens that meat, which has been paid for (if the poisonous draught it procures them can be considered as payment), is left at their lodges until a convenient opportunity occurs of carrying it away. They will rather pass several days without eating than touch the meat thus entrusted to their charge, even when there exists a prospect of replacing it.

The hospitality of the Crees is unbounded. They afford a certain asylum to the half-breed children when deserted by their unnatural white fathers; and the infirm, and indeed every individual in the encampment, share the provisions of a successful hunter as long as they last.

.   .   .   .   .

It has been remarked by some writers that the aboriginal inhabitants of America are deficient in passion for the fair sex. This is by no means the case with the Crees. On the contrary, their practice of seducing each other's wives proves the most fertile source of their quarrels. When the guilty pair are detected, the woman generally receives a severe beating, but the husband is, for the most part, afraid to reproach the male culprit until they get drunk together at the fort; then the remembrance of the offence is revived, a struggle ensues, and the affair is terminated by the loss of a few handfuls of hair. Some husbands, however, feel more deeply the injury done to their honour, and seek revenge even in their sober moments. In such cases it is not uncommon for the offended party to walk with great gravity up to the other, and deliberately seizing his gun or some other article of value, to break it before his face. The adulterer looks on in silence, afraid to make any attempt to save his property. . . .

Although adultery is sometimes punished among the Crees in the manner above described, yet it is no crime provided the husband receives a valuable consideration for his wife's prostitution. Neither is chastity considered as a virtue in a female before marriage. . . .

The Cree women are not in general treated harshly by their hus-

bands, and possess considerable influence over them. They often eat, and even get drunk, in consort with the men; a considerable portion of the labour, however, falls to the lot of the wife. She makes the hut, cooks, dresses the skins, and for the most part carries the heaviest load. But when she is unable to perform her task, the husband does not consider it beneath his dignity to assist her. In illustration of this remark I may quote the case of an Indian who visited the fort in winter. This poor man's wife had lost her feet by the frost and he was compelled, not only to hunt, and to do all the menial offices himself, but in winter to drag his wife with their stock of furniture from one encampment to another. In the performance of this duty, as he could not keep pace with the rest of the tribe in their movements, he more than once nearly perished of hunger.

.   .   .   .   .

Both sexes are fond of, and excessively indulgent to, their children. The father never punishes them and if the mother, more hasty in her temper, sometimes bestows a blow or two on a troublesome child, her heart is instantly softened by the roar which follows, and she mingles her tears with those that streak the smoky face of her darling. It may be fairly said, then, that restraint or punishment forms no part of the education of an Indian child, nor are they early trained to that command over their temper which they exhibit in after years.

.   .   .   .   .

They [the Crees] show great fortitude in the endurance of hunger and the other evils incident to a hunter's life; but any unusual accident dispirits them at once, and they seldom venture to meet their enemies in open warfare, or to attack them even by surprise, unless with the advantage of superiority of numbers. Perhaps they are much deteriorated in this respect by their intercourse with Europeans. Their existence at present hangs upon the supplies of ammunition and clothing they receive from the traders, and they deeply feel their dependent situation. But their character has been still more debased by the passion for spirituous liquors, so assiduously fostered among them. To obtain the noxious beverage they descend to the most humiliating entreaties, and assume an abjectness of behaviour which does not seem natural to them, and of which not a vestige is to be seen in their intercourse with each other. . . .

When a hunter marries his first wife he usually takes up his abode in the tent of his father-in-law, and of course hunts for the family;

but when he becomes a father, the families are at liberty to separate, or remain together, as their inclinations prompt them. His second wife is for the most part the sister of the first, but not necessarily so, for an Indian of another family often presses his daughter upon a hunter whom he knows to be capable of maintaining her well. The first wife always remains the mistress of the tent, and assumes an authority over the others, which is not in every case quietly submitted to.

.   .   .   .   .

Tattooing is almost universal with the Crees. The women are in general content with having one or two lines drawn from the corners of the mouth towards the angles of the lower jaw; but some of the men have their bodies covered with a great variety of lines and figures. It seems to be considered by most rather as a proof of courage than an ornament, the operation being very painful . . . . The lines on the face are formed by dexterously running an awl under the cuticle, and then drawing a cord, dipped in charcoal and water, through the canal thus formed. The punctures on the body are formed by needles of various sizes set in a frame. A number of hawk bells attached to this frame serve by their noise to cover the suppressed groans of the sufferer and, probably for the same reason, the process is accompanied with singing. An indelible stain is produced by rubbing a little finely-powdered willow-charcoal into the punctures.

.   .   .   .   .

The standard of exchange in all mercantile transactions with the natives is a beaver skin, the relative value of which, as originally established by traders, differs considerably from the present worth of the articles it represents, but the Indians are averse to change. The marten, eight musk-rat, or a single lynx or wolverine skin, are eqivalent to one beaver; a silver fox, white fox, or otter, are reckoned two beavers, and a black fox, or large black bear, are equal to four; a mode of reckoning which has very little connection with the real value of these different furs in the European market. Neither has any attention been paid to the original cost of European articles in fixing the tariff by which they are sold to the Indians. A coarse butcher's knife is one skin, a woollen blanket or a fathom of coarse cloth, eight, and a fowling-piece fifteen. The Indians receive their principal outfit of clothing and ammunition on credit in the autumn, to be repaid by their winter hunts; the amount intrusted to each of *the hunters varying with their reputations for industry and skill, from twenty to one hundred and fifty skins. The Indians are generally anxious to pay off the debt thus incurred, but their good intentions are often frustrated by the arts of the rival traders. Each of the Companies keeps men constantly employed travelling over the country during the winter, to collect the furs from the different bands of hunters as fast as they are procured. The poor Indian endeavours to behave honestly, and when he has gathered a few skins sends notice to the post from whence he procured his supplies, but if discovered in the meantime by the opposite party, he is seldom proof against the temptation to which he is exposed. However firm he may be in his denials at first, his resolutions are enfeebled by the sight of a little rum, and when he has tasted the intoxicating beverage they vanish like smoke, and he brings forth his store of furs, which he had carefully concealed from the scrutinizing eyes of his visitors. This mode of carrying on the trade not only causes the amount of furs collected by either of the two companies to depend more on the activity of their agents, the knowledge they possess of the motions of the Indians and the quantity of rum they carry, than upon the liberality of the credits they give, but is also productive of an increasing deterioration of the character of the Indians and will probably, ultimately, prove destructive to the fur trade itself. Indeed the evil has already, in part, recoiled upon the traders; for the Indians, long deceived, have become deceivers in their turn, and not infrequently after having incurred a heavy debt at one post, move off to another, to play the same game . . . . To carry on the contest, the two Companies are obliged to employ a great many servants, whom they maintain often with much difficulty, and always at a considerable expense.*

There are thirty men belonging to the Hudson's Bay Fort at Cumberland, and nearly as many women and children. The inhabitants of the North West Company's House are still more numerous.

On January 18, 1820 Richardson and Hood gave Franklin, Back and Hepburn a hearty sendoff as they set out for the Athabasca country. "At eight in the morning . . . we quitted the fort and took leave of our hospitable friend, Governor Williams. . . . Dr. Richardson, Mr. Hood and Mr. Connolly accompanied us along the Saskatchewan until the snow became too deep for their walking without snowshoes. We then parted from our associates with sincere regret at the prospect of a long separation."

The two companies had furnished Franklin with two carioles and two sledges* together with drivers and dogs. Food sufficient for fifteen days, bedding, an extra suit of outer wear and three changes of underwear filled the carioles and sledges to capacity, so that everyone was obliged to walk. Franklin, Back and Hepburn were well clothed for their first experience of winter travel. Like the traders they wore a hood over their fur cap in strong winds, leather trousers, Indian stockings and mocassins. The outfit was completed by a leather coat with a belt around the waist to which their fire-bag, knife and axe were suspended.

Progress through the heavy snow was so slow that on the first day the party covered only six miles. That night the dogs managed to steal a good part of the supplies from almost underneath Hepburn's head. To add to their troubles, the Englishmen found their first experience on snowshoes quite a test and within three days were suffering greatly from sore ankles. But apart from this difficulty they found much to interest them in winter travel. They were fascinated, for example, by the wolves' method of getting deer:

*The cariole was an ordinary sledge with a leather covering to protect the lower part of the traveller's body. The sledge was eight to ten feet long, made of two or three flat boards which curved up in front, and held together by cross pieces of wood. These vehicles were so thin that if heavily loaded they would bend with the roughness of the track.

We passed the remains of two red-deer, lying at the bases of per-
pendicular cliffs from the summits of which they had, probably, been
forced by the wolves. These voracious animals, who are inferior in
speed to the moose or red-deer, are said frequently to have recourse
to this expedient in places where extensive plains are bounded by
precipitous cliffs. While the deer are quietly grazing, the wolves
assemble in great numbers and, forming a crescent, creep slowly
towards the herd so as not to alarm them much at first. But when
they perceive they have fairly hemmed in the unsuspecting creatures,
and cut off their retreat across the plain, they move more quickly
and with hideous yells terrify their prey and urge them to flight by
the only open way, which is that towards the precipice; appearing to
know that when the herd is once at full speed, it is easily driven over
the cliff, the rearmost urging on those that are before. The wolves
then descend at their leisure and feast on the mangled carcasses.

Heavy snow and severe cold were normal aspects of the journey, but
on the twenty-eighth the snowdrifts were particularly deep and the
northwest wind piercingly cold; several of the party froze their faces,
though they were constantly rubbing them. Three red deer were seen,
but they ran away before the chase could begin. Some fresh meat
would have helped just then; supplies were low and nothing remained
for the dogs except a little burnt leather. Although the men kept going
until a late hour, they had covered only eleven miles when they
camped. "The night was miserably cold; our tea froze in the tin pots
before we could drink it, and even a mixture of spirits and water
became quite thick by congelation; yet, after we lay down to rest, we
felt no inconvenience and heeded not the wolves, though they were
howling within view."

Travelling conditions improved a little, but the food ran out on the
thirtieth. The dogs, in a ravenous state, broke into a deal box containing
tea to get at a small piece of meat that someone had left in it. On
January 31 the men reached Carlton House, a Hudson's Bay post which
afforded them a more than welcome stopover. Mr. Prudens, the manager, received them with the warmth and attention that Governor
Williams' circular was to ensure for them at every post. He quickly set
before them a substantial meal of buffalo steaks; coming after their
recent diet of dried meat and pemmican, it was indeed a feast. The next
priority was to change from the clothes which they had worn for two
solid weeks.

Franklin's ankles were still painfully swollen, so he was prevented from paying an immediate visit to the North West post three miles away. However, Mr. Hallet, the manager, came to see him on February 1 and was given a copy of Mr. McGillivray's circular. He expressed great willingness to help the party in its advance to the Athabasca. Franklin was relieved to be off his snowshoes and to have a week's rest at Carlton House. The Post was pleasantly situated and in summer produced ample returns of wheat, barley, oats and potatoes on its five acres of cultivated land. Moreover, its location gave Franklin and Back a good opportunity to meet members of the Stone Indian tribe. They were of striking appearance, their eyes large and expressive, their noses aquiline, and their teeth white and even. Their foreheads were high and bold, the cheek bones rather high, their figures generally good, their colour a bright copper, and their dress neat. But closer acquaintance with them had taught the traders that they would steal everything that they could lay their hands on, especially horses. In their view, horses were common property sent by the Almighty for the general use of man, though they admitted that the owners had the right to prevent the theft if they could. The Stone Indians were friendly with their neighbours the Crees, the two tribes frequently uniting against the Slave Indians farther to the west. Nearly every summer these tribes went to war and would muster up to 300 or 400 horsemen on each side. There was skilful generalship in both camps; swift attacks were made the moment an advantage was seen. Hand-to-hand encounters were brief and bloody, neither side taking prisoners of either sex but slaying any who survived the initial attack. The dead were immediately scalped, and the brave who finished the day with the most scalps was considered the greatest warrior.

By February 9 Franklin and his party were fit enough to continue their journey from Carlton House, and the carioles and sledges were loaded. Their hosts gave them a warm sendoff and there was the customary salute of muskets.

Before long winter travel became a matter of routine. The distance covered averaged from ten to twenty miles a day, depending on the weather, which varied from gales and deep snow to pleasant sunshine. The two officers and Hepburn now had full control over their snowshoes, and while they were glad to wait two days in mid-February at the Hudson's Bay post at Green Lake for the arrival of a supply of meat, they had no need for the rest. The resident partner at the nearby North West post warned Franklin that meat would be very scarce in the Athabasca area the following summer because widespread sickness among the Indians had kept them from their hunting. Accordingly

Franklin wrote to Richardson telling him to bring as much food from Cumberland House as he could stow in his canoes.

The salute of muskets that honoured the party on its departure from Green Lake was an unusually lively event; since most of the men were away hunting, the guns were fired with the greatest enthusiasm by some of the half-breed women. Fortunately no one was hurt!

Three days' travel brought the party to the two trading posts at Isle à la Crosse, so named because the Indians used to assemble on a nearby island every year to play the game of lacrosse. These were important posts geographically, with good communications to the English River, Athabasca and Columbia districts. Both managers promised to send Franklin supplies of pemmican in the spring and Clark, the Hudson's Bay manager, was able to give him valuable information about the country and the Indians north of Slave Lake. Clark had been far enough north to meet many Eskimos but he had found them so hostile that he made no attempt to trade with them. When the party left on March 5 he accompanied them to the boundary of his district and being an experienced winter traveller showed them how to make camp at night with much greater attention to comfort. During this part of the journey the Aurora Borealis was so brilliant that one night it concealed the brightest stars from sight, and on another seemed to illumine some clouds from behind.

On March 13 Franklin and his companions reached the Methy Portage, twelve miles in length, and had a pleasant ride across it in their carioles. In summer, however, the portage represented a formidable obstacle over which all cargoes had to be carried in passing to and from the Athabasca district. "We afterwards followed the river [the Clearwater] as far as the Pine Portage, when we passed through a very romantic defile of rocks, which presented the appearance of Gothic ruins, and their rude characters were happily contrasted with the softness of the snow and the darker foliage of the pines which crowned their summits." On the morning of the fifteenth, while proceeding along the River, they encountered a strong smell of sulphur and found a quantity of it scattered on the north shore, apparently deposited there by some spring.

From March 19 to 22 Franklin and his party stayed at the North West post of Pierre au Calumet, where John Stuart, the North West Company's senior partner for the Athabasca department, was in charge. Stuart had crossed the continent twice, once reaching the Pacific Ocean by the Columbia River, but he had never been farther north than Great Slave Lake. He had received many reports from the Indians, however, and expressed considerable doubt that Franklin would be able to get experienced voyageurs to accompany him to the Arctic sea. He believed that they feared the Eskimos too much to take the chance. Already one canoe, sent to make trading agreements with the Eskimos living at the mouth of the Mackenzie, had been attacked and everyone in it killed. Nevertheless, Stuart promised to do what he could to remove the voyageurs' fears and undertook to prepare bark and other materials that would be needed in the spring to build two canoes. Franklin was grateful for this promise of help but disturbed to hear of these probable difficulties.

Some of the worst gales, snow and cold of the whole trip were encountered on the last days before the party reached Fort Chipewyan on March 26. In their exhausted state Franklin and the others appreciated all the more the warm welcome given them by the North West partners in charge, Mr. Keith and Mr. Black.

Thus has terminated a winter's journey of eight hundred and fifty-seven miles, in the progress of which there has been a great inter-mixture of agreeable and disagreeable circumstances. Could the amount of each be balanced, I suspect the latter would much pre-ponderate; and among these the initiation into walking in snow-shoes must be considered as prominent. The suffering it occasions can be faintly imagined by a person who thinks upon the inconvenience of marching with a weight of between two and three pounds constantly attached to galled feet and swelled ankles. Perseverance and practice only will enable the novice to surmount this pain.

The next evil is being constantly exposed to witness the wanton and unnecessary cruelty of the men to their dogs, especially those of the voyageurs, who beat them unmercifully, and habitually vent on them the most dreadful and disgusting imprecations. There are other inconveniences which, though keenly felt during the day's journey, are speedily forgotten when stretched out in the encampment before a large fire, you enjoy the social mirth of your companions, who usually pass the evening in recounting their former feats in travelling. At this time the voyageurs are always cheerful and merry, and the only bar to their comfort arises from the frequent interruption occasioned by the dogs, who are constantly prowling about the circle and snatching at every kind of food that happens to be within their reach. . . . But the greatest gratifications a traveller in these regions enjoys are derived from the hospitable welcome he receives at every trading post, however poor the means of the host may be; and from

being disrobed even for a short time of the trappings of a voyager,
and experiencing the pleasures of cleanliness.

In the six and a half months since he had left York Factory Franklin
had covered about 1550 miles in autumn and winter travel. The trip
to Cumberland House had been mostly upstream against strong currents and over difficult portages, while the journey northwest to
Chipewyan had been almost entirely by snowshoe. He could now
begin to make detailed plans for the best use of the approaching
summer, which represented essential preparation for his work along
the Arctic seacoast in the summer of 1821.

With his customary insistence on impartiality between the two
companies Franklin called on Mr. MacDonald, manager of the nearby
Hudson's Bay post of Fort Wedderburne, the day after he reached
Fort Chipewyan. He wasted no time in seeking advice and assistance
from the officials of both posts. Much on his mind was the need for
a good stock of pemmican and other necessities such as canoes. The
officials of both companies readily promised to give him such help.
They also secured useful information for him about the country north
of Great Slave Lake and the Indians to be found there.

When Franklin asked which was the best route to follow north of
the Slave Lake, a half-breed interpreter named Beaulieu stepped forward and with a piece of charcoal sketched on the floor the course
of the Coppermine River as he remembered it. Just as he had finished,
an old Chipewyan Indian called Black Meat entered the room and
recognized Beaulieu's "map." Grabbing the charcoal he made a track
to represent a portion of the Arctic coast which he had followed when
returning from a hostile expedition against the Eskimos. He told
Franklin that the sea was studded with well-wooded islands close to
the shore and was free from ice in July. If true, this was most encouraging. Besides seeking all possible help at Fort Chipewyan, Franklin
had two voyageurs take messages to both companies' posts on Great
Slave Lake telling the officials there of his plans and enlisting their help.

But with the approach of spring Franklin found that he had to play
second fiddle to the demands of the fur trade. The large North West
post of Chipewyan and the much smaller Hudson's Bay post of
Wedderburne were collection centres for furs from the whole Slave
and Peace River areas. In the spring, traders from outlying posts
brought in their winter collection of furs for shipment to Montreal or
York Factory; they returned in the autumn to receive their supply of
goods for the Indians who traded at their posts. The burst of activity

grew throughout the month of May as the traders and voyageurs assembled and the two companies made ready their first brigades of canoes.

One of the problems facing both the fur traders and Franklin in that spring of 1820 was the short supply of food:

> *Mr. Smith assured me that he had only five hundred pounds of meat remaining after the canoes had been despatched, for the use of the men who might travel from the post during the summer, and that five years preceding, there had been thirty thousand pounds in store under similar circumstances. He ascribed this amazing difference more to the indolent habits which the Indians had acquired since the commercial struggle commenced, than to their recent sickness, mentioning in confirmation of his opinion that they could now, by the produce of little exertion, obtain whatever they demanded from either establishment.*

Instructions from head office to give every assistance to the expedition did not mean much to men who were in the middle of a trade, and sometimes a physical, war. Franklin was therefore especially anxious to send word to York Factory requesting immediate shipment of the supplies left there the previous autumn. He also sent by the fur traders a request that Richardson and Hood bring from Cumberland House any supplies available there.

The first brigade of canoes was dispatched for the depot on May 30, and others followed throughout the week. In one of them Franklin sent a box addressed to the Under-Secretary of State in London. The box contained some drawings by Back, a map of the route followed from Cumberland House, some of Franklin's official letters and a fine black beaver pelt that had been presented to him by a partner of the North West Company.

When the dispatching of canoes began, Franklin made an effort to get the ear of both companies' officials in order to arrange for supplies, but distrust between the two companies was so great that neither group of officials would meet in the opponent's post. Not until Franklin had a tent pitched at a point halfway between the two posts did they agree to sit down together with him. They then gave him a good hearing as he outlined his requests for men and supplies, and presents for the natives, but both companies had so exhausted their resources in their competition with each other that there was very little available for him.

At this very discouraging moment some welcome news arrived from the principal chief of the Copper Indians whose encampments were near Great Slave Lake. The chief sent word that he was glad to hear of the plans for the expedition. He offered to accompany the party and to have some of his men act as guides and hunters, but he wanted Mr. Wentzel, a clerk with the North West Company, to come with them. This excellent news had a marked effect on the attitude of some of the voyageurs, who had earlier told Franklin that they would not go north with the expedition. Several now came and volunteered to accompany him. In the course of the next few days six Hudson's Bay men and five North West men were engaged, and Franklin secured permission from the North West Company partners for the release of Wentzel.

Franklin now wrote Wentzel himself, urgently asking that he accept the position, since without him the Copper Indians would probably not agree to come. He also asked Wentzel to join the Indians and keep them from disappearing, should they be tempted to do so if the expedition were delayed.

Ever since Franklin had left York Factory the previous autumn the weather, with few exceptions, had been bad. Now spring had really arrived, and he was amazed at the change in the landscape:

The trees are now in full foliage, and the plants generally in flower, and the whole scene quite enlivening. There can scarcely be a higher gratification than that which is enjoyed in this country in witnessing the rapid change which takes place in the course of a few days in the spring; scarcely does the snow disappear from the ground before the trees are clothed with thick foliage, the shrubs open their leaves and put forth their variegated flowers, and the whole prospect becomes animating.

The canoe that was being built for the expedition was finished on July 1. It was thirty-two and a half feet long, and four feet, ten inches at its greatest width, with seventy-three hoops of thin cedar and a layer of cedar laths within the frame. These flimsy vessels of birch bark were capable of carrying a crew of five or six men, in addition to provisions and baggage—about 3300 pounds altogether. Though such a canoe weighed 300 pounds, two experienced men could carry it over portages, often at a run. While it could easily be damaged—even a slight blow from a sharp object would pierce it—it could be repaired quickly with the gum or pitch and birch bark and pine roots that were always carried.

*July 13. This morning Mr. Back and I had the sincere gratification
of welcoming our long-separated friends, Dr. Richardson and Mr.
Hood, who arrived in perfect health with two canoes, having made a
very expeditious journey from Cumberland, notwithstanding they
were detained near three days in consequence of the melancholy loss
of one of their bowmen, by the upsetting of a canoe in a strong
rapid . . . .*

*The zeal and talent displayed by Dr. Richardson and Mr. Hood, in
the discharge of their several duties since my separation from them,
drew forth my highest approbation. These gentlemen had brought all
the stores they could procure from the establishments at Cumberland
and Isle à la Crosse; and at the latter place they had received ten bags
of pemmican from the North-West Company, which proved to be
mouldy, and so totally unfit for use that it was left at the Methye
Portage. They got none from the Hudson's Bay post. The voyagers
belonging to that Company, being destitute of provision, had eaten
what was intended for us. In consequence of these untoward circumstances, the canoes arrived with only one day's supply of this most
essential article. The prospect of having to commence our journey
from hence, almost destitute of provision, and scantily supplied with
stores, was distressing to us, and very discouraging to the men. It was
evident, however, that any unnecessary delay here would have been
very imprudent, as Fort Chipewyan did not, at the present time,
furnish the means of subsistence for so large a party, much less was
there a prospect of our receiving a supply to carry us forward. We
therefore hastened to make the necessary arrangements for our
speedy departure. All the stores were demanded that could possibly
be spared from both the establishments; and we rejoiced to find, that
when this collection was added to the articles that had been brought
up by the canoes, we had a sufficient quantity of clothing for the
equipment of the men who had been engaged here, as well as to
furnish a present to the Indians, besides some few goods for the
winter's consumption; but we could not procure any ammunition,
which was the most essential article, or spirits, and but little tobacco.*

Dr. Richardson had brought with him ten men who wished to accompany the expedition to the Arctic sea. As a result, Franklin was able to
discharge seven of the less enthusiastic crewmen. When on July 18 the
expedition left Fort Chipewyan and headed north, it consisted of sixteen voyageurs, the four officers, Hepburn and a Chipewyan woman.
Wentzel and an interpreter were to join the expedition at Great Slave

Lake, along with the Copper Indians. There was enough food for only one day, plus some preserved meat, chocolate, arrowroot and portable soup. These Franklin intended keeping for the journey along the Arctic coast the next summer.

A few miles north of Fort Chipewyan the Stony and Peace rivers join to form the Slave, a magnificent river three-quarters of a mile wide. Here the canoes made good speed until, farther on, they passed through several narrow channels between islands, and at one point the current carried them through a whirlpool. The men camped for the night on the swampy bank of the River but they soon found themselves flooded out by torrents of rain. The storm was followed by such swarms of mosquitoes that the men were forced to strike camp in the pitch darkness and paddle down river until morning. Their attempts at fishing produced only four small trout, and hunger drove them to use a small part of the preserved meat.

A succession of rapids led to serious difficulties. On one occasion two canoes collided so violently that one had its bow crushed. The occupants succeeded in landing, however, and completed their repairs within two hours. Later the same day, while crossing a difficult portage, one of the men carrying a canoe slipped and let it fall on the rocks. Although it was split into two parts, two hours later the broken parts were sewn together and the seams covered with pitch.

The last portage on the route to Slave Lake is called "The Portage of the Drowned." The voyageurs told Franklin the story of how it came to be given that name. They said that on one occasion two canoes had reached the upper end of the portage and the men in them had to decide whether to risk shooting the rapids or not. An experienced guide decided to take his canoe down but told the crew in the other canoe to wait until they heard the shot of his gun. This was to be a signal that he had made the passage and considered it safe for them to follow. The rapids proved to be much more difficult than expected, and it required all the skill of the guide and the furious exertions of the crew to get through safely. As they reached calm water, one of the men sighted a duck, grabbed his gun and fired a shot. The guide, realizing that this would be taken as the signal, rushed back up the portage to try and stop the canoe, but the men had already pushed off into the river. He had the agony of watching what followed: the men lost their nerve in the middle of the rapids, the canoe capsized and every one of the occupants was drowned.

The day after portaging these same rapids the expedition reached the Salt River. Franklin and a few men ascended the River in a light canoe, leaving the rest of the party behind to fish. It was a worthwhile side trip, for the small party filled their casks with salt and shot a buffalo. The men who had remained behind had caught practically no fish, and the sight of the returning canoe, loaded to the gunwales with meat, was the best possible answer to their discouragement. As the expedition continued down the River the voyageurs sang their liveliest songs as they paddled.

O n July 25 the party reached Moose-Deer Island, where both companies maintained trading posts. There was very little food available in either post but Franklin decided to wait for the return of a band of Indian hunters who had been sent out by the posts' officers. Next day the Indians returned, loaded down with game, and the two companies were then able to supply Franklin with 550 pounds of meat. This seemed sufficient to keep his men going until they could reach their Indian hunters farther north.

Three days later they reached the North West post of Fort Providence on the north shore of Great Slave Lake. The Fort was farther north than any of the posts established by the Hudson's Bay Company and here Franklin found Frederick Wentzel waiting for him. Wentzel had agreed to spend the next year with the expedition, taking full responsibility for liaison with the Indians. He was also to supervise the voyageurs and handle the acquisition and distribution of provisions and other stores— always the most thankless of jobs. He was well qualified for his new job: he had lived in the area for twenty years and was fully trusted by the Copper Indians. Moreover, he was able to speak the Chipewyan language and thus keep a check on the accuracy of the interpreters. In Franklin's view he was a decided acquisition.

Wentzel informed Franklin that Chief Akaitcho, or Big-foot, of the Copper Indians was camped nearby with his men. They were ready to travel with the expedition and would come next day for an official meeting.

Wentzel gave Franklin useful advice as to the most fitting way to receive Chief Akaitcho and his men.

As we were informed that external appearances made lasting impressions on the Indians, we prepared for the interview by decorating ourselves in uniform, and suspending a medal round each of our necks. Our tents had been previously pitched and over one of them a silken union flag was hoisted. Soon after noon, on July 30th, several Indian canoes were seen advancing in a regular line, and on their approach, the chief was discovered in the headmost, which was paddled by two men. On landing at the fort, the chief assumed a very grave aspect, and walked up to Mr. Wentzel with a measured and dignified step, looking neither to the right nor to the left at the persons who had assembled on the beach to witness his debarkation, but preserving the same immovability of countenance until he reached the hall, and was introduced to the officers. When he had smoked his pipe, drank a small portion of spirits and water himself, and issued a glass to each of his companions, who had seated themselves on the floor, he commenced his harangue, by mentioning the circumstances that led to his agreeing to accompany the expedition, an engagement which he was quite prepared to fulfil. He was rejoiced, he said, to see such great chiefs on his lands; his tribe were poor, but they loved white men who had been their benefactors; and he hoped that our visit would be productive of much good to them. . . .

In reply to this speech, which I understood had been prepared for many days, I endeavoured to explain the objects of our mission in a manner best calculated to ensure his exertions in our service. With this view, I told him that we were sent out by the greatest chief in the world, who was the sovereign also of the trading companies in the country; that he was the friend of peace, and had the interest of every nation at heart. Having learned that his children in the north were much in want of articles of merchandise, in consequence of the extreme length and difficulty of the present route, he had sent us to search for a passage by the sea, which if found, would enable large vessels to transport great quantities of goods more easily to their lands. That we had not come for the purpose of traffic, but solely to make discoveries for their benefit, as well as that of every other people. . . . That we desired the assistance of the Indians in guiding us, and providing us with food; finally, that we were most positively enjoined by the great chief to recommend that hostilities should cease throughout this country; and especially between the Indians and the Eskimos, whom he considered his children, in common with other natives; and by way of enforcing the latter point more strongly, I assured him that a forfeiture of all the advantages which might be anticipated from the Expedition would be a certain consequence if any quarrel arose between his party and the Eskimos. I also communicated to him that, owing to the distance we had travelled, we

had now few more stores than was necessary for the use of our own
party, a part of these, however, should be forthwith presented to
him; on his return he and his party should be remunerated with cloth,
ammunition, and tobacco, and some useful iron materials, besides
having their debts to the North-West Company discharged.

The chief . . . replied by a renewal of his assurances that he and
his party would attend us to the end of our journey, and that they
would do their utmost to provide us with the means of subsistence.
He admitted that his tribe had made war upon the Eskimos, but said
they were now desirous of peace, and unanimous in their opinion as
to the necessity of all who accompanied us abstaining from every act
of enmity against that nation. He added, however, that the Eskimos
were very treacherous, and therefore recommended that we should
advance towards them with caution.

A lengthy conference now took place about the best route to be followed. The Chief's guides drew a map on the floor with charcoal showing a chain of twenty-five small lakes, about half of them connected by
a river that flowed into Great Slave Lake near Fort Providence. There
was considerable argument between the guides as to the course followed
by the Coppermine River, but agreement was finally reached. One of
these guides, who was Akaitcho's older brother, said that as a young
man he had accompanied Mr. Hearne on his journey to the Coppermine
mouth and clearly remembered the massacre of the Eskimos by the
Indians. However, none of the Indians could give Franklin more than a
vague and unsatisfactory impression of the Arctic coastline, since none
of them had travelled more than three days along the coast east of the
Coppermine.

Akaitcho proposed that the expedition's winter base should be situated on a certain lake about three days' journey south of the Coppermine. Reindeer passed the place in the autumn and spring, there were
fish in the lake and there was plenty of wood at hand for construction
and firewood. He said that depending on the pace set by Franklin's
canoes, it should take about twenty days to reach this lake.

To mark the end of the conference Franklin approached Akaitcho
and placed his medal round his neck. The other officers then presented
their medals to the Chief's elder brother and to the two guides. This
expression of friendship, made with some ceremony in the presence of
the hunters, gave the Indian leaders enormous satisfaction, though they
were careful not to show any visible expression of pleasure. They did

say, however, that they would treasure the medals for the rest of their lives.

Chief Akaitcho had impressed Franklin with his intelligence. When told of Parry's expedition by sea in search of a northwest passage, he asked why such a passage had not been discovered long ago—if one actually existed. Franklin was completely honest in all that he said, not only because this was his way, but also because it would have been fatal to have been found lying. It would have destroyed forever the Indians' confidence in him.

We presented to the chief, the two guides, and the seven hunters. who had engaged to accompany us, some cloth, blankets, tobacco, knives, daggers, besides other useful iron materials, and a gun to each; also a keg of very weak spirits and water, which they kept until the evening, as they had to try their guns before dark, and make the necessary preparations for commencing the journey on the morrow. The Indians, however, did not leave us on the next day, as the chief was desirous of being present, with his party, at the dance, which was given in the evening to our Canadian voyagers. They were highly entertained by the vivacity and agility displayed by our companions in their singing and dancing: and especially by their imitating the gestures of a Canadian voyager who placed himself in the most ludicrous postures; and whenever this was done, the gravity of the chief gave way to violent bursts of laughter.

Half way through the evening the party was brought to an abrupt halt by a fire that completely destroyed Franklin's tent. Some embers which had been put inside to smoke out the mosquitoes had ignited. Hepburn, fortunately, had decided to miss the party and was asleep on Franklin's bed. Beside the bed was stacked a supply of gunpowder. Hepburn woke just in time to get the gunpowder, Franklin's baggage and himself clear of the flames. Franklin's immediate fear was that the Indians, with their superstitions about omens, might decide that the expedition was ill-fated and leave him. Akaitcho seemed to read his thoughts and said that he hoped no future misfortune would be hidden from him. His main concern seemed to be that the flag had been burned, but Franklin assured him that it could be repaired. It had been a close call—if the stores had been destroyed, the expedition would probably have been held up for another year. Franklin said a prayer of thanks and agreed with Wentzel that the dancing should start again to reassure the Indians.

*August 1 [1820]—This morning the Indians set out, intending to
wait for us at the mouth of the Yellow Knife River. We remained
behind to pack our stores, in bales of eighty pounds each, an operation which could not be done in the presence of these Indians, as they
are in the habit of begging for every thing they see. Our stores consisted of two barrels of gunpowder, one hundred and forty pounds of
ball and small shot, four fowling-pieces, a few old trading guns, eight
pistols, twenty-four Indian daggers, some packages of knives, chisels,
nails, and fastenings for a boat; a few yards of cloth, some blankets,
needles, looking-glasses, and beads; together with nine fishing-nets,
having meshes of different sizes. Our provision was two casks of flour,
two hundred dried reindeer tongues, some dried moose meat, portable
soup, and arrowroot, sufficient on the whole for ten days' consumption, besides two cases of chocolate, and two canisters of tea. We
engaged another Canadian voyager at this place, and the Expedition
then consisted of twenty-eight persons, including the officers, and the
wives of three of our [Canadian] voyagers, who were brought for the
purpose of making shoes and clothes for the men at the winter
establishment; there were also three children, belonging to two of
these women.*

Fort Providence was the most northerly fur trading post that the
party was to encounter. They were now venturing into territory never
before seen by Europeans and they were in high spirits as they set out
in three canoes, with an additional small one for the women. On
August 3 they caught up with Akaitcho and his hunters camped on the
"River of the Toothless Fish" (named Yellow Knife River by the
traders). Here they were quickly surrounded by a fleet of seventeen
Indian canoes. Akaitcho was paddled by his slave, a young Dog-Rib
Indian whom he had taken from his people by force. When he thought
he was not being watched, however, the Chief would take a paddle
himself, and a few days later he was paddling his canoe quite openly
and even carrying it over portages. Several of the canoes were paddled
by women, who were always quarrelling and making a great noise.
From time to time their husbands tried to shut them up with a few
blows from their paddles, but with little effect. (Franklin does not say
when these other women joined the expedition but Akaitcho and his
hunters seem to have had their families with them at least part of the
time. They probably did a certain amount of coming and going.)

The Indians had the advantage over Franklin's men at the portages,
for they carried only their small canoes, while the women and children

carried their clothes and provisions. This meant that they could cover a portage with a single trip. In contrast, Franklin's men had to make four trips to get their canoes and heavy cargoes across. Tired as they were at the end of day, however, the officers and men took turns standing guard throughout the night. This served both to prevent their being surprised by strangers and to show the Indians that they were constantly on the alert. Akaitcho was impressed by the system and said that he would sleep without anxiety even when they reached Eskimo territory, since no enemy could surprise them.

> On August 5th we continued the ascent of the river [Yellowknife].
> . . . It flows between high rocky banks on which there is sufficient
> soil to support pines, birch, and poplars. Five portages were crossed,
> then the Rocky Lake, and we finished our labours at the end of the
> sixth portage. The issue of dried meat for breakfast this morning had
> exhausted all our stock; and no other provision remained but the
> portable soups, and a few pounds of preserved meat. At the recom-
> mendation of Akaitcho, the hunters were furnished with ammuni-
> tion, and desired to go forward as speedily as possible to the part
> where the reindeer were expected to be found; and to return to us
> with any provision they could procure. He also assured us that in
> our advance towards them we should come to lakes abounding in
> fish. Many of the Indians being also in distress for food, decided on
> separating from us, and going on at a quicker pace than we could
> travel.

Fishing was poor for the next few days, portages more frequent, and spirits correspondingly low. Some of the reserve supply of food was issued but it was not enough to satisfy the men's hunger. At last, on the thirteenth, exhausted from labouring on so inadequate a diet, they broke into open rebellion. For several days they had been murmuring at the smallness of their rations and had tried to get hold of all the food that still remained, which they would have eaten at one sitting. Now they said that they would go no farther unless more food was given them. Franklin regarded their conduct as unpardonable, especially since signal fires had just been seen, indicating that the hunters had made a kill and that food awaited them. Speaking in the strongest terms, he told them insubordination was too dangerous to be permitted and assured them that he would inflict the heaviest punishment on any who refused to continue or tried in any way to delay the expedition. Having been told that a voyageur would invariably try to find out how far he could go in bullying a new master and would cause endless trouble if he once gained the slightest ascendency, Franklin now felt compelled to assert his authority. But that night he wrote in his journal, "I must admit, however, that the present hardships of our companions were of a kind which few could support without murmuring, and no one could witness without a sincere pity for their sufferings."

After Franklin's lecture, the party moved on, crossing seven lakes during the day and making as many portages. Just as the men were making camp for the night, four hunters arrived with two reindeer. After a huge meal there was only enough meat left for the next day, but all signs of discontent had gone. As it turned out, there was to be enough food on the rest of the journey to the winter base, for two days later the hunters brought in the carcasses of seventeen reindeer. A happy twenty-four hours were spent drying the meat, with the women in charge of the operation. They stripped the meat from the bones and dried it over a slow fire in the sun, a process made easier by the fact that the temperature went up to seventy-seven degrees.

Having provided an ample supply of meat for the moment, Akaitcho suggested that he and his men push on to the proposed site for the winter base, some six days' travel ahead. He also asked permission to go off for ten days in order to supply his family with winter clothing. Franklin thought this was a reasonable request and granted it, but he had one of the interpreters go with Akaitcho to discourage him from overstaying his leave.

> Previous to his departure the chief warned us to be constantly on guard against the grizzly bears, which he described as being numerous in this vicinity, and very ferocious . . . . We afterwards learned that the only bear in this part of the country is the brown bear, and that they by no means possess the ferocity which the Indians ascribe to them with their usual love of exaggeration. The fierce grizzly bear . . . is not found on the barren grounds.

On Sunday, August 20, Franklin and his companions reached the site suggested by the Indians for their winter base. That afternoon they assembled for divine service, thanking God for having brought them so far on their journey. They had travelled 553 miles from Fort Chipewyan and had made portages totalling twenty-one miles since leaving Fort Providence. Since the men had to cross each portage four times with a load of 180 pounds, and return three times to reload, it meant that they had walked about 150 miles.

> We determined on placing the house on the summit of the bank,

which commands a beautiful prospect of the surrounding country. The view in the front is bounded at the distance of three miles by round-backed hills; to the eastward and westward lie the Winter and Round-rock Lakes, which are connected by the Winter River, whose banks are well clothed with pines, and ornamented with a profusion of mosses, lichens, and shrubs.

A fire was built on the south side of the River as a signal to the Chief that Franklin and his party had arrived, but a strong wind fanned the flames and the whole wood caught fire. For three days the men choked on the smoke that enveloped them.

The first morning after their arrival at the site, the voyageurs were divided into two work groups: one to cut wood for building a store-house, the other to bring in the meat as hunters procured it. The second group returned to camp in a few hours with carcasses of seven reindeer. Franklin now sent word to Akaitcho, asking him to come to the camp at once and bring whatever meat he had procured. Franklin had decided to proceed to the Coppermine River immediately and he needed the Chief's cooperation.

On the morning of the 25th, we were surprised by some early symptoms of the approach of winter; the small pools were frozen over, and a flock of geese passed to the southward. In the afternoon, however, a fog came on, which afterwards changed into rain, and the ice quickly disappeared. We suffered great anxiety all the next day respecting John Hepburn, who had gone to hunt before sunrise on the 25th, and had been absent ever since. About four hours after his departure the wind changed, and a dense fog obscured every mark by which his course to the tents could be directed, and we thought it probable he had been wandering in an opposite direction to our situation, as the two hunters, who had been sent to look for him, returned at sunset without having seen him. Akaitcho arrived with his party, and we were greatly disappointed at finding they had stored up only fifteen reindeer for us. St. Germain informed us that having heard of the death of the chief's brother-in-law, they had spent several days in bewailing his loss, instead of hunting. We learned also, that the decease of this man had caused another party of the tribe, who had been sent by Mr. Wentzel to prepare provision for us on the banks of the Copper-Mine River, to remove to the shores of the Great Bear Lake, distant from our proposed route. Mortifying as these circumstances were, they produced less painful

sensations than we experienced in the evening, by the refusal of
Akaitcho to accompany us in the proposed descent of the Copper-
Mine River. When Mr. Wentzel, by my direction, communicated to
him my intention of proceeding at once on that service, he desired a
conference with me upon the subject, which being immediately
granted, he began by stating that the very attempt would be rash and
dangerous, as the weather was cold, the leaves were falling, some
geese had passed to the southward, and the winter would shortly set
in; and that, as he considered the lives of all who went on such a
journey would be forfeited, he neither would go himself, nor permit
his hunters to accompany us. He said there was no wood within
eleven days' march, during which time we could not have any fire,
as the moss, which the Indians use in their summer excursions, would
be too wet for burning, in consequence of the recent rains; that we
should be forty days in descending the Copper-Mine River, six of
which would be expended in getting to its banks, and that we might
be blocked up by the ice in the next moon; and during the whole
journey the party must experience great sufferings for want of food,
as the reindeer had already left the river.

He was now reminded that these statements were very different
from the account he had given, both at Fort Providence and on the
route hither; and that up to this moment we had been encouraged by
his conversation to expect that the party might descend the Copper-
Mine River accompanied by the Indians. He replied, that at the
former place he had been unacquainted with our slow mode of
travelling, and that the alteration in his opinion arose from the
advance of winter.

We now informed him that we were provided with instruments
by which we could ascertain the state of the air and water, and that
we did not imagine the winter to be so near as he supposed; however,
we promised to return on discovering the first change in the season.
He was also told that all the baggage being left behind, our canoes
would now of course travel infinitely more expeditiously than anything he had hitherto witnessed. Akaitcho appeared to feel hurt that
we should continue to press the matter further, and answered with
some warmth: "Well, I have said everything I can urge to dissuade
you from going on this service, on which, it seems, you wish to
sacrifice your own lives, as well as the Indians who might attend you:
however, if after all I have said you are determined to go, some of
my young men shall join the party, because it shall not be said, that
we permitted you to die alone after having brought you hither; but

from the moment they embark in the canoes, I and my relatives shall lament them as dead."

We could only reply to this forcible appeal, by assuring him and the Indians who were seated around him, that we felt the most anxious solicitude for the safety of every individual, and that it was far from our intention to proceed without considering every argument for and against the proposed journey.

We next informed him that it would be very desirable to see the river at any rate, that we might give some positive information about its situation and size in our next letters to the Great Chief and that we were very anxious to get on its banks, for the purpose of observing an eclipse of the sun, which we described to him, and said would happen in a few days. He received this communication with more temper than the preceding, though he immediately assigned as a reason for his declining to go, that "the Indians must now procure a sufficient quantity of deer-skins for winter clothing for themselves, and dresses for the Canadians, who would need them if they had to travel in the winter." Finding him so averse to proceed, and feeling at the same time how essential his continuance with us was, not only to our future success, but even to our existence during the winter, I closed the conversation here, intending to propose to him next morning some modification of the plan, which might meet with his approbation. Soon after we were gone, however, he informed Mr. Wentzel, with whom he was in the habit of speaking confidentially, that as his advice was neglected, his presence was useless, and he should, therefore, return to Fort Providence with his hunters after he had collected some winter provision for us. Mr. Wentzel having reported this to me, the night was passed in great anxiety, and after weighing all the arguments that presented themselves to my mind, I came reluctantly to the determination of relinquishing the intention of going any distance down the river this season.

Actually, Franklin did realize that winter was fast approaching and this helped him reach the decision not to go on. But if Akaitcho had agreed to participate, he would have persisted in the attempt. Next morning when he told the officers that he had given up his plan, they agreed that he was right in doing so. They suggested, however, that a small party should be sent as far as the Coppermine to discover its distance from the camp and its size. Franklin immediately accepted this alternative and decided to send Back and Hood as soon as possible in a light canoe.

That same morning, August 27, the officers experienced a sample of what Franklin called the Indians' "versatility." It made them very uneasy, since it involved Hepburn's safety. On reaching camp the night before, the Indians had expressed great concern when they heard he was missing and volunteered to go in search of him first thing next morning. But hearing of Franklin's argument with their chief, they changed their minds and next morning showed no interest in going. Franklin finally persuaded three hunters and a boy to set out and in the afternoon they were successful in finding Hepburn, who was brought back to camp in an exhausted condition. When the fog had descended on the twenty-fifth he had found himself lost. He had had a partridge and some berries to eat, and later on he had shot a deer, but by then his nervous tension was so great that he could not eat, and took only the tongue, and the skin for protection against the wind and the rain. He had become very upset to think that the party would have to delay their departure for the Coppermine on his account, or else leave without him. But a hearty supper and a long night's sleep restored him to his customary health and good spirits.

When Franklin told Akaitcho of his plan to go only as far as the Coppermine, rather than try to descend it, the Chief gave immediate approval and said that he would send two hunters with the party to supply food and act as guides. Franklin's next objective was to get the Indians out to their hunting grounds to procure meat for the winter and deer fat for making pemmican. He had them supplied with ammunition, clothing and other needed articles, and instructed them to leave without delay.

Akaitcho came into our tent this evening [August 28] at supper, and made several pertinent inquiries respecting the eclipse, of which we had spoken last night. He desired to know the effect that would be produced, and the cause of it, which we endeavoured to explain; and having gained this information, he sent for several of his companions, that they might also have it repeated to them. They were most astonished at our knowing the time at which this event should happen, and remarked that this knowledge was a striking proof of the superiority of the whites over the Indians. We took advantage of this occasion to speak to them respecting the Supreme Being, who ordered all the operations of nature, and to impress on their minds the necessity of paying strict attention to their moral duties, in obedience to His will. They readily assented to all these points, and Akaitcho assured us that both himself and his young men would exert themselves in obtaining provision for us, in return for the interesting communications we had just made to them.

Back and Hood left for the Coppermine on August 29, taking with them an interpreter, a hunter and eight voyageurs. On September 6 Franklin moved his tent to the top of a hill three miles from camp where he would be in a better position to observe the eclipse, which he calculated would occur next morning. But all that next day the heavens were completely blotted out by a heavy snowstorm and nothing could be seen. During this period he watched for any change in the weather. It seemed to him that the wind strengthened and that the snow fell in heavier flakes.

Although he had already dispatched Hood and Back, Franklin's keenness to see the Coppermine for himself now got the better of him, and a few days later he and Dr. Richardson set out on foot. With them went an elderly guide called Keskarrah, one of the voyageurs and Hepburn. The first night out they camped under four ancient pines that stood six to seven feet high. They had cut off a few branches to make their beds and were about to cut down one of the trees for firewood when the guide protested in sign language that they should leave it standing. The trees, he said, had long been landmarks for his people. Franklin complied and they settled for a fire made of the roots of a dwarf birch. The two officers went to bed without undressing, for they had only one blanket each. Keskarrah, however, stripped to the skin, toasted his body for a short time over the embers of the fire and then curled himself under his deerskin and rags. He was asleep in no time. Franklin noted in his journal that Indians often undressed completely for the night, even when lying in the open air.

During the next few days of walking, the five men were wet and cold most of the time but they had plenty to eat, since Keskarrah shot several deer. On the afternoon of the third day the party stood on the banks of the Coppermine. The main channel was deep, with high, rocky banks, and the surrounding country was well wooded with spruce. It promised well for the next summer.

Satisfied at having seen the river that would carry him to the Arctic sea, Franklin turned back toward the camp. It was only September 13 but winter was fast setting in with snow and frost, and the return walk was rigorous. On the last day the five men walked twenty-two miles with nothing to eat, but back at the base a substantial meal of reindeer steaks revived them, and they enjoyed comparing notes with Back and Hood.

For the next nine months Franklin and his men were to be based in the two log houses that were now under construction, to which they gave the name Fort Enterprise. The men had almost completed the officers' house when on September 30 a heavy rainfall washed the greater part of the mud off the roof. The Indians were surprised to see the rain, since they considered winter to have started early in the month.

Most of the men were fully employed on the construction work, but two were appointed to fish and others were occasionally sent out to the hunters to bring in meat. The voyageurs liked being chosen to fetch the meat, though it was hard work, for it gave them the chance to help themselves to the fattest and most delicate parts of the deer. Toward the end of the month the reindeer began to leave the barren lands and move to the vicinity of the camp on their way south to the woods. The hunters were therefore able to kill more deer, and additional men had to be taken off construction to bring in meat.

While the building was going on the whole party lived in canvas tents, which were very cold, though a fire was kept burning in front of them. On October 6 the officers were at last able to move into their house. The building measured fifty by twenty-four feet and was divided into a hall, three bedrooms and a kitchen. The floor was laid with planks roughly squared with axes; the windows were covered with parchment made from deerskin, while the walls and roof were plastered with clay that froze the moment it was put on and then cracked badly. Though the wind blew in from every direction, the house was comfortable compared to the tents, and the officers were glad to move in. The large chimney, lined with clay, drew well and a blazing fire did a world of good, especially for Dr. Richardson, who had a sore throat that was getting steadily worse in the tent. In the house he soon recovered, in spite of the drafts.

To begin with the officers slept on the floor but the men soon proved themselves as skilled at making furniture as at building houses. Besides their axes, all they had to work with were their crooked knives, made from old files tempered by heat. These the Indians and voyageurs used as plane, chisel and auger; they were adequate to make snowshoes, the frames for canoes, wooden bowls and spoons—and now beds, tables and chairs.

On the 7th we were gratified by a sight of the sun, after it had been obscured for twelve days. On this and several following days the meridian sun melted the light covering of snow or hoar frost on the lichens, which clothe the barren grounds, and rendered them so tender as to attract great herds of reindeer to our neighbourhood. On the morning of the 10th I estimated the numbers I saw during a short walk, at upwards of two thousand. They form into herds of different sizes, from ten to a hundred, according as their fears or accident induce them to unite or separate.

.   .   .   .   .

The herds of reindeer are attended in their migrations by bands of wolves, which destroy a great many of them. The Copper Indians kill the reindeer in the summer with the gun, or taking advantage of a favourable disposition of the ground, they enclose a herd upon a neck of land, and drive them into a lake, where they fall an easy prey; but in the rutting season and in the spring, when they are numerous on the skirts of the woods, they catch them in snares. The snares are simple nooses, formed in a rope made of twisted sinew, which are placed in the aperture of a slight hedge, constructed of the branches of trees. This hedge is so disposed as to form several winding compartments, and although it is by no means strong, yet the deer seldom attempt to break through it. The herd is led into the labyrinth by two converging rows of poles, and one is generally caught at each of the openings by the noose placed there. The hunter, too, lying in ambush, stabs some of them with his bayonet as they pass by, and the whole herd frequently becomes his prey. Where wood is scarce, a piece of turf turned up answers the purpose of a pole to conduct them towards the snares.

The reindeer has a quick eye, but the hunter by keeping to leeward and using a little caution, may approach very near; their apprehensions being much more easily roused by the smell than the sight of any unusual object. Indeed their curiosity often causes them to come

close up and wheel around the hunter; thus affording him a good
opportunity of singling out the fattest of the herd, and upon these
occasions they often become so confused by the shouts and gestures
of their enemy, that they run backwards and forwards with great
rapidity, but without the power of making their escape.

•   •   •   •   •

The Dog-Rib Indians have a mode of killing these animals, which
though simple, is very successful. The hunters go in pairs, the fore-
most man carrying in one hand the horns and part of the skin of the
head of a deer, and in the other a small bundle of twigs, against
which he, from time to time, rubs the horns, imitating the gestures
peculiar to the animal. His comrade follows treading exactly in his
footsteps, and holding the guns of both in a horizontal position, so
that the muzzles project under the arms of him who carries the head.
Both hunters have a fillet of white skin round their foreheads, and
the foremost has a strip of the same kind round his wrists. They
approach the herd by degrees, raising their legs very slowly, but
setting them down somewhat suddenly, after the manner of a deer,
and always taking care to lift their right or left feet simultaneously.
If any of the herd leave off feeding to gaze upon this extraordinary
phenomenon, it instantly stops, and the head begins to play its part
by licking its shoulders, and performing other necessary movements.
In this way the hunters attain the very centre of the herd without
exciting suspicion, and have leisure to single out the fattest. The
hindmost man then pushes forward his comrade's gun, the head is
dropped, and they both fire nearly at the same instant. The herd
scampers off, the hunters trot after them; in a short time the poor
animals halt to ascertain the cause of their terror, their foes stop at
the same instant, and having loaded as they ran, greet the gazers with
a second fatal discharge. The consternation of the deer increases, they
run to and fro in the utmost confusion, and sometimes a great part of
the herd is destroyed within the space of a few hundred yards.

The weather was getting colder every day and the lakes in the area
were now completely frozen. The reindeer began to move away toward
the south, but this made little difference to the hunting because the
ammunition was almost completely used up. The Indians had by then
brought in the carcasses of 100 deer, together with 1000 pounds of suet
and some dried meat. In addition, about eighty deer were cached at
different places some distance from the fort. It was risky leaving them

there, though they were protected by loads of wood or stone, because the wolves or wolverines would sometimes smell the meat and get at it. But for the moment it was a necessity because the men had to concentrate on completing their house before the weather became too cold.

When the time came to make snowshoes a few men were briefly taken off construction work to collect birch for making the frames. Once these were completed, the women netted them and then went on to prepare leather for winter clothing. Robes made of reindeer skin were secured from the Indians and issued to those of the men who would be involved in winter travel. These skins were lighter and warmer than blankets but could only be used in winter, for moisture spoiled the skin.

As the weather got colder the fishing grew steadily worse and by the end of the month they had to give it up altogether. By that time they had caught 1200 whitefish averaging two to three pounds each. The fish froze as they were taken from the nets but they seemed to come to life again when placed before the fire. Franklin noted that he had seen a carp "recover so far as to leap about with much vigour" even after it had been in a frozen state for thirty-six hours.

On October 18 Back and Wentzel, with an interpreter and several Indians, left for Fort Providence. The supplies from Cumberland House should have reached that post by then, and they were badly needed at Fort Enterprise. Back was directed to secure any additional supplies available at the Great Slave Lake posts, and if the Cumberland House supplies had *not* arrived, he was to continue to Fort Chipewyan and pick up everything available there. Ammunition was essential for the party's existence. Tobacco was needed for the voyageurs and the Indians, especially if the friendship of the latter was to be retained. Blankets, cloth and iron work were needed almost as badly. Wentzel accompanied Back; he knew the traders at the different posts and it seemed likely that he would be able to get more from them. As always when anyone went out, letters were sent along, addressed to the Colonial Office and the Admiralty in London.

Akaitcho and his party of hunters arrived at the Fort on October 26. The deer by then had moved farther south and hunting was over for the season. Franklin was very unhappy at having extra mouths to feed but he could not send the Indians back to the woods because he had no ammunition to give them. He knew that they were accustomed to maintain themselves in the woods for a large part of the year without firearms, but Akaitcho's men showed no desire to move on so long as there seemed to be ample supplies of meat in the storehouse. From time to time they would tell the officers how keen they were to go hunting and would ask for ammunition, knowing that there was none available.

By the end of October the men had finished their house and moved in. It measured thirty-four by eighteen feet and was divided into two rooms. The officers' house, men's house and storeroom were now complete; together they formed three sides of a quadrangle.

> We had become anxious [mid-November] to hear of the arrival of Mr. Back and his party at Fort Providence. The Indians, who had calculated the period at which a messenger ought to have returned from thence to be already passed, became impatient when it had elapsed, and with their usual love of evil augury tormented us by their melancholy forebodings. At one time they conjectured that the whole party had fallen through the ice; at another, that they had been waylaid and cut off by the Dog-Ribs. In vain did we urge the improbability of the former accident, or the peaceable character of the Dog-Ribs, so little in conformity with the latter. "The ice at this season was deceitful," they said, "and the Dog-Ribs, though unwarlike, were treacherous." These assertions, so often repeated, had some effect upon the spirits of our Canadian voyagers who seldom weigh any opinion they adopt; but we persisted in treating their fears as chimerical, for had we seemed to listen to them for a moment, it is more than probable that the whole of our Indians would have gone to Fort Providence in search of supplies, and we should have found it extremely difficult to have recovered them.

Finally, on November 23, Belanger, who had accompanied Back as interpreter, burst into the house so covered in ice as to be scarcely recognizable. He had been sent back to announce the safe arrival of the party at Fort Providence and to bring the mail. He had walked non-stop for thirty-six hours after leaving his Indian companions in the rear. "We welcomed him with the usual shake of the hand, but were unable to give him the glass of rum which every voyageur receives on his arrival at a trading post." As soon as his packet had thawed sufficiently to be opened, the officers eagerly attacked their English letters, even though the most recent ones had been written more than six months earlier.

The interpreter brought unpleasant news concerning their supplies. Governor Williams had shipped ten bales of their stores from York Factory, each of them weighing ninety pounds. Of these, the five most essential ones had been abandoned on the banks of the Saskatchewan. When overtaken at the Grand Rapids by some North West Company canoes the officer to whom the supplies had been entrusted had insisted that the Nor' Westers take half his load, since it was all "intended for the service of Government." The North West men had replied that their instructions were to carry the stores westward only from Cumberland House. They had a canoe waiting there for that purpose, they said, but could carry nothing extra until then, since their canoes were fully loaded. After this argument, the Hudson's Bay officer had dumped the bales containing the ammunition and tobacco on the beach and continued on his way with no thought of the serious consequences for Franklin and his party.

The Indians who had assembled to watch the packet being opened quickly understood the situation about the lost bales, accepting the bad news with unexpected calmness. Franklin used the occasion to speak to them. He minimized the negative points and emphasized the positive news that two Eskimo interpreters had reached Great Slave Lake and were on their way to join the expedition. The Indians were impressed that he had the influence to bring two Eskimos such a great distance. Akaitcho understood the situation perfectly. He was a very shrewd man, often surprising Franklin by the correctness of his judgement of people and by his ability to separate what they said from what they actually did.

In addition to letters the packet contained some London newspapers which told of the death of George III and the proclamation of George IV as King. Franklin kept this news from the Indians in case the death of their "Great Father" should lead them to fear that the promises made in his name would not now be carried out.

The Indians who had been travelling with Belanger arrived next day at the post. They brought word that Weeks, the post manager at Fort Providence, was spreading derogatory stories about the expedition. He had told them, they claimed, that Franklin and his companions were not officers of a great king, as they pretended to be, but "a set of dependant wretches." He said that they were trying to live off the Indians, who stood no chance of being repaid for their services. Akaitcho went immediately to Franklin with the whole story and said that, personally, he did not believe it.

I then pointed out to him that Mr. Wentzel, with whom they had long been accustomed to trade, had pledged the credit of his Company for the stipulated rewards to the party that accompanied us, and that the trading debts due by Akaitcho and his party had already been remitted, which was of itself a sufficient proof of our

influence with the North-West Company. I also reminded Akaitcho
that our having caused the Eskimos to be brought up at a great
expense was evidence of our future intentions, and informed him
that I should write to Mr. Smith, the senior trader in the depart-
ment, on the subject, when I had no doubt that a satisfactory ex-
planation would be given. The Indians retired from the conference
apparently satisfied, but this business was in the end productive of
much inconvenience to us, and proved very detrimental to the
progress of the Expedition.

On November 28 Franklin sent St. Germain, an interpreter, with a
party of eight voyageurs and four Indian hunters to Fort Providence
for additional supplies. With them went letters to the Hudson's Bay
and North West officials at other posts requesting supplies. A stray
dog that had attached itself to St. Germain went with the party, and
though the voyageurs had plenty to eat, they killed and ate it on their
first night out. Franklin later noted in his journal, "A dog is considered
delicate eating by the voyageurs."

The Indians, forty of them including the women and children, were
by now eating Franklin out of house and home and in early December
they were finally persuaded to move on. Franklin gave them a hundred
balls which had been brought from Fort Providence by Belanger, along
with a fishing net.

Keskarrah, the guide . . . remained behind, with his wife and
daughter. The old man has become too feeble to hunt, and his time
is almost entirely occupied in attendance upon his wife, who has
been long affected with an ulcer on the face, which has nearly
destroyed her nose.

Lately he made an offering to the water spirits, whose wrath he
apprehended to be the cause of her malady. It consisted of a knife,
a piece of tobacco, and some other trifling articles, which were tied
up in a small bundle, and committed to the rapid with a long
prayer. He does not trust entirely, however, to the relenting of the
spirits for his wife's cure, but come daily to Dr. Richardson for
medicine.

Upon one occasion he received the medicine from the Doctor
with such formality, and wrapped it up in his reindeer robe with
such extraordinary carefulness, that it excited the involuntary
laughter of Mr. Hood and myself. The old man smiled in his turn,
and as he always seemed proud of the familiar way in which we

were accustomed to joke with him, we thought no more upon the
subject. But he unfortunately mentioned the circumstance to his
wife, who imagined in consequence, that the drug was not produc-
tive of its usual good effects, and they immediately came to the
conclusion that some bad medicine had been intentionally given to
them. The distress produced by this idea was in proportion to their
former faith in the potency of the remedy, and the night was spent
in singing and groaning. Next morning the whole family were cry-
ing in concert, and it was not until the evening of the second day
that we succeeded in pacifying them. The old woman began to feel
better, and her faith in the medicine was renewed.

While speaking of this family, I may remark that the daughter,
whom we designated Green-stockings from her dress, is considered
by her tribe to be a great beauty. Mr. Hood drew an accurate por-
trait of her, although her mother was averse to her sitting for it.
She was afraid, she said, that her daughter's likeness would induce
the Great Chief who resided in England to send for the original. The
young lady, however, was undeterred by any such fear. She has
already been an object of contest between her countrymen, and
although under sixteen years of age, has belonged successively to
two husbands, and would probably have been the wife of many
more, if her mother had not required her services as a nurse.

December was the coldest month experienced by the members of the
expedition during their three years in North America. The average
for the month was twenty-nine degrees below zero and one day the
temperature went down to fifty-seven below. Fortunately there was
very little wind, so that the woodcutters and others who had to go
out suffered no ill effects as they went about their daily work. They
wore reindeer shirts, leather mitts lined with wool, and fur caps. But
they had no protection for their faces, nor needed any, since there
was no wind. However, the intense cold caused the trees to freeze to
their centres and become as hard as stone. Every day some of the
axes were broken, and by the end of the month only one was left.
This was put into the sole charge of the best woodsman, who managed
to keep it in service until the men returned from Fort Providence
bringing a fresh supply.

A thermometer hanging in the officers' bedroom about sixteen feet
from the fire occasionally registered fifteen below, even when the
fire was blazing, and one morning before the fire was lit it registered
forty below. The sun would peep out over a small ridge of hills at

half-past eleven and sink below it at half-past two. For twenty-eight
nights in December the northern lights appeared with varying degrees
of brilliance, and the beauty of the moon was uncanny. It barely disappeared below the horizon in twenty-four hours. Often there was a
halo showing around it, the same phenomenon observed round the
candles in the bedrooms.

The officers never found time hanging heavy on their hands. Franklin
re-checked all the observations made along the route during the year.
Hood worked on his maps, and on the birds, plants and fish he had
sketched earlier. Dr. Richardson managed to get specimens of the
different kinds of moss in the neighbourhood from under the snow,
and to study the mineral formations. They all spent a good deal of
time writing up their journals and read and re-read the newspapers
and magazines received earlier from England. There were endless dis-
cussions and many guesses as to what was happening in the outside
world and when the next batch of letters would reach them. Sometimes they paid a visit to the woodsmen or walked a mile or two along
the River. Often at night they joined the men in the hall and took part
in their games, which usually continued to a late hour.

Sunday was always a day of rest. The woodsmen were expected to
bring in enough wood on Saturday to last until Monday. The whole
party put on their best clothes and all attended divine service. Though
the voyageurs were Roman Catholics and could hardly understand a
word of English, they always attended the service and behaved with
great dignity. Franklin often regretted that he had not brought a
French Prayer Book with him but he did the best he could and always
had the Lord's Prayer and the Creed read in French.

*Our diet consisted almost entirely of reindeer meat, varied twice
a week by fish, and occasionally by a little flour, but we had no
vegetables of any description. On the Sunday mornings we drank
a cup of chocolate, but our greatest luxury was tea (without sugar),
of which we regularly partook twice a day. With reindeer's fat, and
strips of cotton shirts, we formed candles; and Hepburn acquired
considerable skill in the manufacture of soap, from the wood-ashes,
fat and salt. The formation of soap was considered as rather a
mysterious operation by our voyageurs and, in their hands, was
always supposed to fail if a woman approached the kettle in which
the ley was boiling. Such are our simple domestic details.*

On January 1, 1821 everybody collected in the hall first thing in the morning and wished each other a Happy New Year. A double supply of firewood had been collected and no one did any work. For months the voyageurs had been talking about the traditional New Year's feast, and to the last hour of the day they hoped that the party from Fort Providence would get back with the supplies. The morning had dawned, the hour of the feast had arrived but there was no sign of the men with supplies. A little flour and fat had to serve as the extra makings for the feast and though they were considered great luxuries at that time, with no rum the feast left a lot to be desired!

Finally, on January 15, seven men arrived from Fort Providence bringing with them two kegs of rum, a barrel of powder, sixty pounds of ball, two rolls of tobacco and some clothing. It had taken them twenty-one days to walk from Great Slave Lake and the shoulders of their coats were worn through from the pull of their sledge collars. Each man had carried a load of from sixty to ninety pounds, plus bedding and provisions. And at the beginning of the trip the foodstuffs must have weighed as much again. There was shouting, joking and general rejoicing when a cask of rum was opened and the promised New Year issue doled out.

The spirits, which were proof, were frozen, but after standing at the fire for some time they flowed out with the consistency of honey. The temperature of the liquid, even in this state, was so low as instantly to convert into ice the moisture which condensed on the surface of the dram-glass. The fingers also adhered to the glass, and would, doubtless, have been speedily frozen had they been kept in contact with it; yet each of the voyageurs swallowed his dram without experiencing the slightest inconvenience, or complaining even of the toothache.

At the end of the party one of the Indians who had travelled with the men told Franklin that the voyageurs had opened one of the casks along the way and spent two days drinking. Franklin knew very well the hardships endured by the voyageurs and always tried to lessen them, but it distressed him that they had broken their trust in this way. He decided that a voyageur could not be trusted far when it came to food or spirits.

As they were pretty well aware that such a circumstance could not long be concealed from us, one of them came the next morning with an artful apology for their conduct. He stated that as they

knew it was my intention to treat them with a dram on the com-
mencement of the new year, they had helped themselves to a small
quantity on that day, trusting to my goodness for forgiveness; and
being unwilling to act harshly at this period, I did forgive them,
after admonishing them to be very circumspect in their future
conduct.

Immediately after the arrival of the supplies, some ammunition and a
small present of rum were sent to Akaitcho.

At the end of January Wentzel arrived back from Fort Providence
with the two Eskimo interpreters. Their real names were Tattannoeuck
and Hoeootoerock, meaning The Belly and The Ear, but the traders at
Churchill had given them the easier names of Augustus and Junius. It
was a great help that Augustus could speak English.

On comparing the language of our two Eskimos with a copy of
St. John's Gospel, printed for the use of the Moravian Missionary
Settlements on the Labrador coast, it appeared that the Eskimos who
resort to Churchill speak a language essentially the same with those
who frequent the Labrador coast.

.   .   .   .   .

Upon the map being spread before Augustus, he soon compre-
hended it, and recognised Chesterfield Inlet to be "the opening into
which salt waters enter at spring tides, and which receives a river
at its upper end."

About this time, disquieting word reached Franklin that Akaitcho's
confidence in him was being shaken by some of the things Weeks had
been saying about the expedition. He sent the Chief some powder and
shot and a keg of diluted spirits, along with assurances of his regard,
and was relieved a few days later when fresh supplies of meat were
brought in from Akaitcho.

In spite of this, the food situation was becoming serious. The storehouse was nearly empty and the men's rations had to be cut from
eight pounds a day to five. Some men were sent out to bring in the
meat that had been cached earlier in the winter but they returned to
report that more than half the deposits had been taken by wolves or
wolverines. Wolves were prowling about the house every night, sometimes becoming so bold as to jump on the kitchen roof in search of
food.

On March 5 some men who had been sent to Great Slave Lake in early February returned with the balance of the stores—flour, sugar, tobacco and powder. With them came a letter from Weeks denying that he had said anything negative about the expedition. He even claimed to have urged Akaitcho to stay with the expedition when he was thinking of pulling out. One of the hunters, having learned of the letter, expressed amazement that Weeks would dare to make such a complete denial of his previous charges; he had personally heard Weeks make such charges, he said. Whatever Weeks had or had not told Akaitcho, the Chief was evidently recovering his good spirits. St. Germain came in from his camp to report that he had left Akaitcho in good humour, with no thought of leaving the expedition.

Franklin had been observing the customs and nature of the Copper Indians and on March 18 he inserted an account of their origin and way of life in his journal.

> I shall now give a brief account of the Copper Indians. . . . They were originally a tribe of the Chipewyans, and, according to their own account, inhabited the south side of Great Slave Lake, at no very distant period. Their language, traditions, and customs are essentially the same with those of the Chipewyans, but in personal character they have greatly the advantage of that people; owing, probably to local causes, or perhaps to their procuring their food more easily and in greater abundance. They hold women in the same low estimation as the Chipewyans do, looking upon them as a kind of property, which the stronger may take from the weaker, whenever there is just reason for quarrelling, if the parties are of their own nation, or whenever they meet, if the weaker party are Dog-Ribs or other strangers. They suffer, however, the kinder affections to show themselves occasionally; they, in general, live happily with their wives, the women are contented with their lot, and we witnessed several instances of strong attachment. Of their kindness to strangers we are fully qualified to speak; their love of property, attention to their interests, and fears for the future, made them occasionally clamorous and unsteady; but their delicate and humane attention to us, in a season of great distress, at a future period, are indelibly engraven on our memories. Of their notions of a Deity, or future state, we never could obtain any satisfactory account; they were unwilling, perhaps, to expose their opinions to the chance of ridicule. Akaitcho generally evaded our questions on these points,

but expressed a desire to learn from us, and regularly attended Divine Service during his residence at the fort, behaving with the utmost decorum.

This leader, indeed, and many others of his tribe, possess a laudable curiosity, which might easily be directed to the most important ends; and I believe that a well-conducted Christian mission to this quarter would not fail of producing the happiest effect. Old Keskarrah alone used boldly to express his disbelief of a Supreme Deity, and state that he could not credit the existence of a Being whose power was said to extend everywhere, but whom he had not yet seen, although he was now an old man. The aged sceptic is not a little conceited, as the following exordium to one of his speeches evinces: "It is strange that I never meet with any one who is equal in sense to myself."

.   .   .   .   .

Few of this nation have more than one wife at a time, and none but the leaders have more than two. Akaitcho has three, and the mother of his only son is the favourite. They frequently marry two sisters, and there is no prohibition to the intermarriage of cousins, but a man is restricted from marrying his niece.

The last war excursion they made against the Eskimos was ten years ago, when they destroyed about thirty persons, at the mouth of what they term Stony-Point River, not far from the mouth of the Copper-Mine River. They now seem desirous of being on friendly terms with that persecuted nation, and hope through our means, to establish a lucrative commerce with them. Indeed, the Copper Indians are sensible of the advantages that would accrue to them, were they made the carriers of goods between the traders and Eskimos.

At the time of Hearne's visit, the Copper Indians being unsupplied with firearms, were oppressed by the Chipewyans; but even that traveller had occasion to praise their kindness of heart. Since they have received arms from the traders, the Chipewyans are fearful of venturing upon their lands; and all of that nation, who frequent the shores of Great Slave Lake, hold the name of Akaitcho in great respect. The Chipewyans have no leader of equal authority amongst themselves.

The number of the Copper Indians may be one hundred and ninety souls, viz., eighty men and boys, and one hundred and ten women and young children. There are forty-five hunters in the tribe.

The adherents of Akaitcho amount to about forty men and boys; the rest follow a number of minor chiefs. . . . The Thlingcha-dinneh, or Dog-Ribs, or . . . Slaves, inhabit the country to the westward of the Copper Indians, as far as Mackenzie's River. They are of a mild, hospitable, but rather indolent disposition; spend much of their time in amusements, and are fond of singing and dancing. In this respect, and in another, they differ very widely from most of the other aborigines of North America. I allude to their kind treatment of the women. The men do the laborious work, while their wives employ themselves in ornamenting their dresses with quill-work, and in other occupations suited to their sex. Mr. Wentzel has often known the young married men to bring specimens of their wives' needle-work to the forts, and exhibit them with much pride. Kind treatment of the fair sex being usually considered as an indication of considerable progress in civilisation, it might be worth while to inquire how it happens that this tribe has stepped so far beyond its neighbours.

. . . . .

When bands of Dog-Ribs meet each other after a long absence, they perform a kind of dance. A piece of ground is cleared for the purpose, if in winter of the snow, or if in summer of the bushes; and the dance frequently lasts for two or three days, the parties relieving each other as they get tired. The two bands commence the dance with their backs turned to each other, the individuals following one another in Indian file, and holding the bow in the left hand, and an arrow in the right. They approach obliquely, after many turns, and when the two lines are closely back to back, they feign to see each other for the first time, and the bow is instantly transferred to the right hand, and the arrow to the left, signifying that it is not their intention to employ them against their friends.

George Back arrived from Fort Chipewyan on March 17 after an absence of five months. During that time he had travelled approximately 1100 miles on snowshoes, sleeping under the open sky with no covering but a blanket and deerskin. The temperature had often dropped to forty degrees below zero and once plunged to fifty-seven below. In his journal Back gave Franklin a full report of the situations that he had encountered. Franklin inserted the account at this point in his own narrative of the expedition:

> On quitting Fort Enterprise [October 18, 1820] with Mr. Wentzel and two voyageurs accompanied by two hunters and their wives, our route lay across the barren hills. We saw during the day a number of deer, and occasionally a solitary white wolf; and in the evening halted near a small knot of pines. . . . Early the next morning we continued our march, sometimes crossing small lakes (which were just frozen enough to bear us), and at other times going large circuits, in order to avoid those which were open. The walking was extremely bad throughout the day; for independent of the general unevenness of the ground, and the numberless large stones which lay scattered in every direction, the unusual warmth of the weather had dissolved the snow, which not only kept us constantly wet, but deprived us of a firm footing, so that the men, with their heavy burdens, were in momentary apprehension of falling. . . . We made about twelve miles this day. The night was fine, and the Aurora Borealis so vivid, that we imagined, more than once, that we heard a rustling noise like that of autumnal leaves stirred by the wind; but after two hours of attentive listening, we were not entirely convinced of the fact.

Next day fog slowed the progress of the party and forced an early encampment.

The cracking of the ice was so loud during the night as to resemble thunder, and the wolves howled around us. We were now at the commencement of the woods, and at an early hour, on the 21st, continued our journey over hills for three miles, when the appearance of some deer caused us to halt, and nearly the remainder of the day was passed in hunting them . . . .

The surrounding country was extremely rugged; the hills divided by deep ravines, and the valleys covered with broken masses of rocks and stones; yet the deer fly (as it were) over these impediments with apparent ease, seldom making a false step, and springing from crag to crag with all the confidence of the mountain goat. After passing Reindeer Lake, (where the ice was so thin as to bend at every step for nine miles,) we halted, perfectly satisfied with our escape from sinking into the water.

.   .   .   .   .

On the 27th we crossed two lakes, and performed a circuitous route, frequently crossing high hills to avoid those lakes which were not frozen; during the day one of the women made a hole through the ice, and caught a fine pike, which she gave to us; the Indians would not partake of it, from the idea (as we afterwards learnt), that we should not have sufficient for ourselves: "We are accustomed to starvation," said they, "but you are not."

.   .   .   .   .

On the 30th we set out with the expectation of gaining the Slave lake in the evening; but our progress was again impeded by the same causes as before, so that the whole day was spent in forcing our way through thick woods and over swamps covered with snow. We had to walk over pointed and loose rocks, which sliding from under our feet made our path dangerous, and often threw us down several feet on sharp-edged stones lying beneath the snow. Once we had to climb a towering, and almost perpendicular rock, which not only detained us, but was the cause of great anxiety for the safety of the women, who being heavily laden with furs, and one of them with a child at her back, could not exert themselves with the activity which such a task required. Fortunately nothing serious occurred, though one of them once fell with considerable violence. During the day one of the hunters broke through the ice, but was soon extricated; when it became dark we halted near the Bow String Portage, greatly disappointed at not having reached the lake. The weather was cloudy, accompanied with thick mist and snow. The

Indians expected to have found here a bear in its den, and to have made a hearty meal of its flesh: indeed it had been the subject of conversation all day, and they had even gone so far as to divide it, frequently asking me what part I preferred; but when we came to the spot—oh! lamentable! it had already fallen a prey to the devouring appetites of some more fortunate hunters, who had only left sufficient evidence that such a thing had once existed, and we had merely the consolation of realising an old proverb. One of our men, however, caught a fish which, with the assistance of some weed scraped from the rocks [tripe de roche] . . . made us a tolerable supper; it was not of the most choice kind, yet good enough for hungry men. While we were eating it I perceived one of the women busily employed scraping an old skin, the contents of which her husband presented us with. They consisted of pounded meat, fat, and a greater proportion of Indians' and deers' hair than either; and though such a mixture may not appear very alluring to an English stomach, it was thought a great luxury after three days' privation in these cheerless regions of America. Indeed had it not been for the precaution and generosity of the Indians, we must have gone without sustenance until we reached the fort.

    •   •   •   •   •

. . . at noon [November 2] we arrived at Fort Providence, and were received by Mr. Weeks, a clerk of the North-West Company, in charge of the establishment. I found several packets of letters for the officers, which I was desirous of sending to them immediately; but as the Indians and their wives complained of illness and inability to return without rest, a flagon of mixed spirits was given them, and their sorrows were soon forgotten. In a quarter of an hour they pronounced themselves excellent hunters, and capable of going anywhere; however, their boasting ceased with the last drop of the bottle, when a crying scene took place, which would have continued half the night, had not the magic of an additional quantity of spirits dried their tears, and once more turned their mourning to joy. It was a satisfaction to me to behold these poor creatures enjoying themselves, for they had behaved in the most exemplary and active manner towards the party, and with a generosity and sympathy seldom found even in the more civilised parts of the world: and the attention and affection which they manifested towards their wives evinced a benevolence of disposition and goodness of nature which could not fail to secure the approbation of the most indifferent observer.

The accounts I here received of our goods were of so unsatis-
factory a nature, that I determined to proceed, as soon as the lake
was frozen, to Moose-Deer Island, or if necessary to the Athabasca
Lake, both to inform myself of the grounds of the unceremonious
and negligent manner in which the Expedition had been treated, and
to obtain a sufficient supply of ammunition and other stores, to
enable it to leave its present situation, and proceed for the attain-
ment of its ultimate object.

Having sent one of the men and some Indians back to Fort Enterprise
with the mail and some ammunition, Back continued to Moose-Deer
Island, and on December 10 reached the North West Company's post,
where his fears of negligence were confirmed. Only five packages had
reached the post. These included three kegs of rum, part of which
had already been consumed by the voyageurs, a keg of flour and thirty-
five pounds of sugar—instead of the expected sixty pounds. The two
most needed commodities, ammunition and tobacco, had been left
behind. Back rounded up absolutely everything at the post that would
be of use to the expedition and had it shipped immediately to Fort
Enterprise, but it represented only half of what was needed. There
seemed no alternative but to continue to Fort Chipewyan and try
there to secure additional supplies. The post manager at Moose-Deer
Island told him it was useless to go, that there was nothing to spare at
Chipewyan, and even if there were, supplies had never been transported such long distances during the winter. He said that while he
might manage to supply Back with one team of dogs to get him there,
they could not possibly bring him back and he would find none available at the other end.

Refusing to listen to all the objections, Back set out on December
23 with two voyageurs. It was a terrible journey. In his journal he
described the last two days of the year:

Our journey these days was by far the most annoying we had yet
experienced; but, independent of the vast masses of ice that were
piled on one another, as well as the numerous open places about
the rapids (and they did not a little impede us), there was a strong
gale from the north-west, and so dreadfully keen that our time was
occupied in rubbing the frozen parts of the face, and in attempting
to warm the hands, in order to be prepared for the next operation.
Scarcely was one place cured by constant friction than another was
frozen; and though there was nothing pleasant about it, yet it was

laughable enough to observe the dexterity which was used in chang-
ing the position of the hand from the face to the mitten, and vice
versa. One of the men was severely affected, the whole side of his
face being nearly raw. Towards sunset I suffered so much in my
knee and ankle, from a recent sprain, that it was with difficulty I
could proceed with snow-shoes to the encampment on the Stony
Islands. But in this point I was not singular: for Beauparlant was
almost as bad, and without the same cause.

In spite of the difficulties, Back and his companions made it to Chipewyan in ten days, instead of the sixteen he had been told it would
take. They had in fact set a record for winter travel. There was little
of what Back had come for at either the North West or Hudson's Bay
post, but additional supplies were expected to arrive shortly at the
latter post, so he settled in for a wait of several weeks.

During this time of enforced idleness Back made good friends among
the fur traders. One of the North West partners told him of an experience that he had had with the Aurora Borealis. The story impressed
Back so much that he included it in his journal:

He was travelling in a canoe in the English River, and had landed
near the Kettle Fall, when the coruscations of the Aurora Borealis
were so vivid and low that the voyageurs fell on their faces, and
began praying and crying, fearing they should be killed; he himself
threw away his gun and knife, that they might not attract the
flashes, for they were within two feet from the earth, flitting along
with incredible swiftness, and moving parallel to its surface. They
continued for upwards of five minutes, as near as he could judge,
and made a loud rustling noise, like the waving of a flag in a strong
breeze. After they had ceased, the sky became clear, with little wind.

Back remained at Fort Chipewyan for five weeks. Although some laden
sledges came to the post during that time, he was unable to obtain any
supplies for the expedition beyond the few available when he had first
arrived. Before leaving he presented both companies with a list of the
goods the expedition would need in the coming year.

On his arrival at Fort Enterprise on March 17, Back received a warm
welcome. The vivid way he described his adventures came as a breath
of fresh air to the rather stale atmosphere at the Fort, and while the
news he brought was far from satisfactory, it was best to know where
the expedition stood.

CHAPTER 8 ❖ ❖ ❖ ❖ ❖ ❖   SPRING AT FORT ENTERPRISE

Throughout the month of March there was reasonably fine weather at the Fort, although one day the temperature fell to forty-nine below. By the end of the month the winter stock of deer meat had been consumed and the residents of Fort Enterprise had to draw on supplies intended for use during the coming summer. Fishing under the ice contributed only two or three small fish a day. One day a message arrived from The Hook, the senior chief of the Copper Indians after Akaitcho. The Hook offered to supply the expedition with a quantity of dried meat in the early summer, provided he received goods and ammunition in return. It would be made available at a point on the Coppermine River, he said. Franklin very much wanted the meat but he lacked the goods and ammunition for such an exchange. He sent word to The Hook that he would be glad to pay by notes on the North West Company post.

At about this time several incidents came to Franklin's attention that made him suspect the reliability of the interpreters. Their talks with the Indians had apparently made them fear the dangers involved in exploring the Arctic sea and they had begun to encourage the hunters not to bring in too much meat. Their idea was that a shortage of food might hold the expedition back in the spring. The other voyageurs looked up to the interpreters with some deference and there was real danger of their becoming disaffected. When Franklin tackled St. Germain, who seemed to be the chief offender, he denied the charge. He did admit, however, that he had told Akaitcho he was being neglected and that the small quantity of rum given him was an insult. Later, Franklin observed in his journal:

Although perfectly convinced of his baseness, I could not dispense with his services; and had no other resource but to give him a serious

admonition and desire him to return to his duty; after endeavouring
to work upon his fears by an assurance that I would certainly
convey him to England for trial if the Expedition should be stopped
through his fault. He replied, "It is immaterial to me where I lose
my life, whether in England or in accompanying you to the sea,
for the whole party will perish." After this discussion, however, he
was more circumspect in his conduct.

When in late March Akaitcho visited the Fort, Franklin decided to
take the Chief into his confidence. He showed him the drawings and
maps that were about to be sent to England and went thoroughly into
his plans for the future. Akaitcho appreciated this mark of confidence
and gave his opinion that all the unfavourable rumours circulating
about the expedition were false. Taking advantage of the friendly
atmosphere, Franklin pointed out that in view of the all-too-short
open season he could not afford any delays; and a large quantity of
meat would have to be secured before they set out. Akaitcho promised that he and his young men would do everything possible to help.
He then agreed to accompany the expedition to the mouth of the
Coppermine, and provided no Eskimos were encountered would continue some distance along the coast. In spite of his fear of the Eskimos,
he wanted to make a friendly contact with them. It was an encouraging interview.

On April 4 the last of the supplies arranged for by Back arrived
from Fort Providence. The winter accumulation of journals, maps,
drawings and observations were packed in a box with letters addressed
to the Secretary of State for Colonial Affairs and sent to Fort Providence to be forwarded to London. Franklin wrote to Governor
Williams at York Factory, asking him to send a schooner up the north
coast of Hudson Bay to Wager Bay with supplies of food and clothing, in case the expedition should succeed in reaching that point.
(This must have seemed like a perfectly sensible request to Franklin,
for the only map in his possession—reproduced at the front of the
book—suggested that Wager Bay was directly accessible from the
Arctic sea. The map at the back of the book, which includes the coastline and islands mapped by Franklin and by those who went in search
of him after 1847, shows how impossible was his goal.)

There was now almost no food left in the storehouse and everyone
was put on short rations. The Indian women and children suffered
most. Franklin had urged them to move to Akaitcho's camp where

they would be more certain to receive food, but most of them were old and sick and reluctant to join a hunting camp that was often on the move. Nor did they want to leave Dr. Richardson and the medicine he gave them every day. They preferred to dig in the snow on the site of the autumn camp and look for bones, deer feet, bits of hide and other scraps.

When we beheld them gnawing the pieces of hide, and pounding the bones, for purpose of extracting some nourishment from them by boiling, we regretted our inability to relieve them, but little thought that we should ourselves be afterwards driven to the necessity of eagerly collecting these same bones a second time from the dunghill.

The long wait for spring, coupled with the short rations, was depressing the men. To divert them from their problems and help cheer them up Franklin organized sliding parties down the steep river bank, even though such activity increased their appetites. The sledges went at a great speed and often turned over. It was good fun, but Franklin sprained his knee when a fat Indian woman drove her sledge over him. The ice in the river was still five feet thick when they measured it on April 21, while that on the lake was six and a half feet thick.

A moose was killed on April 22 and that brought relief for the moment. Then Keskarrah killed a deer and the same night a good supply of meat arrived from Akaitcho's camp. Next morning Wentzel sent every available man out to the camp to bring more meat in as fast as the Indians procured it. Dr. Richardson went off to collect specimens of rocks and returned a few days later with the news that the reindeer were advancing toward them from the south. Patches of sandy ground began to appear through the snow near the house and the first days of May were fine and warm. On May 8 the first large housefly was seen, a sure sign of spring and one that gave everyone a topic of conversation for the rest of the day. Next day the approach of spring was still more agreeably confirmed by the appearance of a merganser duck, two gulls and some loons. Blueberries, crowberries, eyeberries and cranberries that had been covered and protected by the snow all winter were found and gathered in quantities.

The women and children and all but four of the men were sent to live with Akaitcho so that less meat would have to be brought from his camp to the Fort. Wentzel put some of these women to work, sending them into the woods to collect resin from the spruce trees. The gum was needed to repair the canoes, and he promised to pay them well for it.

When Wentzel returned to the Fort, Franklin had a frank talk with him about his summer plans. He intended to reduce the size of his party on arrival at the Arctic coast, keeping only enough men to handle two canoes. The fewer mouths to feed, the better. Wentzel had told him earlier that he wished to go no farther than the mouth of the Coppermine. Franklin now said that it would be invaluable to have him return from that point with the Indians, making sure that they left deposits of meat along the route and especially back at Fort Enterprise.

On May 21 two of Akaitcho's young men arrived to announce the approach of their chief and to ask that he be honoured by a salute. This was evidently going to be an official visit, which meant using precious ammunition to fire off muskets. Franklin had to agree, though he hated wasting the powder. Ammunition was sent back to the Chief so that he could return the salute. Franklin also sent him some tobacco, vermilion, a comb and a looking glass. The flag was flying at the Fort when Akaitcho arrived at eleven, and as he approached, muskets were discharged by some of the voyageurs. The young men with Akaitcho returned the compliment.

Preceded by his standard bearer, the Chief advanced with slow and stately step to the door of the house, where Franklin and Wentzel received him. He was not painted himself but his party had daubed themselves with vermilion, the old men with a spot on the right cheek and the young men with a spot on the left. On entering the house, the Chief sat down on a chest, while the others sat in a circle on the floor. The pipe was passed round several times and a bowl of spirits and water was placed on the floor with a few small presents of cloth, blankets, shirts, etc. for the Chief's acceptance and distribution. Though the quantity was small, it represented a considerable proportion of what was left.

Akaitcho then began a speech which indicated he had lost the good humour of his March visit. He first wanted to know whether any of the white men would actually return to his country if a passage by sea was discovered. On being told that it was probable but not certain, he said he hoped that suitable presents would be sent to him and his people, ". . . for the great Chief who commands where all the goods come from, must see from the drawings and descriptions of us and our country that we are a miserable people." Franklin replied that as long as the Chief fulfilled his engagements he would be remembered.

Akaitcho then complained that Weeks had refused to honour Franklin's notes. How, he asked, could he expect the promised large rewards to be paid after Franklin had left the country, if notes for trifling amounts were not accepted when he was still near at hand. He had come to the conclusion that both trading companies were hostile to the expedition and that neither would honour the notes given to the Indians. He also maintained that he was given too little honour as chief, that the rum was too weak and the presents too few, and that he had not been given a new chief's outfit that spring, as he had in previous years. He underlined his complaints by refusing to accept the goods now laid before him.

Franklin refused to give an inch. He made no apologies. Complaints about Week's conduct could not be discussed profitably at such a distance from his post, he said, and no dependence could be placed on the rumours floating about. He himself had heard many stories about Akaitcho that were to his discredit but he had not believed them. The rum sent to Akaitcho, similar to what the great men in England drank, was, he insisted, actually stronger than the spirits he had generally received. He added that when the Chief had agreed to accompany the expedition it had been fully explained to him that his reward would come at the *end* of the journey. Akaitcho should know that it was impossible for him to carry large quantities of goods as the traders did. He reminded the Chief that his debts to the trading companies had already been cancelled. Then Franklin went on the attack. He said Akaitcho's charges were made to cover up his own failure to supply a large quantity of meat, and that the Chief's complaints were groundless in comparison with the real injury the expedition was sustaining from a shortage of supplies.

At this point Akaitcho shifted his ground and said that the white men would inevitably lose their lives if they tried to make a voyage along the sea coast. Since these were the exact words used earlier by the interpreters, it was clear that they had been influencing the Chief against the expedition and had probably told him that there were hidden supplies of goods and rum in the Fort. He now accepted a meal and seemed ready to forget his complaints provided he was given more presents. He was a bit shaken when told that he had already been offered every drop of rum remaining at the Fort and every article of clothing, etc. that could be spared. He decided to do nothing until his older brother, Humpy, arrived. His young men had had enough of waiting, however, and came forward for their share of the rum—a big step toward reconciliation.

All the next day Akaitcho stayed in his tent, and although they were in good spirits, his young men refused to go hunting. Franklin went ahead with his preparations for departure, though he had no assurance that the Chief and his hunters would go with him. On May 25 the voyageurs were issued with additional clothing and other necessities, while a few blankets, some cloth, iron work and trinkets were put aside to be used as gifts for the Eskimos. The two Eskimo interpreters, Augustus and Junius, were given laced dresses. Junius especially was overjoyed to receive his new clothing.

Two of Akaitcho's brothers, Humpy and Annoethai-yazzeh, arrived that afternoon with the rest of his people. There were now thirty hunters in the encampment, together with thirty-one women and sixty children. The rest of the Copper Indians were farther down the Coppermine River with The Hook. Annoethai-yazzeh had sixteen of his eighteen children with him.

The next two days of discussion were crucial for the whole future of the expedition. In the first session that evening all the old complaints were repeated, and the only visible progress was the reaction of Akaitcho's two brothers, who accused him of being greedy. Next morning while the Indians had a caucus of their own, Franklin had the canoes taken out of their winter storage and a start was made at repairing them. The full conference resumed in the afternoon, with the Chief still refusing to accept the presents. He complained that blankets, kettles and daggers were not included and angrily accused Wentzel of giving goods to the voyageurs that should have gone to the Indians. Wentzel kept his temper and simply reminded Akaitcho that he had agreed not to expect any goods until his return. The Chief said that he had made no such agreement but lost considerable ground when his brother Humpy spoke up and said that he had been present when this point had been agreed upon. Following Humpy's declaration one of the guides added, "I do not expect anything here. I have promised to accompany the white people and I will therefore go, confidently relying upon receiving the stipulated reward on my return."

Surprised, Akaitcho abruptly changed his tactics and launched into a diatribe against the treatment he had received from the fur traders.

I immediately refused to discuss this topic, as foreign to our present business, and desired Akaitcho to recall to memory what he had told

me on our first meeting, that he considered me the father of every
person attached to the Expedition, in which character it was surely
my duty to provide for the comfort and safety of the voyageurs as
well as the Indians. The voyageurs, he knew, had a long journey to
perform, and would in all probability be exposed to much suffering
from cold on a coast destitute of wood; and, therefore, required a
greater provision of clothing than was necessary for the Indians, who,
by returning immediately from the mouth of the river, would reach
Fort Providence in August and obtain their promised rewards. Most
of the Indians appeared to assent to this argument.

Akaitcho, however, now began to raise questions about the wealth
of the two fur companies. Franklin refused to be drawn into such
discussion and reminded the Chief once again of his goal. "Our thoughts
. . . are fixed solely on the accomplishment of the objects for which we
came to the country. Our success depends much on your furnishing us
with provision speedily, that we may have all the summer to work; and
if we succeed a ship will soon bring goods in abundance to the mouth
of the Coppermine River." Again the Indians talked things over among
themselves. Then Akaitcho made one last request; he asked that he be
given two or three kettles and some blankets as additional presents for
his young men. He was told that there was not a single kettle to spare,
but the officers promised to give a blanket each from their own beds.

Dinner was then brought in, and as usual the leading men received a
share of the food. When conversation was resumed the Chief renewed
his request for goods, but now it became obvious that he was out to get
everything he possibly could from Franklin, leaving him without the
means to make gifts to the Eskimos and the Indians. Franklin firmly
refused every request. Finally Akaitcho made a bad mistake: angrily
addressing his young men he said, "There are too few goods for me to
distribute. Those that mean to follow the white people to the sea may
take them." The guides and most of the hunters quickly stepped
forward to accept their share before the Chief could change his mind.
The hunters then asked Wentzel for ammunition so that they could
hunt in the morning—and the strike was over!

That night the Indians sat around watching the officers and voyageurs
play various games until two in the morning. Franklin was keen to
occupy the voyageurs with some form of amusement, not only to keep
them happy, but also to keep them from talking over the differences
that had occurred between the Indians and himself. The games involved
a certain amount of exercise, which was especially good for Hood. He

had kept to the house all winter to concentrate on his drawings and other duties, and his health had suffered. In his journal Franklin admitted regretfully that he could only watch the games from the sidelines, since he was still lame from the sliding accident. Next day many of the Indians showed their renewed friendliness by attending divine service.

On May 29 Akaitcho came up to Franklin with a smile on his face. Realizing that he had been out of step with his young men, he had decided to cooperate. He told Franklin not to think the worse of him because of his demands, saying it was the custom to do this, and as chief he had to speak up for all his people. He saw now, he said, that he had not been deceived, that there really were no hidden supplies, and he would therefore ask for nothing more. He was ready to set out for the Coppermine as soon as the route was passable, but farther north the snow was still too deep and the moss too wet to make fires. He then accepted the dress that he had refused earlier and next day appeared in the outfit that Franklin had given him the previous autumn. During the preceding days he had been dressing in rags to demonstrate his poverty, but when this tactic brought no results he decided that he should show off some of his possessions to the strangers who were arriving every day.

But when the opportunity arose, the Chief tried one more trick on Franklin. He told him that two old men had just arrived with some meat and that they wanted to barter. Akaitcho knew how badly Franklin wanted to increase his meat supply and he craftily waited to see if goods would be produced from a hidden store in return for the food. Franklin replied that he needed the meat but had nothing with which to barter. All he could do was give the men notes on the North West Company for whatever goods they desired. The men accepted his conditions, and Akaitcho was further convinced.

> *I have deemed it my duty to give the details of the tedious conversations we had with Akaitcho, to point out to future travellers, the art with which these Indians pursue their objects, their avaricious nature, and the little reliance that can be placed upon them when their interests jar with their promises. In these respects they agree with other tribes of northern Indians; but as has been already mentioned, their dispositions are not cruel, and their hearts are readily moved by the cry of distress.*

On June 4 Dr. Richardson led an advance party to Point Lake. With him were fifteen voyageurs and eight Indians, several of them women. Each man had to carry eighty pounds of supplies and an equal amount of personal baggage.

These Indians set a great value upon medicine, and made many demands upon Dr. Richardson on the prospect of his departure. He had to make up little packets of the different articles in his chest, not only for the leader, but for each of the minor chiefs, who carefully placed them in their medicine bags, noting in their memories the directions he gave for their use. The readiness with which their requests for medical assistance were complied with, was considered by them as a strong mark of our good intentions towards them; and the leader often remarked that they owed much to our kindness in that respect; that formerly numbers had died every year, but that not a life had been lost since our arrival among them.

.   .   .   .   .

I had intended to send the canoes by the first party, but they were not yet repaired, the weather not being sufficiently warm for the men to work constantly at them, without the hazard of breaking the bark. This day one of the new trading guns, which we had recently received from Fort Chipewyan, burst in the hands of a young Indian; fortunately, however, without doing him any material injury. This was the sixth accident of the kind which had occurred since our departure from Slave Lake. Surely this deficiency in the quality of the guns, which hazards the lives of so many poor Indians, requires the serious consideration of the principals of the trading Companies.

After Richardson had left, the Indians struck their tents and the women, boys and old men departed. Akaitcho and the hunters left in the afternoon with the intention of joining Richardson at Point Lake. Before they got into their canoes Franklin reminded Akaitcho once more, in the hearing of his men, that he was depending on him to store a good supply of meat in the house before September, to be available for the expedition on its return. The Chief again promised to do so and suggested that it would be safer to store the meat in the cellar. He had watched the stripping of the rooms and storehouse, and as he left he said with a smile, "I see now that you have really no goods left . . . and therefore I shall not trouble you any more, but use my best endeavours to prepare provision for you, and I think if the animals are tolerably numerous, we may get plenty before you can embark on the river."

While the Indians were packing up this morning, one of the women absconded. She belongs to the Dog-Rib tribe and had been taken by force from her relations by her present husband, who treated her very harshly. The fellow was in my room when his mother announced the departure of his wife and received the intelligence with great composure, as well as the seasonable reproof of Akaitcho. "You are rightly served," said the chief to him, "and will now have to carry all your things yourself, instead of having a wife to drag them."

.   .   .   .   .

On the 5th the Dog-Rib woman presented herself on a hill at some distance from the house, but was afraid to approach us, until the interpreter went and told her that neither we nor the Indian who remained with us, would prevent her from going where she pleased. Upon this she came to solicit a fire-steel and kettle. She was at first low-spirited, from the non-arrival of a countrywoman who had promised to elope with her, but had probably been too narrowly watched. The Indian hunter, however, having given her some directions as to the proper mode of joining her own tribe, she became more composed, and ultimately agreed to adopt his advice of proceeding at once to Fort Providence, instead of wandering about the country all summer in search of them, at the imminent hazard of being starved.

By June 12 the Winter River was almost clear of ice. On the following day the voyageurs returned, having left Richardson on the borders of Point Lake. They brought a letter from Richardson in which he explained that the snow was deeper near his camp than it had been at any time during the past winter around Fort Enterprise, and that the ice had just begun to decay on Point Lake. Though the voyageurs were very tired when they arrived and had eaten nothing for twenty-four hours, they were in good spirits and anxious to start back next morning with the balance of the stores.

All the preparatory stages were now over; the main operation could begin. On June 14, 1821, Franklin and the balance of his men left their winter base and headed toward the Coppermine and, ultimately, the Arctic sea. Sleds for transporting the canoes over ice had been finished the night before. Each one was hauled by four men and two dogs. They followed the water course to the River, though it was longer than overland, because it was a safer route for the canoes. Ice was still a major problem. To reach the mouth of the Coppermine from Fort Enterprise the party was to travel 334 miles, and for 117 miles of this distance they had to drag the canoes and supplies over ice. But they could afford to wait no longer if they were to reach the sea that summer.

The work of closing up the Fort had given the men great satisfaction. They had been waiting for ten months and were keen to get away. In one of the rooms Franklin had left a box containing his journal, written up to that morning, as well as charts and drawings. Wentzel was to take the box to Fort Chipewyan when he got back, and from there it would be sent to England. At his suggestion, a drawing of a man holding a dagger had been fixed to the door in hopes that it might keep the Indians from breaking in.

The pace was slow, for the men were loaded with packs weighing about 180 pounds each. Where there was ice, they dragged their packs on makeshift sleighs made of sticks and deer horns. They were constantly wet, since the ice had broken along the shores of the lake, but the temperature on the second day out went up to eighty-two degrees, so they did not suffer. The hunters had been sent on ahead to Marten Lake to recover two deer cached there, but when Franklin caught up with them he was dismayed to learn that the meat had been taken by wolverines. That night the men's supper had to be taken from their scanty supply of dried meat. There was not enough wood in the area to build a decent fire and the northwest wind blew through their blankets, so they passed a cold and miserable night; next morning they were glad to leave their frigid beds and set off at five a.m.

The party advanced over the ice of Marten Lake, finding the surface smooth enough to have the dogs drag the canoes. The animals set such a pace that the men had a hard time keeping up. In the afternoon Franklin left the canoe party in Wentzel's charge and set out in search of one of the crewmen, Antonio Fontano, who had strayed during the morning. The search lasted two and a half days, impeded by snow storms and violent gales. The missing crewman was eventually found on the north shore of an extensive lake after the search party had crossed its surface, waist deep in the water that covered the ice:

We had the happiness of finding Fontano at this place. The poor fellow had passed the three preceding days without tasting food, and was exhausted by anxiety and hunger. His sufferings were considered to have been a sufficient punishment for his imprudent conduct in separating from us, and I only admonished him to be more cautious in future.

The severe travel conditions, plus a diet limited to two deer, had brought the men to a state of exhaustion when on June 21 they reached Dr. Richardson's tent on Point Lake. Akaitcho and his hunters were also camped there. Richardson informed Franklin that the Chief had used up all his ammunition without contributing any provision whatever.

On the following morning I represented to Akaitcho that we had been greatly disappointed by his conduct, which was so opposite to the promise of exertion he had made on quitting Fort Enterprise. He offered many excuses, but finding they were not satisfactory, admitted that the greater part of the ammunition had been given to those who accompanied the women to the Beth-see-to [a temporary camp], and promised to behave better in future. I then told him that I intended in future to give them ammunition only in proportion to the meat which was brought in, and that we should commence upon that plan by supplying him with fifteen balls, and each of the hunters with ten.

The number of our hunters was now reduced to five, as two of the most active declined going any further, their father, who thought himself dying, having solicited them to remain and close his eyes.

The extreme difficulty of advancing through the winterbound country with canoes and supplies, and yet the absolute necessity of doing so
if the expedition was to reach the Arctic that season, presented Franklin
with a bleak prospect:

> The ice on the lake was still six or seven feet thick, and there was
> no appearance of its decay except near the edges; and as it was
> evident that by remaining here until it should be removed, we might
> lose every prospect of success in our undertaking, I determined on
> dragging our stores along its surface, until we could come to a part
> of the river where we could embark; and directions were given this
> evening for each man to prepare a train for the conveyance of his
> portion of the stores.

> The wind having abated in the night, we prepared for starting at an
> early hour [June 25]. The three canoes were mounted on sledges and
> nine men were appointed to conduct them, having the assistance of
> two dogs to each canoe. The stores and provisions were distributed
> equally among the rest of our men, except a few small articles which
> the Indians carried. The provision consisted of only two bags of
> pemmican, two of pounded meat, five of suet, and two small bundles
> of dried provision, together with fresh meat sufficient for our supper
> at night. It was gratifying to witness the readiness with which the
> men prepared for and commenced the journey, which threatened to
> be so very laborious, as each of them had to drag upwards of one
> hundred and eighty pounds on his sledge.

That day Franklin and his party advanced six miles. Already several
of the men were suffering from an inflammation of the thigh. The
twenty-sixth was extremely hot and the lameness of the men increased.

> The dogs too showed symptoms of great weakness and one of them
> stretched himself obstinately on the ice and was obliged to be
> released from the harness. . . . The sufferings of the people in this
> early stage of our journey were truly discouraging to them. . . . I
> therefore determined on leaving the third canoe, which had been
> principally carried to provide against any accident happening to the
> others. By this we gained three men to lighten the loads of those who
> were most lame, and an additional dog for each of the other canoes.
> . . . It rained heavily during the night and this was succeeded by a

dense fog on the morning of the 28th. . . . The surface of the ice,
being honeycombed by the recent rains, presented innumerable sharp
points, which tore our shoes and lacerated the feet at every step. The
poor dogs, too, marked their path with their blood.

On June 30, sixteen days after leaving Fort Enterprise, the canoes
were loaded and launched in the water for the first time. The river on
which the men found themselves was about two hundred yards wide,
and they ventured to hope that from that point to the Coppermine
there would be open water. But ice soon blocked the way, and the
canoes had to be placed once again on the sledges. It was dangerous
work, crossing ice so badly decayed that the men had to spread out
widely to avoid breaking through. There were succeeding lengths of
this badly weakened ice, followed by stretches of open water where
they again embarked in the canoes.

To make matters worse, the guide was not sure of his route and took
them up wrong channels more than once. Finally he admitted that he
did not know where to find the Coppermine. Accompanied by two
others in the party, he climbed a high hill to see if it was visible from
there. Later in the afternoon they returned with the good news that
they had seen the River. First dragging the canoes, then paddling them,
Franklin and his much relieved crew finally reached the Coppermine
and encamped at a point where it was two hundred yards wide, ten
feet deep, free of ice and flowing swiftly toward the Arctic sea.

We embarked at nine a.m. on July 2nd, and descended a succession
of strong rapids for three miles. We were carried along with extraor-
dinary rapidity, shooting over large stones, upon which a single
stroke would have been destructive to the canoes; and we were also
in danger of breaking them, from the want of the long poles which
lie along their bottoms and equalise their cargoes, as they plunged
very much, and on one occasion the first canoe was almost filled with
the waves. But tnere was no receding after we had once launched
into the stream, and our safety depended on the skill and dexterity
of the bowmen and steersmen.

The battle with nature was unremitting but Franklin had his troubles
with human nature as well. That night as the men were working on the
canoes, the hunters came in from the bush in a great state. They had
found a dog that had escaped from the party a few days earlier and
when they saw that it wore no harness, they jumped to the conclusion

that the whole party must have drowned in some rapid. Panic-stricken, they had thrown away much of their luggage and all of a large supply of meat. Then they had run in search of their leader, Long-legs. One of Franklin's men having encountered them in full flight, brought them to the camp to face Akaitcho. The Chief talked sternly to them for losing their heads and especially for throwing away the meat. The men made a profound apology and set out with Akaitcho in a chastened mood for a good hunting area thirty miles farther on.

When the necessary repairs to the canoes had been completed, Franklin instructed the bowmen in future to examine every rapid before descending it. If there was the least danger, the ammunition, guns and instruments were to be put ashore and carried along the bank, so that the members of the party would have a means of keeping themselves alive if the canoes were lost.

> At four in the morning of July 4th we embarked and descended a succession of very agitated rapids, but took the precaution of landing the articles mentioned yesterday, wherever there appeared any hazard; notwithstanding all our precautions the leading canoe struck with great force against a stone, and the bark was split, but this injury was easily repaired, and we regretted only the loss of time.

As the River widened, the current lessened and the party encountered an accumulation of drift ice over which the canoes and cargoes had to be carried. At one point the ice gave way and three men were thrown into the water. No harm came to them, but their canoe barely escaped being crushed.

Shortly after this accident, one of the Indians was seen sitting on the riverbank. On learning from him that Akaitcho and his hunters had gone after a herd of musk ox, the party encamped to await the results, having advanced twenty-four and a half miles. Before long the hunters came in with the good news that they had killed eight musk ox, four of them full grown. The whole party immediately went with the hunters to help bring in the meat.

> The musk oxen, like the buffalo, herd together in bands, and generally frequent the barren grounds during the summer months, keeping near to the banks of the rivers, but retire to the woods in winter. They seem to be less watchful than most other wild animals, and when grazing are not difficult to approach, provided the hunters go against the wind; when two or three men get so near a herd as to

fire at them from different points, these animals, instead of separating or running away, huddle closer together, and several are generally killed; but if the wound is not mortal they become enraged and dart in the most furious manner at the hunters, who must be very dexterous to evade them. They can defend themselves by their powerful horns against the wolves and bears, which as the Indians say, they not unfrequently kill.

The officers had treated Akaitcho with some coolness after his failure to provide meat at Point Lake. However, the large supply that he and his men had now produced led Franklin and the others to speak to him more warmly when he came to see them. For his part, he tried to get back into their good books by running down his fellow chief, The Hook. He told them, "I am aware that you consider me the worst man of my nation; but I know The Hook to be a great rogue, and I think he will disappoint you."

On July 6 the expedition camped at the foot of a range of hills which seemed to be from 1200 to 1500 feet high. Franklin regarded these as the first hills he had seen that could properly be called mountains, probably a continuation of the Stony Mountains, which Hearne had crossed. Many plants were in flower near the tents but Dr. Richardson preferred to climb high up in the hills to collect his specimens. The party advanced fifty miles that day, an achievement which put everyone in good spirits.

Next morning they embarked at four a.m. with the temperature at forty degrees. The canoes glided swiftly downstream until seven when they arrived at The Hook's encampment and landed to pay him a visit. This chief, ranking second after Akaitcho among the Copper Indians, had with him only three hunters and a few old men with their families, the rest of his band being at their hunting ground on Bear Lake. His brother, Long-legs, and Keskarrah had joined him a few days earlier and had told him of Franklin's need for meat. As soon as Franklin landed, he decorated The Hook with a medal similar to the ones he had given to the other leaders. He was relieved that The Hook came straight to the point when he began his speech.

The Hook said he had heard that the expedition needed food and had therefore told his women to collect all the meat available and give it to the white men. He was sorry that they had so little but his people were giving all they had. "We are too much indebted to the white people to allow them to want food on our lands, while we have any to give them. Our families can live on fish until we can secure more meat, but the season is too short to allow of your delaying. . . ." He then called on the women to bring the meat. There was enough to make three and a half bags of pemmican. Franklin wished he could reward such kindness with a large present, but all he could spare was fifteen charges of ammunition for The Hook and his senior men. In addition, he gave them an order on the North West Company for clothing. Anxious as always about his return journey from the sea, Franklin asked The Hook to make deposits of dried meat along the River, marking the places well. The Indians warned Franklin against the treachery of the Eskimos. They also cautioned against going too far along the Arctic coast because of gales and high seas. The Hook's manner was very friendly and he seemed sincere in wishing to give every assistance. It meant a great deal for him to meet Dr. Richardson, since he had been an invalid for several years. The Doctor examined him and gave him some advice, as well as a supply of medicine.

Continuing down river, the party came to signs of a recent Indian encampment. Here they landed and made a signal fire. The signal was quickly answered, and soon three old Indians and their families appeared. It seemed that for the past year they had supported themselves with bow and arrow with such success that they freely offered the party about seventy pounds of dried meat, together with the skins of six moose for making shoes. The offer became somewhat less exciting when it developed that the meat was cached far beyond their reach on Great Bear Lake. However, the Indians promised to bring the meat to the Coppermine and deposit it at a clearly marked spot for the use of the party on the return journey.

Re-embarking, the crews continued their descent of the Coppermine. The current became increasingly strong as the river bed narrowed to about 120 yards in width. At eleven in the morning they came to a rapid that the Indians had been describing for days as being totally impassable for canoes. For three-quarters of a mile the River descended through a narrow, crooked channel between perpendicular cliffs that rose 150 feet above it. The water, confined within this chasm, dashed furiously past the projecting rocks and discharged itself in a sheet of foam. The canoes were therefore lightened of their cargo and succeeded in making the passage without accident.

Beyond this difficult stretch, the country became flat and sandy. The Copper Mountains could be seen about twelve miles to the northeast. The hunters were sent out for game in the direction of the Mountains but were warned not to light fires in case there were Eskimos around. The River had now become shallow and was filled with jagged rocks.

The men tried tracking, but the mosquitoes were such a torment that they got back into the canoes and used poles to get through the shallows.

We rejoined our hunters at the foot of the Copper Mountains, and found they had killed three musk oxen. This circumstance determined us on encamping to dry the meat, as there was wood at the spot. We availed ourselves of this delay to visit the Copper Mountains in search of specimens of the ore, agreeably to my Instructions; and a party of twenty-one persons, consisting of the officers, some of the voyageurs, and all the Indians, set off on that excursion. We travelled for nine hours over a considerable space of ground, but found only a few small pieces of native copper. The range we ascended was on the west side of the river, extending W.N.W. and E.S.E. The mountains varied in height from twelve to fifteen hundred feet. . . . The uniformity of the mountains is interrupted by narrow valleys traversed by small streams. The best specimens of metal we procured were among the stones in these valleys, and it was in such situations that our guides desired us to search more carefully. It would appear that when the Indians see any sparry substance projecting above the surface, they dig there; but they have no other rule to direct them, and have never found the metal in its original repository. Our guides reported that they had found copper in large pieces in every part of this range, for two days' walk to the north-west, and that the Eskimos come hither to search for it. The annual visits which the Copper Indians were accustomed to make to these mountains, when most of their weapons and utensils were made of copper, have been discontinued since they have been enabled to obtain a supply of ice chisels and other instruments of iron by the establishment of trading posts near their hunting grounds. . . .

The impracticability of navigating the river upwards from the sea, and the want of wood for forming an establishment, would prove insuperable objections to rendering the collection of copper at this part worthy of mercantile speculation.

On July 12 the guides told Franklin that they had probably reached Eskimo country and that the party should light fires only with the greatest caution. "Throughout this day's voyage the current was very strong. . . . Large masses of ice twelve or fourteen feet thick were still adhering to many parts of the banks, indicating the tardy departure of winter from this inhospitable land, but the earth around them was rich with vegetation."

That evening two musk ox were killed. While waiting to carry the meat back to the camp the Indians were suddenly attacked by a bear. When the animal sprang at them, they were too flustered to do anything except grab their guns and fire in its general direction. Everyone missed except Akaitcho, who kept his head, took careful aim and shot the animal dead. The Indians themselves would not eat the bear meat but they gave the choice pieces to the officers and Hepburn, who found it excellent.

At this point Akaitcho proposed that two of his hunters should go on ahead and try to make contact with the Eskimos. There were now signs of them about—such as the marks of their stone axes on stumps of trees. Franklin turned Akaitcho's proposal down, convinced that the way the Indians had formerly treated the Eskimos made them the worst possible ambassadors of peace. He decided that the two Eskimo interpreters should be the ones to go, much to their delight. The officers had become very fond of the two men and were concerned for their safety, but the Eskimos prepared for their mission in the highest spirits and without the slightest show of fear. They put on the Eskimo clothes that had been made for them at Fort Enterprise, concealed the pistols on their persons and took some beads, looking glasses and other presents to help conciliate their countrymen. They were instructed to tell the Eskimos that the white men had come to bring peace between them and their enemies, and also to discover a passage by which large ships could bring them all manner of goods. They were told not to mention the presence of the Indians; instead, they should try to bring some of the Eskimos back with them to meet the white men.

Several times during the evening the officers climbed a hill nearby, hoping to catch sight of Augustus and Junius, but there was no sign. All night they took turns standing watch. On the first watch Dr. Richardson was roused from his thoughts by an indistinct sound and saw nine wolves advancing toward him in a crescent formation. They apparently intended to drive him into the river but when he stood up they stopped in their tracks, and when he advanced, they made way for him to pass and gain the tents. Though he had his gun, he had no wish to use it in case there were Eskimos within earshot.

When in the morning there was still no sign of Augustus and Junius, Franklin decided to go and look for them. Several hours of argument were required to make the Indians agree to remain behind, though he told them that word would be sent back immediately if a good contact were made with the Eskimos. Akaitcho registered his displeasure by becoming a prophet of doom: the two messengers were already dead; the Eskimos had already been warned of their coming and were lying in wait; neither group could withstand them if they separated; their only safety was in remaining together. In the end, he agreed to stay behind provided Wentzel stayed also.

The current was fast, but not dangerously so, as the party paddled downstream. Franklin had hoped to catch sight of the sea once he passed through a range of high hills, but all that met his eye was yet another series of hills. In the evening, Junius appeared with the news that he and Augustus had found four Eskimo tents beside a waterfall. From the description Franklin decided that the cascade must be the "Bloody Fall" about which Samuel Hearne had written. Junius and Augustus had been on the other side of the River when they saw the tents. Augustus had called out to the Eskimos and tried to tell them about the white men and their desire to give them presents. The roar of the Coppermine made it impossible for the natives to hear very well, but one of them crossed in his canoe and heard the whole message. Though he would not land, he listened to all that Augustus had to say before returning to his companions.

> We now encamped, having come fourteen miles. After a few hours' rest, Junius set off again to rejoin his companion, being accompanied by Hepburn, who was directed to remain about two miles above the fall to arrest the canoes on their passage, lest we should too suddenly surprise the Eskimos. About ten p.m. we were mortified by the appearance of the Indians with Mr. Wentzel, who had in vain endeavoured to restrain them from following us. The only reason assigned by Akaitcho for his conduct was that he wished for a reassurance of my promise to establish peace between his nation and the Eskimos.

In the morning Franklin put an end to the Chief's renewed demands to proceed by telling him that the Indians would receive no rewards whatever if they moved before he sent word back that the Eskimos were ready to meet them. Some of the men then embarked in the two canoes, while two officers and the rest of the party—without the Indians— walked along the shore to lighten the canoes. It was well that they did; farther downstream they came upon some unexpected rapids and both canoes were nearly swamped.

Below the rapids Franklin found Augustus talking to an Eskimo. The moment the Eskimo saw the party, he crossed the Coppermine to rejoin his companions and they all fled. According to Augustus' account, there were four men and four women in the party. They had been friendly and had seemed pleased to hear about the white men, but the memories of the massacres inflicted by the Indians were still fresh in their minds and they were easily frightened away. Franklin crossed the River to their camp and decided to wait, in hopes that they would return. It was extremely important to him to win their confidence, since they were probably the only ones who could give him information about the Arctic coastline.

Under the covering of their tents were observed some stone kettles and hatchets, a few fish spears made of copper, two small bits of iron, a quantity of skins, and some dried salmon, which was covered with maggots and half putrid. The entrails of the fish were spread out to dry. A great many skins of small birds were hung up to a stage, and even two mice were preserved in the same way. Thus it would appear that the necessities of these poor people induce them to preserve every article that can be possibly used as food. Several human skulls which bore the marks of violence, and many bones were strewed about the ground near the encampment, and as the spot exactly answers the description given by Mr. Hearne of the place where the Chipewyans who accompanied him perpetrated the dreadful massacre on the Eskimos, we had no doubt of this being the place, notwithstanding the difference in its position as to latitude and longitude given by him, and ascertained by our observation. We have, therefore, preserved the appellation of Bloody Fall, which he bestowed upon it.

(Fifty years earlier, in 1771, Hearne had described the massacre in graphic terms which conveyed the full horror of the scene. The Indians, as they lay in ambush, had performed the ceremonies thought necessary before an engagement, painting their faces, cutting their hair and removing all extra clothing so that they could move more quickly. By that time it was one in the morning and the Eskimos were asleep in their tents. The Indians fell upon the poor, unsuspecting creatures and began their bloody butchery as Hearne looked on helplessly. The victims, men, women and children—as many as twenty of them—ran out of their tents stark naked and tried to escape, but without success. Hearne's revulsion was increased when a young girl of about eighteen

was killed so near him that when the first spear entered her side she fell
at his feet and twisted herself around his legs so that he could hardly
free himself from her dying hold. He pleaded for her life but the two
murderers took no notice until they had struck both their spears
through her body into the ground. They then looked scornfully at him
and asked him if he wanted an Eskimo wife.*)

In his journal Franklin described his encounter with the Eskimos:

> On the morning of the 16th [July] three men were sent up the river
> to search for dried wood to make floats for the nets. Adam, the
> interpreter, was also despatched with a voyageur to inform Akaitcho
> of the flight of the Eskimos. We were preparing to go down to the sea
> in one of the canoes, leaving Mr. Back to await the return of the men
> who were absent; but just as the crew were putting the canoe in the
> water, Adam returned in the utmost consternation and informed us
> that a party of Eskimos were pursuing the men whom we had sent
> to collect floats. The orders for embarking were instantly counter-
> manded, and we went with a party of our men to their rescue. We
> soon met our people returning at a slow pace, and learned that they
> had come unawares upon the Eskimo party, which consisted of six
> men, with their women and children, who were travelling towards
> the rapid with a considerable number of dogs carrying their baggage.
> The women hid themselves on the first alarm, but the men advanced,
> and stopping at some distance from our men, began to dance in a
> circle tossing up their hands in the air and accompanying their
> motions with much shouting, to signify . . . their desire of peace. Our
> men saluted them by pulling off their hats and making bows, but
> neither party was willing to approach the other; and at length, the
> Eskimos retired to the hill from whence they had descended when
> first seen. We proceeded in the hope of gaining an interview with
> them. . . . We were led to their baggage, which they had deserted, by
> the howling of the dogs; and on the summit of a hill we found, lying
> behind a stone, an old man who was too infirm to effect his escape
> with the rest. He was much terrified when Augustus advanced, and
> probably expected immediate death; but that the fatal blow might
> not be unrevenged, he seized his spear and made a thrust with it at
> his supposed enemy. Augustus, however, easily repressed the feeble
> effort and soon calmed his fears by presenting him with some pieces
> of iron and assuring him of his friendly intentions. Dr. Richardson

*A Journey from Prince of Wales' Fort in Hudson's Bay to the northern ocean
—1769, 1770, 1771, 1772, Samuel Hearne (London, 1795)

and I then joined them and, after receiving our presents, the old man was quite composed and became communicative. His dialect differed from that used by Augustus, but they understood each other tolerably well.

The old man's name was Terregannoeuck, or the White Fox. He told Franklin that reindeer frequented the Arctic coast during the summer, fish were plentiful at the mouths of the rivers, and seals numerous; and there was plenty of driftwood along the shore. His tribe, the Deer-Horn Eskimos, were now busy salting salmon and would move westward later and pass the winter in igloos. As a token of goodwill he gave pieces of meat to everyone. It was highly tainted but they forced themselves to eat it to show their friendship. Franklin used the opportunity to tell the old man that he was accompanied by Copper Indians who had come to make peace with his nation. The old man replied that he would be happy to see the end of hostility between his people and the Indians and that he would welcome them. Adam was sent immediately to Akaitcho to tell him that he might now join the rest of the party.

The countenance of Terregannoeuck was oval . . . and had nothing very different from a European face, except in the smallness of his eyes, and, perhaps, in the narrowness of his forehead. His complexion was very fresh and red, and he had a longer beard than I had seen on any of the aboriginal inhabitants of America. It was between two and three inches long, and perfectly white. His face was not tattooed. His dress consisted of a shirt, or jacket with a hood, wide breeches, reaching only to the knee, and tight leggins sewed to the shoes, all of deers' skins. The soles of the shoes were made of seal-skin, and stuffed with feathers instead of socks. He was bent with age, but appeared to be about five feet ten inches high. . . . Whenever Terregannoeuck received a present, he placed each article first on his right shoulder, then on his left; and when he wished to express still higher satisfaction, he rubbed it over his head. He held hatchets and other iron instruments in the highest esteem. On seeing his countenance in a glass for the first time, he exclaimed, "I shall never kill deer more," and immediately put the mirror down.

Akaitcho and the Indians arrived in the evening. They had seen a band of Eskimos the day before and had tried to communicate with them, but while the Eskimos did not seem hostile, they were too frightened to come close. In fact, Terregannoeuck's aged wife was the only one who would return to where the old man was now lying. She told him that the rest of the party had gone to join other Eskimos who were fishing in a river to the west. The old man seemed unconcerned at being left behind and offered the white men some more meat, but when they went to the place where he had concealed it they found it was too putrid to eat.

> In the afternoon [July 17] a party of nine Eskimos appeared on the east bank of the river, about a mile below our encampment, carrying their canoes and baggage on their backs; but they turned and fled as soon as they perceived our tents. The appearance of so many different bands of Eskimos terrified the Indians to such a degree that they determined on leaving us the next day, lest they should be surrounded and their retreat cut off. I endeavoured, by the offer of any remuneration they would choose, to prevail on one or two of the hunters to proceed, but in vain; and I had much difficulty even in obtaining their promise to wait at the Copper Mountains for Mr. Wentzel and the four men, whom I intended to discharge at the sea.
>
> The fears which our interpreters, St. Germain and Adam, entertained respecting the voyage, were now greatly increased, and both of them came this evening to request their discharges. . . . St. Germain even said that he had understood he was only engaged to accompany us as long as the Indians did, and persisted in this falsehood until his agreement to go with us throughout the voyage had been twice read to him. As these were the only two of the party on whose skill in hunting we could rely, I was unable to listen for a moment to their desire of quitting us, and lest they should leave us by stealth, their motions were strictly watched. This was not an unnecessary precaution, as I was informed that they had actually laid a plan for eloping; but the rest of the men knowing that their own safety would have been compromised had they succeeded, kept a watchful eye over them.

Next day Akaitcho and the Indians left, after Franklin had once again reminded them of their promise to leave a good supply of meat at Fort Enterprise. They renewed their promise, and agreed also to deposit as much meat as possible along the Coppermine as they made their way back.

The party now set out for the Arctic sea; by evening they had covered nine miles and camped at the mouth of the River. It was about a mile wide at this point and very shallow. Many islands of considerable height filled the horizon to the north. Toward the east, there seemed to be a chain of islands surrounded by solid ice, but there was an open channel between the ice and the shore. The water was of a clear, green colour and decidedly salty, and there appeared to be a rise and fall in the water of about four inches. There was plenty of driftwood along the shore, and seals, gulls, duck and partridges were to be seen.

The voyageurs began to complain of the cold the moment the wind changed to the northwest. Their first sight of the sea and the seals had amused them, but depression set in soon after. Their terror at the prospect of a voyage through the icy sea in frail birch-bark canoes was skilfully exploited by the two interpreters, who were still demanding their discharge. In contrast, Hepburn was overjoyed to reach salt water again and was a great help to the officers in getting the voyageurs back into a happier frame of mind.

The despatches being finished were delivered this evening [July 19] to Mr. Wentzel, who parted from us at eight p.m. with . . . [four voyageurs] whom I discharged for the purpose of reducing our expenditure of provision as much as possible. The remainder of the party, including officers, amounted to twenty persons. I made Mr. Wentzel acquainted with the probable course of our future proceedings and mentioned to him that if we were far distant from this river when the season or other circumstances rendered it necessary to put a stop to our advance, we should, in all probability, be unable to return to it and should have to travel across the barren grounds towards some established post: in which case I told him that we should certainly go first to Fort Enterprise, expecting that he would cause the Indians to place a supply of dried provision there, as soon as possible after their arrival in its vicinity. My instructions to him were that he should proceed to Point Lake, transport the canoe that was left there to Fort Enterprise, where he was to . . . forward the box containing the journals, etc. with the present despatches, by the next winter packet to England. But before he quitted Fort Enterprise, he was to be assured of the intention of the Indians to lay up the provision we required, and if they should be in want of ammunition for that purpose to procure it if possible from Fort Providence, or the other forts in Slave Lake. . . . I also requested him to ascertain from Akaitcho and the other leading Indians where their different parties would be hunting in the months of September and October, and to leave this in-

formation in a letter at Fort Enterprise, for our guidance in finding them, as we should require their assistance. Mr. Wentzel was furnished with a list of the stores that had been promised to Akaitcho and his party . . . as well as with an official request to the North-West Company that these goods might be paid to them on their next visit to Fort Providence, which they expected to make in the latter part of November. I desired him to mention this circumstance to the Indians as an encouragement to exertion in our behalf, and to promise them an additional reward for the supply of provision they should collect at Fort Enterprise.

Franklin noted that the position of the mouth of the River, according to his observations, differed widely from the position assigned to it by Hearne, but the accuracy of Hearne's description convinced him that they were on the same ground. He therefore named the most conspicuous cape in the explorer's honour. He named another cape after Sir Alexander Mackenzie. A river that flows into the sea to the west of the Coppermine he named after Dr. Richardson.

Franklin and his nineteen men now prepared to embark on the Arctic sea. For the officers and Hepburn, it was a return to their natural environment to be at sea again. It was as Franklin put it, "an element more congenial with our habits than the fresh-water navigations with their numerous difficulties."

Franklin was impatient to embark immediately but a northeast gale accompanied by thunder storms held the party where it was for a day and a half. The fishing was so poor that he decided to dip into the precious supply of dried meat, even though there was only enough for fifteen days. The officers would have gone to bed without dinner but it seemed necessary to give the voyageurs a good meal on their first night at the sea in order to raise their spirits. The voyageurs struck Franklin as happy-go-lucky in outlook. If there was food available, they wanted to have a feast, with no thought that tomorrow they might starve. They considered it no disgrace to be caught stealing food from the common store, though it was much better not to be caught. In this case, the meal put the men in a much happier frame of mind. Along with the meat there was a little salt, a luxury that had been served for some time as a substitute for bread and vegetables. The meal was rounded out by an Indian tea plant which, when boiled, produced a drink that smelled like rhubarb.

The wind moderated on the morning of July 21, but dense fog kept the men from embarking until noon, when they commenced their voyage eastward along the Arctic coast.

Soon afterwards we landed on an island where the Eskimos had erected a stage of drift timber and stored up many of their fishing implements and winter sledges, together with a great many dressed seal, musk ox, and deer skins. Their spears headed with bone, and many small articles of the same material, were worked with extreme neatness, as well as their wooden dishes and cooking utensils of stone; and several articles, very elegantly formed of bone, were evidently intended for some game, but Augustus was unacquainted with their use. We took from this deposit four seal-skins to repair our shoes, and left in exchange a copper-kettle, some awls and beads.

That first day they paddled thirty-seven miles, advancing between the coastline and a crowded range of islands. The temperature ranged between forty-three and forty-five degrees. After observing the foam floating on the water between the islands they decided that there was a tide but they were unable to detect whether it was rising or falling. There was very little ice, though the "blink" of it could be seen to the north, and there was one small iceberg in the distance. The day was well rounded out when St. Germain killed a fat deer on one of the islands, the first one they had seen all summer in really good condition. At the end of the day they found a good place to camp where the shoreline sloped down to the sea and was well covered with vegetation. In contrast, the islands opposite were rocky and barren and had high cliffs. On the beach they found one piece of sea-weed and the only mussel shells they were to encounter along the whole coast. But much more important was the appearance of driftwood. It seemed to have drifted with a current from the mouth of the Mackenzie, since there had been none coming down the Coppermine. At every halt Hepburn was given the job of setting up a pole and measuring the rise and fall of the sea.

Next morning Franklin and his crew embarked at four, hoisted sail to take advantage of a light breeze, and continued until eleven when they landed for breakfast. As they advanced, the coastline changed from having a "friendly" aspect to a much rougher and rockier appearance. Loose formations of ice appeared, but the men were able to navigate the canoes through them until evening. Occasional soundings indicated that the water was deep enough to allow large ships to navigate between the islands and the coast.

During the night an offshore wind drove the ice away from the coast, opening a channel a mile wide, and for the first nine miles next morning they made good time. The wind then turned against them and blew with such strength that they were forced to take shelter at the mouth of a river. The fishing nets were set out but they produced only one whitefish and a few bull-heads.

This part of the coast is the most sterile and inhospitable that can be imagined. One trap-cliff succeeds another with tiresome uniformity, and their debris cover the narrow valleys that intervene, to the exclusion of every kind of herbage. From the summit of these cliffs the ice appeared in every direction.

By eight p.m. the wind had subsided enough to allow the men to re-embark. Soon after, the two interpreters killed a reindeer on an island. By four in the morning the ice had closed in on the canoes once again and the men were forced to land.

They started off again at eleven, paddling close to shore against a strong wind. The coast was now indented by a series of deep bays, and they made the mistake several times of following the shoreline around the bays instead of cutting straight across. A thunderstorm forced them to camp at the mouth of a river which Franklin named after their good friend Wentzel. Earlier in the day he had named an island after Hepburn, much to the latter's embarrassment and delight. It had been a difficult day, but they had paddled thirty-one miles.

> At noon [July 25] the wind coming from a favourable quarter tempted us to proceed, although the fog was unabated. We kept as close as we could to the main shore, but having to cross some bays, it became a matter of doubt whether we had not left the main, and were running along an island. Just as we were endeavouring to double a bold cape, the fog partially cleared away and allowed us an imperfect view of a chain of islands on the outside and of much heavy ice which was pressing down upon us. The coast near us was so steep and rugged that no landing of the cargoes could be effected, and we were preserved only by some men jumping on the rocks and thrusting the ice off with poles. There was no alternative but to continue along this dreary shore, seeking a channel between the different masses of ice which had accumulated at the various points. In this operation both the canoes were in imminent danger of being crushed by the ice, which was now tossed about by the waves that the gale had excited. We effected a passage, however, and keeping close to the shore, landed at the entrance of Detention Harbour, at nine p.m., having come twenty-eight miles.

For the next three days they could not move a foot. Franklin had some of the men carry the canoes and cargo a mile and a half across a point of land, but the ice was just as solid on the other side. In any case, the operation was ordered mainly to keep the men busy and thus give them less time to worry. Others were sent out hunting, but though they saw a few deer they failed to make a kill. It was encouraging, however, to know that there was still some wildlife about. The food situation was bad. Two bags of pemmican were found to have gone mouldy from being wet, and the beef had been cured so badly that it was almost impossible to eat. But the officers worried less about the condition of the food than the fact that it was being used up so quickly, and the area they were now entering offered small chance of replenishing it: "The land around Cape Barrow, and to Detention Harbour, consists of steep craggy mountains of granite, rising so abruptly from the water's edge as to admit of few landing-places even for a canoe. The higher parts attain an elevation of one thousand four hundred or one thousand five hundred feet; and the whole is entirely destitute of vegetation."

Most of the driftwood in the area was pine or balsam and must have been in the water a long time, for the bark was completely worn off and the ends rubbed smooth. There was a sharp frost at night, and a layer of ice formed in the kettles placed in the tents. In spite of the cold nights, the mosquitoes were terrible during the day.

By noon on Sunday, July 29, the ice seemed to be loosening, so after divine service Franklin decided to try and make a break, spurred on by the fact that they had burnt all the available driftwood. An offshore wind came up just as they pushed off, and the men managed to open a passage along the shore by pushing the ice away with their poles. It was tricky work, moving the canoes through the narrow passage without piercing the bark on sharp corners of ice, and in seven hours they moved ahead only three miles, but without seriously damaging the boats. Another hour and a half of this painful progress and they were through another large field of floating ice. With great relief they landed to repair the canoes and eat a well-deserved meal. The country there was less desolate and had grassy hills that sloped down to the beach. It was a picturesque and welcome sight.

By the next day their stock of food was down to an eight-day supply. The two Eskimos were sent up a nearby river with Hepburn to try to find native Eskimos, while the hunters went out after deer. The rest of the party paddled the canoes upstream to the foot of a small waterfall where they made camp and put down four nets. Franklin subsequently named the river after Robert Hood, but as a river it was a disappointment. There was no driftwood, and the nets yielded only one salmon and five whitefish. Fortunately, the hunters returned with two small deer and a brown bear. The voyageurs would not eat the bear, since it appeared to have been sick, but the officers boiled the paws and found them excellent.

Later that morning they embarked and ran along the eastern shore of Arctic Sound, which Franklin named Banks Peninsula. Before them lay a large sheet of water. There was no way of being sure whether it was another bay or simply a passage between the shore and a series of islands, so the men landed and climbed a high hill. From there it appeared that the second theory was the right one. Consequently, Franklin decided to follow the shoreline. Meantime, the hunters had killed four more reindeer, all young and lean, but very welcome.

They continued paddling until midnight, not having sighted any driftwood along the shore, but when they finally saw some on an island, they landed and made camp. The day's difficulties were climaxed when during the night a heavy gale blew down their tents. Although Arctic Sound was decidedly inhospitable at that moment, Franklin decided that it would provide the best anchorage for ships that he had encountered since leaving the mouth of the Coppermine. Deer were numerous in the area and there were musk ox up the Hood River, while the sandy bottom of the bays promised good fishing.

The gale continued to blow fiercely and it was not until ten p.m. on August 2 that the party could embark and continue along the coast. The direction continued to be toward the southeast, and Franklin began to fear that they were being led into a deep inlet. Though they landed frequently and climbed a high hill it was impossible to clarify their position. After three days in this state of uncertainty they were mortified to reach the end of their "channel"—an inlet terminating in a good-sized river! Franklin named the river, unwelcome as it was, after George Back, but the name was not retained. He was consoled somewhat for the loss of so much time by the success of the hunters, who came in with the first musk ox killed since reaching the sea, and a bear. The bear was in excellent condition and the voyageurs forgot their earlier prejudice against eating its meat and found it greatly to their taste. The nets soon yielded a variety of fish—salmon trout, some round fish, tittameg, star fish, herring and a flat fish rather like plaice.

Five days were needed to travel up the eastern shore of the inlet, which Franklin named after the Secretary of State, Lord Bathurst. The men encountered a good deal of rain, several gales and intermittent fogs, but they paddled on stubbornly as long as wind and water permitted. Two large bears and a cub supplemented the pemmican during these days. By following the coast of the inlet instead of paddling straight across, Franklin and his men had paddled 174 miles and used up nine precious days. There was some value, however, in having made this involuntary detour, for they had discovered several harbours suitable for ships, especially one near the mouth of Back's River.

On August 11 they rounded Point Everitt and began sailing eastward once again, but a strong breeze and a heavy swell made the canoes

pitch wildly and greatly slowed them down. Spotting some deer in a
valley near the shore, the whole party landed and St. Germain and
Adam succeeded in killing three of them. Small and lean as they were,
they gave the men enormous encouragement, as they had begun to
fear that the deer had already left the coast for the south. Eighteen
miles farther on they camped at a spot that had evidently been visited
recently by Eskimos. It was a small bay that Franklin named after his
friend Captain David Buchan, and it was sufficiently well sheltered to
provide safe anchorage for sailing ships.

> Embarking at four on the morning of the 12th, we proceeded
> against a fresh piercing north-east wind, which raised the waves
> to a height that quite terrified our people, accustomed only to the
> navigation of rivers and lakes. We were obliged, however, to per-
> severe in our advance, feeling as we did that the short season for
> our operations was hastening away; but after rounding Cape Croker
> the wind became so strong that we could proceed no farther. The
> distance we had made was only six miles on a north-east by east
> course. The shore on which we encamped is formed of the debris
> of red sandstone, and is destitute of vegetation. The beach furnished
> no drift wood, and we dispensed with our usual meal rather than
> expend our pemmican. . . .
>
> Though the wind was not much diminished [August 13], we were
> urged by the want of firewood to venture upon proceeding. We
> paddled close to the shore for some miles, and then ran before the
> breeze with reefed sails, scarcely two feet in depth. Both the canoes
> received much water, and one of them struck twice on sunken rocks.
> At the end of eighteen miles we halted to breakfast in a bay which
> I have named after Vice-Admiral Sir William Johnstone Hope, one
> of the Lords of the Admiralty.

Later that morning the party turned northward from the main coast
and soon found itself in an extensive bay on the underside of what
came to be known as Kent Peninsula.

> On August 14th we paddled the whole day along the northern
> shores of the sound [Melville Sound], returning towards its mouth.
> The land which we were now tracing is generally so flat, that it
> could not be described from the canoes at the distance of four
> miles, and is invisible from the opposite side of the sound, otherwise
> a short traverse might have saved us some days.

.   .   .   .   .

On the following morning the breeze was fresh and the waves rather high. In paddling along the west side of Parry's Bay we saw several deer, but owing to the openness of the country the hunters could not approach them. They killed, however, two swans that were moulting, several cranes and many gray geese. . . . In the evening, having rounded Point Beechy . . . we were exposed to much inconvenience and danger from a heavy rolling sea; the canoes receiving many severe blows and shipping a good deal of water, which induced us to encamp at five p.m. opposite to Cape Croker, which we had passed on the morning of the 12th; the channel which lay between our situation and it, being about seven miles wide. We had now reached the northern point of entrance into this sound, which I have named in honour of Lord Viscount Melville, the first Lord of the Admiralty. . . . Shortly after the tents were pitched, Mr. Back reported from the steersmen that both canoes had sustained material injury during this day's voyage. I found on examination that fifteen timbers of the first canoe were broken, some of them in two places, and that the second canoe was so loose in the frame that its timbers could not be bound in the usual secure manner, and consequently there was danger of its bark separating from the gunwales if exposed to a heavy sea. Distressing as were these circumstances, they gave me less pain than the discovery that our people, who had hitherto displayed in following us through dangers and difficulties no less novel than appalling to them, a courage beyond our expectations, now felt serious apprehensions for their safety, which so possessed their minds that they were not restrained even by the presence of their officers from expressing them. Their fears, we imagined, had been principally excited by the interpreters, St. Germain and Adam, who from the outset had foreboded every calamity; and we now strongly suspected that their recent want of success in their hunting excursions had proceeded from an intentional relaxation in their efforts to kill deer in order that the want of provision might compel us to put a period to our voyage.

As a matter of fact Franklin had been coming round on his own to the view that the expedition would have to turn back. Almost every day now they had to battle heavy winds—a sure sign of the end of the season. Driftwood for fuel had become almost non-existent, and there was now only a three-day supply of pemmican. Reindeer were still seen occasionally but the ground was so flat that the hunters could not get near enough to kill them. In any case, it seemed likely that they would be migrating south any day. Franklin had set his mind on reaching Repulse Bay on the northwest coast of Hudson Bay, but the time lost in paddling around the inlets and bays had convinced him that it could not be done. Moreover, they were steadily getting away from any trading posts and thus increasing the length and difficulty of their return journey.

The officers agreed that it was time to turn back, and the men were overjoyed. But first Franklin wanted to take four more days to try and estimate the trend of the coast eastward. He was so desperately keen to complete his mission that even at that point if he had encountered a band of Eskimos he would probably have arranged to pass the winter with them.

Next morning the men paddled with fresh spirit. Rounding a cape about noon, they found the coast trending to the north-north-east, and for the first time they were in the open sea with no islands in sight. The voyageurs were amazed at the spectacle. That night, violent squalls of wind and rain blew the tents down three times and huge waves pounded the beach. The voyageurs were terrified by their first experience of the open sea. The one good feature of their campsite was the abundance of driftwood, which showed that they had finally escaped from the bays.

Bad weather kept the party at the same spot for the next few days. The food allowance was cut to a handful of pemmican and a small cup of soup per day. Not content to wait idly for the chance of embarking, Franklin set out on foot with Richardson and Back to see what they could find farther to the east. They walked ten to twelve miles along the coast, which seemed to trend more directly to the east and continued to be flat. The most easterly spot reached before turning back they named Point Turnagain, and it is so named on the map today.

When the many perplexing incidents which occurred during the survey of the coast are considered, in connection with the shortness of the period during which operations of the kind can be carried on, and the distance we had to travel before we could gain a place of shelter for the winter, I trust it will be judged that we prosecuted the enterprise as far as was prudent, and abandoned it only under a well-founded conviction that a farther advance would endanger the lives of the whole party and prevent the knowledge of what had been done from reaching England. The active assistance I received from the officers, in contending with the fears of the men, demands my warmest gratitude.

Our researches, as far as they have gone, favour the opinion of those who contend for the practicability of a North-West Passage. The general line of coast probably runs east and west, nearly in the latitude assigned to Mackenzie's River, the Sound into which Kotzebue entered, and Repulse Bay; and I think there is little doubt of a continued sea in or about that line of direction. The existence of whales too, on this part of the coast, evidenced by the whalebone we found in Eskimo Cove, may be considered as an argument for an open sea; and a connection with Hudson's Bay is rendered more probable from the same kind of fish abounding on the coasts we visited, and on those to the north of Churchill River. . . . The portion of the sea over which we passed is navigable for vessels of any size; the ice we met, particularly after quitting Detention Harbour, would not have arrested a strong boat. The chain of islands affords shelter from all heavy seas, and there are good harbours at convenient distances.

Every man in the expedition now had one aim in life—to get back to Fort Enterprise. But a succession of gales, heavy rain, frost and snow kept the party where it was for another four days. On the nineteenth, Belanger and Michel were sent out with Junius to search for a deer that Augustus had killed. When Junius returned that night he had some of the meat but he had lost track of his companions in the fog. Next day the thermometer registered freezing, snow covered the ground and flights of geese were passing to the south. It was a chilling prospect. Franklin sent out all available men to search for the two missing men, and most fortunately they succeeded in finding them. They had suffered greatly from the cold, but what was worse for the expedition, they had thrown away all the remaining meat. Next day the hunters were completely unsuccessful in a day-long search for game, and that night the men had only a handful of pemmican each, after which only half a bag remained.

Even in these dire straits Franklin never forgot the purpose of his mission. When Augustus returned empty-handed from an all-night chase after a deer, he reported that he had walked several miles beyond Point Turnagain. Though the sea was finally calm enough to allow embarkation and the men were longing to be off, Franklin had Augustus draw on the ground a map of the coast beyond the Point; he then copied the map in his journal before setting off.

It was August 22.* The canoes were launched and the men paddled with such spirit that they had covered twenty miles before noon. Franklin had originally planned to return as he had come, along the coast to the mouth of the Coppermine River, but now he felt compelled to alter his plans:

*In a journal footnote Franklin observed, "It is a curious coincidence that our expedition left Point Turnagain on August 22nd—on the same day that Captain Parry sailed out of Repulse Bay. The parties were then distant from each other 539 miles.

We had already found that the country, between Cape Barrow and the Copper-Mine River would not supply our wants . . . besides, at this advanced season we expected the frequent recurrence of gales, which would cause great detention if not danger in proceeding along that very rocky part of the coast.

I determined, therefore, to make at once for Arctic Sound, where we had found the animals more numerous than at any other place; and entering Hood's River, to advance up that stream as far as it was navigable, and then to construct small canoes out of the materials of the larger ones, which could be carried in crossing the barren grounds to Fort Enterprise.

As they paddled along the west coast of Kent Peninsula Franklin threw overboard a sealed tin containing a short account of their progress to date and a rough map. The wind was offshore and it seemed possible that the current might carry the tin to Hudson Bay.

By midday the wind was so strong that they had to land. Everyone immediately went hunting but returned at night empty-handed and drenched. They went to bed with nothing to eat. After passing a comfortless night the men had to wait until the next afternoon before embarking; even then they faced a heavy sea. Arriving at the opening of Melville Sound, they faced a choice: to follow the coastline the way they had come would mean paddling eighty-seven miles, while the distance straight across was only fifteen miles. There was a strong head wind and heavy seas, but the men were more frightened of the prospect of starvation than of drowning, and volunteered to head directly across. There were times when they had to paddle desperately to keep the canoes from turning broadside to the waves, which were so high that the top of the mast of one canoe could not always be seen from the other, but somehow they got across the Sound.

On the other side, a heavy surf was beating on a high, rocky shoreline. The canoes were fast drifting on shore and there seemed to be no protected spot where they could land. Then an open beach, free of rocks, came into sight and they managed to haul the canoes up through the surf with no serious damage. They could find no game on the beach but there were lots of berries, and the gales had blown away the mosquitoes!

Embarking at three in the morning the party arrived at the eastern entrance of Bathurst Inlet and paddled straight across to Barry's Island. There the hunters' success in killing three deer enabled Franklin and his men to conserve their last meal of pemmican. Next morning when two more deer were killed they were reprieved once again from immediate want of food.

Rounding Point Wollaston at the top of Banks Peninsula, the party sailed southward to Hood River and paddled upstream as far as the first rapid.

> *Here terminated our voyage on the Arctic Sea, during which we had gone over six hundred and fifty geographical miles. Our Canadian voyagers could not restrain their joy at having turned their backs on the sea, and passed the evening in talking over their past adventures with much humour and no little exaggeration. The consideration that the most painful, and certainly the most hazardous, part of the journey was yet to come did not depress their spirits at all. It is due to their character to mention that they displayed much courage in encountering the dangers of the sea, magnified to them by their novelty.*

Before proceeding up river next morning Franklin gave to the whole area of Arctic and Melville sounds and Bathurst Inlet the name of George IV's Coronation Gulf, in honour of the new king's coronation. He hoisted the Union Jack on a high point of land where it could be seen by passing ships and deposited a tin box containing a letter which outlined their journey so far and the course they meant to follow to Great Slave Lake. As presents for the Eskimos he deposited a variety of articles made of iron, some beads, looking glasses and the like. Then, at eight in the morning, August 26, the canoes headed up river.

The next two days brought the men only thirteen miles nearer their destination. So many shoals and rapids intervened that the canoes had to be carried most of the way. But still the food supply was adequate: a small deer was killed and there were quantities of berries, and the second day on the river produced ten whitefish and one trout.

> *In the evening we encamped at the lower end of a narrow chasm through which the river flows for upwards of a mile. The walls of this chasm are upwards of two hundred feet high, quite perpendicular, and in some places only a few yards apart. The river precipitates itself into it over a rock, forming two magnificent and picturesque falls close to each other. The upper fall is about sixty feet high, and the lower one at least one hundred; but perhaps considerably more, for the narrowness of the chasm into which it fell prevented us from seeing its bottom, and we could merely discern the top of the spray far beneath our feet. The lower fall is*

divided into two by an insulated column of rock which rises about forty feet above it. The whole descent of the river at this place probably exceeds two hundred and fifty feet. . . . I have named these magnificent cascades "Wilberforce Falls," as a tribute of my respect for that distinguished philanthropist and Christian.

The magnitude of these falls and the difficulty of approach made further use of the large canoes impossible. The next four days were therefore spent in taking them apart and building two small canoes out of the materials. The intention was that each would serve to transport three persons across rivers and lakes and yet be light enough to be carried overland by one man.

Franklin had told the men of his intention to travel as directly as possible to Point Lake, just north of Fort Enterprise and a distance of 149 miles as the crow flies. It was necessary now for all of them to lighten their loads drastically, leaving behind every non-essential. Franklin set an example by packing in boxes all the stores, books, etc. that were not absolutely needed and depositing them in a place where he hoped they would be found later. He then divided between the men the leather intended for making shoes and gave to each a pair of socks and what remained of the warm clothing. He gave them one of the officers' tents as well.

The morning of August 31 was warm and fine as the party set out. Each of the two newly-constructed canoes was carried by one man. The others carried about ninety pounds each of supplies and equipment—ammunition, nets, axes, ice chisels, astronomical instruments, clothing, blankets and three kettles. Progress was made at the rate of about a mile an hour, including rests. In the evening the hunters killed a musk ox and the men enjoyed a hearty meal. They could take with them only a little of the meat that was left over, for they were already heavily laden.

Snow fell on the second day after they had left the falls. High winds made it very difficult to carry the canoes, and they were frequently damaged when the men carrying them fell down. The country now began to get hilly and the small stones covering the ground cut through the men's soft moose-skin shoes, causing great pain. Having advanced about eleven miles under these conditions, the party made camp and some men were sent out to fetch a musk ox and a deer that St. Germain and Augustus had killed. The temperature during the day had stood at about thirty-five degrees. There was no wood for a fire but some moss served the same purpose.

Next morning Franklin viewed the countryside from the top of a hill and decided that the course of the Hood River lay too far to the west to be followed any longer; they must strike out in a more southerly direction toward Point Lake. Accordingly, on September 3 they crossed the River a little farther on, by lashing the two canoes together, and entered a barren country broken only by small lakes and marshes.

By the next night the suffering that was to mark the return journey had already begun. For supper the men ate the last of their pemmican and a little arrowroot. One of them had an inflamed knee and all were exhausted, but there were no complaints. Rain began about midnight and changed at dawn to snow, accompanied by a violent gale. They had nothing to eat and no means of making a fire, so the party stayed in bed all that day and the day after as the storm continued to rage.

> . . . our tents were completely frozen, and the snow had drifted around them to a depth of three feet, and even in the inside there was a covering of several inches on our blankets. Our suffering from cold, in a comfortless canvas tent in such weather, with the temperature at 20°, and without fire, will easily be imagined; it was, however, less than that which we felt from hunger.

Though conditions were little better on the morning of the seventh, the officers decided that winter might actually be setting in and that they must move on without delay. They were all weak from lack of food and their clothes were frozen stiff. It took a long time to pack up the frozen bedclothes and tents, for no one could keep his hands out of his mitts for more than a few minutes.

> Just as we were about to commence our march I was seized with a fainting fit, in consequence of exhaustion and sudden exposure to the wind; but after eating a morsel of portable soup, I recovered so far as to be able to move on. I was unwilling at first to take this morsel of soup, which was diminishing the small and only remaining meal for the party; but several of the men urged me to it, with much kindness. The ground was covered a foot deep with snow, the margins of the lakes were encrusted with ice . . . but the ice not being sufficiently strong to bear us, we frequently plunged knee-deep in water. Those who carried the canoes were repeatedly blown down by the violence of the wind . . . on one of these occasions, the largest canoe was so much broken as to be rendered utterly unserviceable. This we felt was a serious disaster, as the

remaining canoe having through mistake been made too small, it
was doubtful whether it would be sufficient to carry us across a
river. . . . As there was some suspicion that Benoit, who carried the
canoe, had broken it intentionally . . . we closely examined him on
the point; he . . . insisted that it was broken by his falling accident-
ally; and as he brought men to attest the latter fact, who saw him
tumble, we did not press the matter further.

When the men had first murmured against carrying both canoes they
had been told how necessary it would be to have two, in case the
party should have to separate in search of game, or if it were decided
to send the best walkers on ahead in search of the Indians. Now, however, there were no such options. Since nothing could be done to
repair the canoe, a good fire was built from the wreckage and the last
of the soup and arrowroot cooked. After three days without food this
was a skimpy meal, but it gave each man a little energy. The party
now began to advance through the snow in Indian file, the voyageurs
taking turns breaking a trail and Hood following in second place as
"navigator."

The plight of the expedition grew progressively worse. For food
the men began to collect the lichen called *tripe de roche*. It was barely
edible, even after having been boiled, but it gave a brief feeling of
nourishment. Taken often, however, it caused abdominal cramps. One
day the party ate half a partridge each with some tripe de roche;
another day they had a whole partridge each. On September 9 Junius
brought in four pounds of meat—the remains of a deer that had been
partly eaten by wolves—and this, along with two hares, furnished
supper for the whole party. But on the sixth day since anyone had
eaten a real meal, the hunters brought in a large musk ox. It took
only a few minutes to skin and cut up the animal. The famished men
devoured the contents of the stomach on the spot, and the raw in-
testines, which they next attacked, were pronounced excellent.

I do not think that we witnessed through the course of our journey
a more striking proof of the wise dispensation of the Almighty, and
of the weakness of our own judgment than on this day. We had
considered the dense fog which prevailed throughout the morning as
almost the greatest inconvenience that could have befallen us. . . .
Yet this very darkness enabled the party to get to the top of the hill
which bounded the valley wherein the musk oxen were grazing
without being perceived. Had the herd discovered us and taken alarm,

*our hunters in their present state of debility would in all probability
have failed in approaching them.*

As the men grew weaker, the distance covered each day inevitably
decreased. The snow was now from one to three feet deep and hidden
rocks frequently tripped them. Many of the party became ill after the
large meal of musk ox. Some of the men began to lose hope and threw
away useful equipment, including three of the fishing nets. This was a
disaster, for it meant that they had cut themselves off from one of their
chief sources of food. At the same time they were growing steadily
weaker. Franklin now realized that half measures would not do. To
save their strength for walking they would have to leave behind
practically everything except their guns and ammunition.

> *This morning [September 14] the officers being assembled round a
> small fire, Perrault presented each of us with a small piece of meat
> which he had saved from his allowance. It was received with great
> thankfulness, and such an act of self-denial and kindness being totally
> unexpected in a voyager filled our eyes with tears.*

That same day two deer were killed. One was eaten immediately, the
second cut up and distributed among the men. Their strength thus
renewed, they were better able to face the next difficulty: a river, 300
yards wide flowing with great rapidity through a broken, rocky
channel.

> *Having searched for a part where the current was most smooth, the
> canoe was placed in the water at the head of a rapid, and St. Germain,
> Solomon Belanger, and I embarked in order to cross. We went from
> the shore very well, but in mid-channel the canoe became difficult to
> manage under our burden as the breeze was fresh. The current drove
> us to the edge of the rapid, when Belanger unluckily applied his
> paddle to avert the apparent danger of being forced down it, and lost
> his balance. The canoe was overset in consequence in the middle of
> the rapid. We fortunately kept hold of it, until we touched a rock
> where the water did not reach higher than our waists; here we kept
> our footing, notwithstanding the strength of the current, until the
> water was emptied out of the canoe. Belanger then held the canoe
> steady while St. Germain placed me in it, and afterwards embarked
> himself in a very dexterous manner. It was impossible, however, to
> embark Belanger, as the canoe would have been hurried down the
> rapid the moment he should have raised his foot from the rock on*

which *he* stood. We were, therefore, compelled to leave him in his perilous situation. We had not gone twenty yards before the canoe, striking on a sunken rock, went down. The place being shallow, we were again enabled to empty it, and the third attempt brought us to the shore. In the meantime Belanger was suffering extremely, immersed to his middle in the centre of a rapid, the temperature of which was very little above the freezing-point, and the upper part of his body covered with wet clothes, exposed in a temperature not much above zero to a strong breeze. He called piteously for relief and St. Germain on his return endeavoured to embark him, but in vain. The canoe was hurried down the rapid, and when he landed he was rendered by the cold incapable of further exertion, and Adam attempted to embark Belanger, but found it impossible. An attempt was next made to carry out to him a line, made of the slings of the men's loads. This also failed, the current acting so strongly upon it as to prevent the canoe from steering, and it was finally broken and carried down the stream. At length, when Belanger's strength seemed almost exhausted, the canoe reached him with a small cord belonging to one of the nets, and he was dragged perfectly senseless through the rapid. By the direction of Dr. Richardson he was instantly stripped, and being rolled up in blankets, two men undressed themselves and went to bed with him: but it was some hours before he recovered his warmth and sensations. . . .

It is impossible to describe my sensation as I witnessed the various unsuccessful attempts to relieve Belanger. The distance prevented my seeing distinctly what was going on, and I continued pacing up and down on the rock on which I landed, regardless of the coldness of my drenched and stiffening garments. The canoe, in every attempt to reach him, was hurried down the rapid and was lost to view among the rocky islets with a rapidity that seemed to threaten certain destruction; once indeed I fancied that I saw it overwhelmed in the waves. Such an event would have been fatal to the whole party. Separated as I was from my companions, without gun, ammunition, hatchet, or the means of making a fire, and in wet clothes, my doom would have been speedily sealed. My companions, too, driven to the necessity of coasting the lake, must have sunk under the fatigue of rounding its innumerable arms and bays which, as we have learned from the Indians, are very extensive. By the goodness of Providence, however, we were spared at that time. . . .

During the crossing Franklin had lost his portfolio containing his complete journal from the departure from Fort Enterprise up to that day, as well as all his astronomical and meteorological observations. Dr. Richardson, Back and Hood had kept detailed journals of their own, and Franklin was able at a later date to rewrite his account with their help. But the scientific observations had not been copied and all that information was lost.

Next morning the whole party was successfully ferried across the river, one at a time. Even Belanger had recovered sufficiently to be able to proceed. In the afternoon Perrault came upon a herd of deer and after a long chase killed a fine male. That night the men were all in good spirits, cheered by their success in crossing the river and optimistic at having enough meat left over for a good meal next day.

But the cheer and optimism were short-lived. Next day the country became still more rugged, the hills separated by ravines that were as exhausting to descend as they were to climb. By the end of the day the party was worn out, though the distance covered was only eleven miles. And on the following day there was only one meal—some pieces of singed hide and a little tripe de roche.

These would have satisfied us in ordinary times, but we were now almost exhausted by slender fare and travel, and our appetites had become ravenous. We looked, however, with humble confidence to the Great Author and Giver of all good, for a continuance of the support which had hitherto been always supplied to us at our greatest need.

.   .   .   .   .

The reader will probably be desirous to know how we passed our time in such a comfortless situation: the first operation after en-camping was to thaw our frozen shoes, if a sufficient fire could be made, and dry ones were put on; each person then wrote his notes of the daily occurrences, and evening prayers were read; as soon as supper was prepared it was eaten, generally in the dark, and we went to bed, and kept up a cheerful conversation until our blankets were thawed by the heat of our bodies, and we had gathered sufficient warmth to enable us to fall asleep. On many nights we had not even the luxury of going to bed in dry clothes, for when the fire was insufficient to dry our shoes we durst not venture to pull them off, lest they should freeze so hard as to be unfit to put on in the morning. . . .

By the twentieth, Hood was too weak to continue as second man in line, so Richardson took over. Franklin, too, fell behind as the voyageurs put forth a burst of speed in the hope of reaching Point Lake by evening.

> *We had not seen either deer or their tracks through the day, and this circumstance, joined to the disappointment of not discovering the lake, rendered our voyageurs very desponding, and the meagre supper of* tripe de roche *was little calculated to elevate their spirits. They now threatened to throw away their bundles and quit us, which rash act they would probably have committed if they had known what track to pursue.*

At noon next day the sun appeared for the first time in six days; the observations that the officers were enabled to take showed them to be six miles off their proper course. Direction was altered immediately to west-south-west, and guns were fired to notify the hunters, who were then out of sight of the main party. Seeing the change of direction, the men jumped to the conclusion that they were lost and became deeply despondent. When the party halted for the night, Dr. Richardson, who had tenaciously clung to his specimens of plants and minerals collected along the seacoast, now admitted that he could carry them no farther and deposited them under a rock.

A fresh breeze on the twenty-third increased the difficulty of carrying the canoe over the hills. Peltier, who had it, fell several times and then refused to carry it any farther. Vaillant was told to take over and he seemed to be doing quite well, so Franklin went forward to catch the rest of the party, which had advanced out of sight during the argument with Peltier. Somehow he missed the track and stumbled about for several hours before turning back. Eventually he ran into Dr. Richardson, who had been gathering tripe de roche and had also missed his way. When finally they came upon the men, they were eating a meal which consisted of pieces of skin and the bones of a deer that had been devoured by wolves months earlier. Several men had also eaten their old shoes!

Peltier and Vaillant now went up to Franklin and reported that the canoe had been broken so badly by another fall that its usefulness had been destroyed, and they had left it behind. "The anguish this intelligence occasioned may be conceived," wrote Franklin, "but it is beyond my power to describe it." The officers tried every argument and threat to get the men to go back for the canoe, even in its present state, but they refused, and the officers did not have the strength to carry it themselves.

> *To their infatuated obstinacy on this occasion a great portion of the melancholy circumstances which attended our subsequent progress may, perhaps, be attributed. The men now seemed to have lost all hope of being preserved; and all the arguments we could use failed in stimulating them to the least exertion.*

By morning rain had almost obliterated the tracks made by the hunters, who had gone on ahead with George Back a short time earlier. Now the men were convinced that they had been deserted by the hunters. In fury, some of the strongest of them began to throw away their packs, saying that they were going to strike out for themselves. The officers succeeded in persuading them to give up this mad scheme, while the promise of a reward induced Belanger to try to catch up with Back and ask him to wait for the main party. Soon after this, a thick fog closed in, but they continued their march and actually overtook Back.

After halting an hour for a meal of "old shoes, and a few scraps of leather," Franklin and his reunited party set out again, hoping to discover whether a stretch of water ahead of them was the Coppermine River. But the fog soon forced them to make camp. Toward evening, as the fog lessened, Augustus went out alone to survey the water. He returned with the distressing intelligence that they were approaching a lake, not a river.

Next morning the hunters killed five small deer and the men's hopes revived, everyone expressing gratitude for this sign of God's provision. The voyageurs urgently asked for a day's rest, saying that they would gain renewed strength if they could quietly enjoy two substantial meals after eight days of famine. It was now September 25, but while the officers knew that every hour was precious at this critical point in the journey, they felt compelled to give in to the men's entreaties. Hood, who had taken over the invidious task of issuing food to the men when Wentzel left the expedition, now distributed the remaining flesh and skin of the deer and the contents of the stomachs in equal portions. Although he always took the smallest portion himself, the men generally grumbled. By midnight they had eaten about a third of their share and having fasted for so many days, they inevitably suffered severe pains.

The Coppermine was finally reached on September 26 near a point where it flowed into Point Lake. If the canoe had still been available the party could have crossed quite easily in spite of the swift current and the proximity of two rapids. Despite the officers' entreaties, the men refused to build a raft from the willows that grew nearby, insisting that the river was not the Coppermine and that such a raft would not work anyway. The officers maintained that it *was* the Coppermine and that Fort Enterprise was only forty miles away. It was only when some of the men came across a few bear-berry plants which they knew did not grow east of the Coppermine, that they began to listen and "deplored their folly and impatience in breaking the canoe."

Franklin had discovered that two of the men had stolen part of the officers' share of food, though it had been no more than that given the men, and the officers were in worse shape physically. But nothing could be done about it. The men no longer dreaded punishment or hoped for reward.

One way or another the River had to be crossed. St. Germain said that he could not possibly build the frame for a canoe with willows. The only alternative was a raft made from pine trees—if any could be found. Before going to bed Franklin asked Back to go on ahead with St. Germain and Beauparlant to hunt. Should he succeed in crossing the River and contacting the Indians, he was to urge them to bring immediate relief to the expedition.

Back and his men set out at six next morning and Franklin left an hour later with the rest of the party in search of pine trees for the raft. By noon they had walked seven or eight miles along the shore of the lake and had come to an arm which ran northeast. It seemed to be leading them back to the barren country they had crossed a few days earlier, so they stopped to consider what to do. Then, close to where they had halted, they found the carcass of a deer. It had been dead some six months, but the meat was no less acceptable for being putrid, and they devoured most of it then and there.

Food always gave the voyageurs a new outlook on life; now they decided that it would be quite possible to cross the River on a raft made of willows. They urged Franklin to return to the River, which was exactly what he wanted to do. First, however, it was necessary to inform the whole party of the change in plans. Crédit and Junius had fallen behind. They would have to be found and notified, along with George Back. Augustus undertook this mission, encouraged to do so by the promise of a reward. The members of the main party then began to retrace their steps and camped for the night in a valley that was well

treed with good-sized willows. Supper consisted of the remains of the
putrid meat, along with blueberries and cranberries laid bare by the
melting snow.

Crédit rejoined the party next day but there was still no sign of
Junius. Reaching the River at a point where it was narowest—about
130 yards in width—the men began immediately to cut willows for the
raft. To spur them on, Franklin offered a reward of 300 *livres** to the
first man who got a line across the River. This would be needed to pull
the raft across. The hunters could be heard in the woods firing away at
partridges but they returned to camp empty-handed. It came to light
later that they often kept partridges that they brought down and ate
them secretly.

The raft was finished by seven on the morning of September 29, but
the willows were so green that it had little buoyancy. Belanger and
Benoit, the two strongest men of the party, were unsuccessful in their
attempts to get it across the River. They had no oars and a pole made
by tying two tent poles together was too short to touch bottom. Dr.
Richardson had brought a paddle from the Arctic sea, but it was not
sufficient to propel the raft against the strong breeze blowing from the
other side. By now all the men were wet up to their waists and suffering
greatly from the cold.

*At this time Dr. Richardson, prompted by a desire of relieving his
suffering companions, proposed to swim across the stream with a
line, and to haul the raft over. He launched into the stream with the
line round his middle, but when he had got a short distance from the
bank his arms became benumbed with cold, and he lost the power of
moving them; still he persevered, and turning on his back, had nearly
gained the opposite bank when his legs also became powerless, and
to our infinite alarm we beheld him sink. We instantly hauled upon
the line and he came again on the surface, and was gradually drawn
ashore in an almost lifeless state. Being rolled up in blankets, he was
placed before a good fire of willows, and fortunately was just able to
speak sufficiently to give some slight directions respecting the manner
of treating him. He recovered strength gradually, and by the blessing
of God was enabled in the course of a few hours to converse, and by
the evening was sufficiently recovered to remove into the tent. We
then regretted to learn that the skin of his whole left side was
deprived of feeling in consequence of exposure to too great heat. He*

*The old French currency of Quebec was apparently still used among the
voyageurs.

did not perfectly recover the sensation of that side until the following
summer. I cannot describe what every one felt at beholding the
skeleton which the Doctor's debilitated frame exhibited. When he
stripped, the voyageurs simultaneously exclaimed, "Ah que nous
sommes maigres."

Further proof of Richardson's courage, if any were needed, was the
discovery that he had stepped on a dagger as he was entering the water.
His foot had been cut to the bone, but even this had not stopped him
from making the attempt.

That night Augustus rejoined the party, having failed to find either
Junius or Back. He had followed Back's tracks until they were lost on
hard ground. Of Junius there had been no sign, but the general feeling
was that he could look after himself in the woods. Morale rose about a
hundred per cent when Crédit brought from the woods a cap that was
identified as having belonged to one of the hunters who had left the
party in the spring. This seemed to the men clear evidence that they
were on the banks of the Coppermine.

A new and more buoyant raft was built on the thirtieth but an
adverse wind was still blowing too strongly to make the attempt at
crossing advisable. October 1 dawned and still the wind was too strong.
Back and his party returned in the afternoon, having found neither
game nor a means of crossing the River. St. Germain now proposed that
he build a canoe, using, instead of birch bark, the canvas that had
covered the bedding. The experiment seemed worth trying, and men
were accordingly sent back to some stands of pine trees to collect gum
for covering the seams.

In the afternoon there was a heavy fall of snow. Crédit brought in
the antlers and backbone of a deer that had been dead since summer.
"The wolves and birds of prey had picked them clean, but there still
remained a quantity of the spinal marrow which they had not been
able to extract. This, although putrid, was esteemed a valuable prize,
and the spine being divided into portions, was distributed equally. After
eating the marrow, which was so acrid as to excoriate the lips, we
rendered the bones friable by burning, and ate them also."

By morning, a foot and a half of snow covered the ground and it was
still very stormy. The men reverted to their mood of hopelessness and
refused even to go out and pick tripe de roche, preferring to do without
rather than make the effort. The party that had gone out for gum
returned empty-handed, but St. Germain said he could still build the
canoe with willows covered by canvas. Accompanied by Adam and

Back he went out to cut willows. Augustus, meantime, went fishing, but a large trout carried away his bait and he had nothing to take its place.

The following day Franklin set out from the campsite with the intention of joining St. Germain at the willows.

> . . . though he was only three quarters of a mile distant, I spent three hours in a vain attempt to reach him, my strength being unequal to the labour of wading through deep snow; and I returned quite exhausted and much shaken by the numerous falls I had got. My associates were all in the same debilitated state, and poor Hood was reduced to a perfect shadow, from the severe bowel complaints which the tripe de roche never failed to give him. Back was so feeble as to require the support of a stick in walking; and Dr. Richardson had lameness superadded to weakness. The voyageurs were somewhat stronger than ourselves, but more indisposed to exertion on account of their despondency. The sensation of hunger was no longer felt by any of us, yet we were scarcely able to converse upon any other subject than the pleasures of eating. We were much indebted to Hepburn at this crisis. The officers were unable from weakness to gather tripe de roche themselves, and Semandrè, who had acted as our cook on the journey from the coast, sharing in the despair of the rest of the voyageurs refused to make the slightest exertion. Hepburn, on the contrary, animated by a firm reliance on the beneficence of the Supreme Being, tempered with resignation to his will, was indefatigable in his exertions to serve us, and daily collected all the tripe de roche that was used in the officers' mess. Mr. Hood could not partake of this miserable fare, and a partridge which had been reserved for him was, I lament to say, this day stolen by one of the men.

The instant St. Germain completed his canoe he launched it and paddled for the other shore, while the rest of the party watched anxiously from the beach. To their intense relief, he landed safely on the other side. The canoe was then hauled back and forth until every man was transported across the River without serious accident. Although it held together, the canoe let in more and more water with each crossing so that the bedding and clothing got thoroughly wet. There was not enough wood on the other side to light a fire and no one could get dry, but in their great relief at being across the river, none of the party seemed to mind.

It is impossible to imagine a more gratifying change than was produced in our voyageurs after we were all safely landed on the southern banks of the river. Their spirits immediately revived, each of the men shook the officers cordially by the hand and declared they now considered the worst of their difficulties over, as they did not doubt of reaching Fort Enterprise in a few days, even in their feeble condition.

Franklin agreed that there was every reason to be grateful, but he felt keenly the absence of the Eskimo Junius, who seemed to have been lost for good. Nor did he have any illusions about the seriousness of their own position. In a desperate bid to get help he ordered Back, with three of the best men, St. Germain, Solomon Belanger and Beauparlant, to separate from the main party and make all possible speed for Fort Enterprise. Most likely the Indians would be waiting there, but if not, then at least they could expect to find a note from Wentzel saying where the Indians were to be found. St. Germain was to leave a portion of any meat he obtained in a secure but conspicuous place along the route.

One day later the main party was on the verge of collapse. Hood, who was now very feeble, was accompanied by Dr. Richardson, the two of them walking very slowly at the rear of the party. Franklin remained near the front, stopping the men from time to time to give the stragglers a chance to catch up. Overcome by weariness, they encamped early, having advanced only six miles. Crédit, who had been carrying the men's tent, was so exhausted that he could no longer stand when they reached the campsite. Tripe de roche disagreed with both him and Vaillant, and they were the first to break down.

As Crédit was very weak in the morning, his load was reduced to little more than his personal luggage, consisting of his blanket, shoes, and gun. Previous to setting out, the whole party ate the remains of their old shoes and whatever scraps of leather they had, to strengthen their stomachs for the fatigue of the day's journey. We left the encampment at nine and pursued our route over a range of bleak hills. The wind having increased to a strong gale in the course of the morning became piercingly cold, and the drift rendered it difficult for those in the rear to follow the track over the heights. . . . Those in advance made as usual frequent halts, yet being unable from the severity of the weather to remain long still, they were obliged to move on before the rear could come up, and the party, of course, straggled very much.

At noon Franklin was told that Crédit and Vaillant could go no
farther. The party halted in a valley among some willows, while Dr.
Richardson went back to them. He found Vaillant about a mile and a
half in the rear and encouraged him in every possible way to try to
rejoin the party. Vaillant tried, but at every step he fell in the deep
snow. The Doctor then went farther back to look for Crédit, but the
track had been obliterated by drifting snow. Returning, he discovered
that Vaillant had moved only a few yards and could barely speak.
Richardson saw that there was nothing more he could do and returned
to Franklin to report the bad news.

J. B. Belanger* was dispatched immediately to help Vaillant and to
carry his pack. Before long he was back with Vaillant's pack, but alone.
He had found the voyageur lying on his back and had been unable to
rouse him. Franklin pleaded with the strongest men of the party to go
to Vaillant and carry him to the fire. Instead of going, they threatened
to throw away their packs and advance on their own to Fort Enterprise.
Such a step would have been fatal to the whole party. Franklin was
able to dissuade them for the moment, but he realized that only an
alternative plan would prevent further threats of mutiny. After the
officers had consulted together, Hood and Richardson proposed to
remain behind with one other man at the first place where they found
tripe de roche sufficient to last them ten days. They were to keep a tent
and everything else that could possibly be left behind. The rest of the
party could then advance more quickly to the Fort and send back help
from there. Franklin dreaded leaving his companions in such a precarious position, but realized it had to be done. The voyageurs, responding to the least prospect of an improvement in their lot, promised to
cooperate fully.

Before moving on, the voyageurs asked if they might leave Vaillant's
blanket and other necessities on the route, though they had little hope
of his ever reaching them.

*The painful retrospection of the melancholy events of the day
banished sleep [that night], and we shuddered as we contemplated
the dreadful effects of this bitterly cold night on our two companions,
if still living. Some faint hopes were entertained of Crédit's surviving
the storm, as he was provided with a good blanket, and had leather
to eat.*

*There were two Belangers in Franklin's party. Solomon Belanger had left two
days earlier with George Back.

Shortly before noon next day the party came to a thicket of small willows and near it a fair quantity of tripe de roche. Dr. Richardson and Hood decided to stop there and Hepburn volunteered to remain with them. The tent was securely pitched, wood was collected and ammunition and all other articles deposited. Only one tent, a little ammunition and personal clothing were taken by the main party. Before leaving, Franklin asked if any of the men felt too weak to continue, for if so they could remain at the camp. No one accepted, though Michel nearly did.

> *After we had united in thanksgiving and prayers to Almighty God, I separated from my companions, deeply afflicted that a train of melancholy circumstances should have demanded of me the severe trial of parting from friends in such a condition, who had become endeared to me by their constant kindness and co-operation, and a participation of numerous sufferings. . . . Previously to our starting, Peltier and Benoit repeated their promises to return to them with provision, if any should be found at the house, or to guide the Indians to them, if any were met.*

Hood's chief purpose in staying behind was obviously to free the rest of the party of the burden that he now represented. Both Richardson and Hepburn were fit enough to have kept up with the rest: the former remained behind because it was in his character to stand by the weak, and the latter because of the zealous attachment that he had always shown toward his officers. About a mile and a quarter farther on, Franklin and his remaining companions came to a fine stand of pine trees and a large deposit of tripe de roche. They wished the three men had waited a little longer to make their encampment.

In the next twenty-four hours Franklin lost four men. They had only advanced five miles when deep snow forced them to make camp. Belanger and Michel had been straggling far behind and when they finally reached camp they were completely exhausted. Belanger burst into tears and said he could go no farther. He begged permission to go back to Richardson's tent. Soon after, Michel made the same request. Despair now spread through the rest of the men, though Franklin tried to put hope into them by saying that they would probably reach Fort Enterprise in four days. For supper they ate a little burnt leather and drank some Labrador "tea." No one had the strength to raise the tent, and since it was too heavy to carry any farther, they cut it up to use for extra covering. The night was bitterly cold and no one slept.

Next morning, Belanger and Michel were still weaker and asked again for permission to return to the tent, where at least there was a supply of tripe de roche. Franklin wearily agreed and gave them a letter to Richardson and Hood suggesting that they move their tent forward into the pines. Observing that Michel was carrying a considerable amount of ammunition, Franklin had him share it with the other men. Before leaving the voyageur asked in detail how to reach Fort Enterprise and requested permission to take Vaillant's blanket if he could find it. He said that he would try to find Vaillant and Crédit.

Minutes later Perrault and Fontano were seized with fits of dizziness and showed other signs of extreme weakness. After taking some tea and a little burnt leather, they recovered enough to want to continue, but the rest of the party, alarmed and dejected by what they had just seen, declared that they could go no farther. Franklin spent about an hour persuading his beaten companions that they *must* move on or forfeit their own lives and the lives of their friends in the tent. They had gained only about two hundred yards when Perrault was again overcome by dizziness. Again everyone halted until he had recovered and agreed to move on. But within ten minutes the dizziness recurred, and Perrault, sobbing, said he could go no farther. Since Belanger and Michel were no more than a quarter of a mile behind, Franklin encouraged him to turn back and join them. By this time Augustus was fed up with all the delays and had walked on out of sight.

The fourth casualty was Fontano. The last straw for him came when they had to cross a lake, its ice blown clear of snow so that they slipped and fell at almost every step. He halted the party twice with spells of fainting and dizziness and then declared that he could not go on. They were two miles beyond the place where they had left Belanger and Michel, but Franklin proposed that he return to the spot, and next day follow their track to the officers' tent.

I cannot describe my anguish on the occasion of separating from another companion under circumstances so distressing. There was, however, no alternative. The extreme debility of the rest of the party put the carrying of him quite out of the question, as he himself admitted; and it was evident that the frequent delays he must occasion if he accompanied us and did not gain strength must have endangered the lives of the whole. By returning he had the prospect of getting to the tent where tripe de roche *could be obtained, which agreed with him better than with any other of the party, and which*

*he was always very assiduous in gathering. After some hesitation he
determined on returning, and set out, having bid each of us farewell
in the tenderest manner. We watched him with inexpressible anxiety
for some time, and were rejoiced to find, though he got on slowly,
that he kept on his legs better than before. Antonio Fontano was an
Italian. . . . and had begged that should he survive I would take him
with me to England and put him in the way of reaching home.*

Only five now remained in the main party—Adam, Peltier, Benoit,
Samandré and Franklin. No word passed between them as they turned
their backs on their friends and continued the slow progress toward
Fort Enterprise. In an hour they camped among some willows and made
supper of tea and a few pieces of leather. The fact that Augustus was
still absent caused no alarm; they felt sure he could look after himself.
They had advanced four and a half miles on that disastrous day, and
now a good fire helped them find some repose and sleep.

Two more days of travel brought the party to the familiar territory
surrounding Fort Enterprise. Despite their cold and hunger, the men's
spirits soared. A large herd of reindeer appeared nearby but Adam, their
only hunter, was too feeble to go after them. As the five approached
Fort Enterprise on October 11 their feelings were a mixture of hope
and fear. So much hinged on what they would find inside the house
that they advanced in complete silence.

*At length we reached Fort Enterprise, and to our infinite disap-
pointment and grief found it a perfectly desolate habitation. There
was no deposit of provision, no trace of the Indians, no letter from
Mr. Wentzel to point out where the Indians might be found. It would
be impossible for me to describe our sensations after entering this
miserable abode, and discovering how we had been neglected: the
whole party shed tears, not so much for our own fate as for that of
our friends in the rear, whose lives depended entirely on our sending
immediate relief from this place.*

*I found a note, however, from Mr. Back, stating that he had
reached the house two days ago, and was going in search of the
Indians at a part where St. Germain deemed it probable they might
be found. If he was unsuccessful, he purposed walking to Fort
Providence. . . . But he doubted whether either he or his party could
perform the journey to that place in their present debilitated state.
It was evident that any supply that could be sent from Fort Providence would be long in reaching us and could not be sufficient to*

enable us to afford any assistance to our companions behind, and that the only relief for them must be procured from the Indians. I resolved, therefore, in going also in search of them; but my companions were absolutely incapable of proceeding, and I thought by halting two or three days they might gather a little strength, while the delay would afford us the chance of learning whether Mr. Back had seen the Indians.

Once the first shock of disappointment had passed, the main priority was to find something to eat. One of the men found a few deerskins, discarded not many months before. Bones were gathered from among the ashes of old fires. The skin and the bones, with some tripe de roche added, would keep them alive for a while. They chose one room to patch up for living quarters. The parchment had been torn from the windows, the wind was blowing in from all sides and the temperature was from fifteen to twenty below. Loose boards were wedged between the cracks. Planks were torn up from the floor of another room and used to build a fire. Later, as they sat around the fire melting ice and singeing some deerskin for their supper, in walked Augustus. They were overjoyed to see him and impressed at his skill in having found his way back alone.

Next morning Franklin's body was so swollen that he could walk no more than a few yards. Adam was in still worse shape: he could not move at all without help. The other four were somewhat better off and went out to collect bones and tripe de roche for the meals. Soup made from boiling the bones seared their mouths when taken alone but it was a bit milder when boiled with tripe de roche. On October 14 Belanger arrived with a note from Back saying that he had found no trace of the Indians. The voyageur was covered with ice and almost unable to speak, having fallen into a rapid on the way to the Fort. The men rubbed him down, changed his clothes and gave him hot soup.

My companions nursed him with the greatest kindness, and the desire of restoring him to health seemed to absorb all regard for their own situation. I witnessed with peculiar pleasure this conduct, so different from that which they had recently pursued, when every tender feeling was suspended by the desire of self-preservation. They now no longer betrayed impatience or despondency, but were com-

posed and cheerful, and had entirely given up the practice of swear-
ing, to which the Canadian voyagers are so lamentably addicted.

Back's failure to find any trace of the Indians convinced Franklin that
they must be on their way to Fort Providence. If they were, he was
certain he could overtake them, since they travelled slowly when
accompanied by their families. In following them he would be in the
vicinity of Reindeer Lake, and the year before the hunters had found
the deer plentiful in that area. Having weighed all possibilities, Franklin
wrote to Back requesting that he join him at Reindeer Lake.

Belanger was not strong enough to leave with the message until the
eighteenth. Meantime, he was very vague in his replies as to the
whereabouts of Back. Franklin suspected that something was wrong
but there seemed no other choice than to let him go. Later, Adam told
Franklin that the vagueness had been part of an attempt to discourage
him from joining Back, since this would have meant more mouths to
feed. Belanger had even tried to persuade Adam, the one remaining
hunter, to slip away with him and take the only kettle still in Franklin's
possession.

It is painful to have to record a fact so derogatory to human nature,
but I have deemed it proper to mention it to show the difficulties we
had to contend with, and the effect which distress had in warping the
feelings and understanding of the most diligent and obedient of our
party; for such Belanger had been always esteemed up to this time.

Franklin had intended taking his five companions with him to Reindeer
Lake, but the plan had to be abandoned, for Adam's body was so
swollen that it was impossible for him to travel. Peltier and Samandré
volunteered to remain behind and care for their companion, leaving
Benoit and Augustus to go with Franklin.

Despite the hopelessness of their situation Franklin did not abandon
the work of the expedition. He wrote up his journal and packed it with
those of the other officers and with the charts and other documents.
He then wrote a covering letter to the Under-Secretary of State in
London and placed the package in Peltier's and Samandré's hands,
instructing them to send it by the first Indians going to Fort Providence
The two voyageurs also promised to send help to their companions in
the rear as soon as it became available. Before leaving he urged on the
three men the importance of eating two meals a day.

*My clothes were so much torn, as to be quite inadequate to screen
me from the wind, and Peltier and Samandre, fearing that I might
suffer on the journey in consequence, kindly exchanged with me
parts of their dress, desiring me to send them skins in return by the
Indians. Having patched up three pair of snow-shoes, and singed a
considerable quantity of skin for the journey, we started on the
morning of the 20th. . . . No language that I can use could adequately
describe the parting scene. I shall only say there was far more
calmness and resignation to the Divine will evinced by every one
than could have been expected. We were all cheered by the hope that
the Indians would be found by the one party, and relief sent to the
other. Those who remained entreated us to make all the haste we
could, and expressed their hope of seeing the Indians in ten or twelve
days.*

It was a pitiful start to what proved a futile effort. On the second day
out Franklin broke his snowshoes by falling between two rocks.
Without them he found it quite impossible to keep up with his companions, and realizing that it would be fatal to delay them, he decided
to return to the Fort. Once again a note was written to Back, this one
explaining why he had to turn back and asking him to send Benoit and
Augustus back to the Fort with meat immediately, should St. Germain
have killed anything. He also wrote a letter to the post manager at Fort
Providence asking for all possible help; if he missed Back, Benoit was to
go straight to the post.

It was as well that Franklin returned to the house. Samandré had
given up and Peltier was left to do everything. They had decided to eat
only one meal a day and were deeply despondent. Franklin took on the
job of cooking and insisted that they eat twice a day whenever anything
was available. The day after his return there was a violent storm,
which so depressed Adam and Samandré that they would not leave their
beds. Devoid of hope, they wept almost constantly and were reluctant
to eat the meals prepared for them. Franklin recognized the seriousness
of their situation but considered that they were fortunate in comparison
with Richardson and the others who had been left behind.

*We perceived our strength decline every day, and every exertion
began to be irksome; when we were once seated the greatest effort
was necessary in order to rise, and we had frequently to lift each
other from our seats; but even in this pitiable condition we conversed*

*cheerfully, being sanguine as to the speedy arrival of the Indians.
We calculated indeed that if they should be near the situation where
they had remained last winter, our men would have reached them
by this day.*

When it became clear that their house would collapse if they took
any more wood from it for fuel, Peltier began to pull down parts of the
adjoining houses. Although they were only twenty yards away, he was
completely exhausted by evening from the extra work involved in
bringing the wood that distance. Even with Franklin and Samandré
helping, they could carry only enough to replenish the fire four times
during the day. The insides of their mouths had by now become so sore
from eating bone soup that they abandoned it altogether and ate only
boiled deerskins.

By October 29 Peltier was in great pain and had only enough strength
to cut a few pieces of wood. They tried to pick some tripe de roche,
but it was frozen solid. While searching for some bones under the snow
Franklin discovered a few pieces of bark. It was a valuable find, since
they had almost no dry wood left to kindle a fire. A herd of reindeer
stayed within half a mile of the house for several hours that day but
no one had the strength to go after it.

*While we were seated round the fire this evening, discoursing
about the anticipated relief, the conversation was suddenly interrupted by Peltier's exclaiming with joy, "Ah! le monde!" imagining
that he heard the Indians in the other room; immediately afterwards,
to his bitter disappointment, Dr. Richardson and Hepburn entered,
each carrying his bundle. Peltier, however, soon recovered himself
enough to express his joy at their safe arrival, and his regret that their
companions were not with them. When I saw them alone my own
mind was instantly filled with apprehensions respecting my friend
Hood and our other companions, which were immediately confirmed
by the Doctor's melancholy communication that Mr. Hood and
Michel were dead. Perrault and Fontano had neither reached the tent
nor been heard of by them. This intelligence produced a melancholy
despondency in the minds of my party, and on that account the
particulars were deferred until another opportunity. We were all
shocked at beholding the emaciated countenances of the Doctor and
Hepburn, as they strongly evidenced their extremely debilitated
state. The alteration in our appearance was equally distressing to
them, for since the swellings had subsided we were little more than*

skin and bone. The Doctor particularly remarked the sepulchral tone of our voices, which he requested us to make more cheerful if possible, unconscious that his own partook of the same key.

While they were talking Hepburn had slipped from the room; he came back carrying a partridge. The Doctor tore the feathers off, held it briefly to the fire and divided it into six portions. Franklin and his companions had not tasted meat for thirty-one days, "unless indeed the small gristly particles which we found occasionally adhering to the pounded bones may be termed flesh." They devoured their shares, and even this small amount revived their spirits. The Doctor tried to give them further encouragement by telling them that Hepburn would probably kill a deer the next day. Then he spoke to them about the state of the room, which was absolutely filthy. Finally, before they all went to bed, he took out his prayer book and Bible and read some prayers and psalms and portions from the scripture.

Hepburn did not kill a deer the next day, nor on any of the days that followed. Several herds roamed tantalizingly near the house but like the rest, he was now too weak to hold a gun steady. The main source of life continued to be the putrid deerskins which the two officers dragged from under the snow. Peltier and Samandré, meanwhile, had become too weak and dispirited even to cut firewood and that task, too, fell to Hepburn.

After our usual supper [October 30] of singed skin and bone soup, Dr. Richardson acquainted me with the afflicting circumstances attending the death of Mr. Hood and Michel, and detailed the occurrences subsequent to my departure from them, which I shall give from his journal in his own words; but I must here be permitted to express the heart-felt sorrow with which I was overwhelmed at the loss of so many companions; especially for that of my friend Mr. Hood, to whose zealous and able co-operation I had been indebted for so much invaluable assistance during the Expedition, while the excellent qualities of his heart engaged my warmest regard. His scientific observations, together with his maps and drawings, evince a variety of talent, which, had his life been spared, must have rendered him a distinguished ornament to his profession, and which will cause his death to be felt as a loss to the service.

After Captain Franklin had bidden us farewell [Dr. Richardson wrote] we remained seated by the fire-side. . . . We had no tripe de roche *that day, but drank an infusion of the country tea-plant, which was grateful from its warmth, although it afforded no sustenance. We then retired to bed, where we remained all the next day, as the weather was stormy. . . . The party, previous to leaving London, had been furnished with a small collection of religious books, of which we still retained two or three of the most portable, and they proved of incalculable benefit to us. We read portions of them to each other as we lay in bed, in addition to the morning and evening service, and found that they inspired us . . . with so strong a sense of the omnipresence of a beneficent God that our situation, even in these wilds, appeared no longer destitute; and we conversed, not only with calmness, but with cheerfulness, detailing with unrestrained confidence the past events of our lives, and dwelling with hope on our future prospects. Had my poor friend been spared to revisit his native land, I should look back to this period with unalloyed delight.*

On the morning of the 29th,* the weather, although still cold, was clear, and I went out in quest of tripe de roche, leaving Hepburn to cut willows for a fire, and Mr. Hood in bed. I had no success . . . but, on my return to the tent, I found that Michel, the Iroquois, had come with a note from Mr. Franklin, which stated that this man and Jean Baptiste Belanger being unable to proceed, were about to return to us, and that a mile beyond our present encampment there was a clump of pine trees, to which he recommended us to remove the tent. Michel informed us that he quitted Mr. Franklin's party yesterday morning, but that having missed his way, he had passed the night on the snow a mile or two to the northward of us. Belanger, he said, being impatient, had left the fire about two hours earlier, and as he had not arrived, he supposed he had gone astray. It will be seen in the sequel that we had more than sufficient reason to doubt the truth of this story.

Michel now produced a hare and a partridge which he had killed in the morning. This unexpected supply of provision was received by us with a deep sense of gratitude to the Almighty for his goodness, and we looked upon Michel as the instrument he had chosen to preserve all our lives. He complained of cold, and Mr. Hood offered to share his buffalo robe with him at night: I gave him one of two shirts which I wore, while Hepburn, in the warmth of his heart, exclaimed, "How I shall love this man if I find that he does not tell lies like the others." Our meals being finished, we arranged that the

*A misprint; Richardson meant October 9.

greatest part of the things should be carried to the pines the next day. . . .

Early in the morning Hepburn, Michel and myself carried the ammunition and most of the other heavy articles to the pines. Michel was our guide, and it did not occur to us at the time that his conducting us perfectly straight was incompatible with his story of having gone astray on his way to us. He now informed us that he had, on his way to the tent, left on the hill above the pines a gun and forty-eight balls, which Perrault had given to him when with the rest of Mr. Franklin's party, he took leave of him. It will be seen, on a reference to Mr. Franklin's journal, that Perrault carried his gun and ammunition with him when they parted from Michel and Belanger. After we had made a fire and drank a little of the country tea, Hepburn and I returned to the tent, where we arrived in the evening, much exhausted with our journey. Michel preferred sleeping where he was, and requested us to leave him the hatchet, which we did, after he had promised to come early in the morning to assist us in carrying the tent and bedding. Mr. Hood remained in bed all day. Seeing nothing of Belanger to-day, we gave him up for lost.

On the 11th, after waiting until late in the morning for Michel, who did not come, Hepburn and I loaded ourselves with the bedding and, accompanied by Mr. Hood, set out for the pines. Mr. Hood was much affected with dimness of sight, giddiness, and other symptoms of extreme debility, which caused us to move very slow and to make frequent halts. On arriving at the pines, we were much alarmed to find that Michel was absent. We feared that he had lost his way in coming to us in the morning, although it was not easy to conjecture how that could have happened, as our footsteps of yesterday were very distinct. Hepburn went back for the tent and returned with it after dusk, completely worn out with the fatigue of the day. Michel too arrived at the same time, and relieved our anxiety on his account. He reported that he had been in chase of some deer . . . and although he did not come up with them, yet that he found a wolf which had been killed by the stroke of a deer's horn, and had brought a part of it. We implicitly believed this story then, but afterwards became convinced from circumstances, the detail of which may be spared, that it must have been a portion of the body of Belanger or Perrault. A question of moment here presents itself; namely, whether he actually murdered these men, or either of them, or whether he found the bodies on the snow. Captain Franklin, who

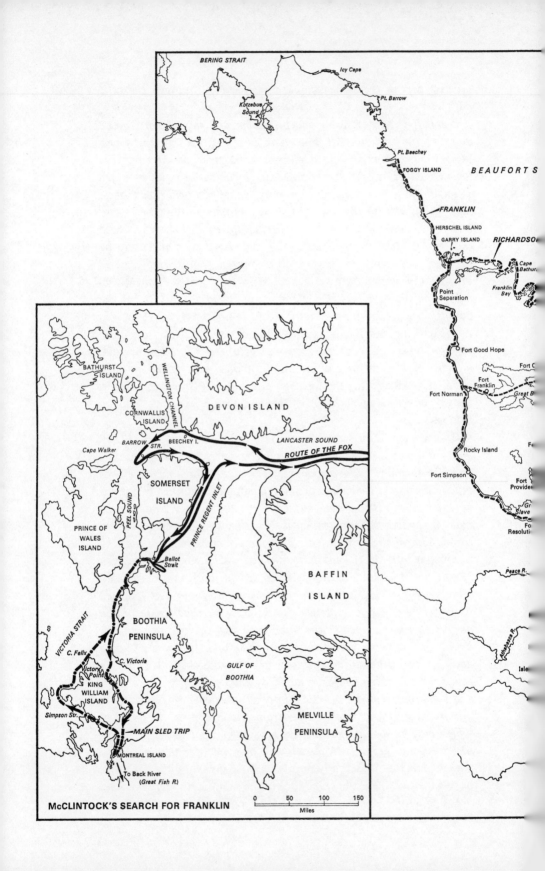

BERING STRAIT

Icy Cape

Pt. Barrow

Pt. Beechey

FOGGY ISLAND

BEAUFORT S

Kotzebue Sound

FRANKLIN

HERSCHEL ISLAND

GARRY ISLAND

RICHARDSO

Cape Bathura

Franklin Bay

Point Separation

Fort Good Hope

Fort C

Fort Franklin

Great B

Fort Norman

Rocky Island

Fe

Fort Simpson

Fort Provide

Gr Slave

Fo Resoluti

Peace R.

Athabasca R.

Isle

BATHURST ISLAND

WELLINGTON CHANNEL

DEVON ISLAND

CORNWALLIS ISLAND

BARROW STR.

Cape Walker

Beechey I.

LANCASTER SOUND

ROUTE OF THE FOX

SOMERSET ISLAND

PEEL SOUND

PRINCE REGENT INLET

PRINCE OF WALES ISLAND

Bellot Strait

BAFFIN ISLAND

VICTORIA STRAIT

BOOTHIA PENINSULA

C. Felix

C. Victoria

Victory Point

KING WILLIAM ISLAND

GULF OF BOOTHIA

Simpson Str.

MAIN SLED TRIP

MELVILLE PENINSULA

MONTREAL ISLAND

To Back River (Great Fish R.)

McCLINTOCK'S SEARCH FOR FRANKLIN

0   50   100   150
Miles

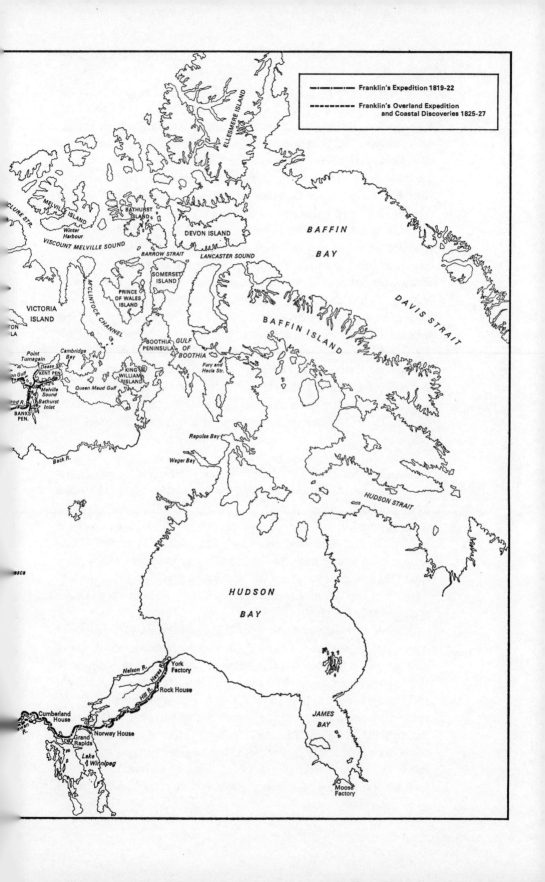

Franklin's Expedition 1819-22
Franklin's Overland Expedition
and Coastal Discoveries 1825-27

ELLESMERE ISLAND

BAFFIN
BAY

DAVIS STRAIT

M°CLURE STR.

MELVILLE ISLAND

Winter Harbour

VISCOUNT MELVILLE SOUND

BATHURST ISLAND

DEVON ISLAND

BARROW STRAIT

LANCASTER SOUND

M°CLINTOCK CHANNEL

SOMERSET ISLAND

PRINCE OF WALES ISLAND

VICTORIA ISLAND

BAFFIN ISLAND

BOOTHIA PENINSULA

GULF OF BOOTHIA

Point Turnagain

Cambridge Bay

on Gulf

Desse Str.

KENT PEN.

Melville Sound

KING WILLIAM ISLAND

Fury and Hecla Str.

ood R.

Bathurst Inlet

BANKS PEN.

Queen Maud Gulf

Back R.

Repulse Bay

Wager Bay

HUDSON STRAIT

asca

HUDSON

BAY

Nelson R.

York Factory

Hayes R.

Hill R.

Rock House

JAMES
BAY

Cumberland House

Norway House

Grand Rapids

Lake Winnipeg

Moose Factory

*is the best able to judge of this matter from knowing their situation
when he parted from them, suggested the former idea, and that both
Belanger and Perrault had been sacrificed. When Perrault turned
back, Captain Franklin watched him until he reached a small group
of willows, which was immediately adjoining to the fire and concealed it from view, and at this time the smoke of fresh fuel was
distinctly visible. Captain Franklin conjectures that Michel having
already destroyed Belanger, completed his crime by Perrault's death
in order to screen himself from detection. Although this opinion is
founded only on circumstances and is unsupported by direct evidence, it has been judged proper to mention it, especially as the
subsequent conduct of the man showed that he was capable of committing such a deed. The circumstances are very strong. It is not
easy to assign any other adequate motive for his concealing from
us that Perrault had turned back, and his request overnight that
we should leave him the hatchet; and his cumbering himself with
it when he went out in the morning, unlike a hunter who makes
use only of his knife when he kills a deer, seem to indicate that he
took it for the purpose of cutting up something that he knew to be
frozen. These opinions, however, are the result of subsequent consideration. We passed this night in the open air.*

*On the following morning the tent was pitched, and Michel went
out early, refused my offer to accompany him, and remained out
the whole day. He would not sleep in the tent at night, but chose
to lie at the fire-side.*

*On the 13th there was a heavy gale of wind, and we passed the
day by the fire. Next day, about two p.m., the gale abating, Michel
set out as he said to hunt, but returned unexpectedly in a very short
time. This conduct surprised us, and his contradictory and evasory
answers to our questions excited some suspicions, but they did not
turn towards the truth.*

*October 15th.—In the course of this day Michel expressed much
regret that he had stayed behind Mr. Franklin's party, and declared
that he would set out for the house at once if he knew the way.
We endeavoured to soothe him and to raise his hopes of the
Indians speedily coming to our relief, but without success. He
refused to assist us in cutting wood, but about noon, after much
solicitation, he set out to hunt. Hepburn gathered a kettle of tripe
de roche, but froze his fingers. Both Hepburn and I fatigued ourselves
much to-day in pursuing a flock of partridges from one part to
another of the group of willows, in which the hut [tent] was situated,*

but we were too weak to be able to approach them with sufficient caution. In the evening Michel returned, having met with no success.

Next day he refused either to hunt or cut wood, spoke in a very surly manner, and threatened to leave us. Under these circumstances, Mr. Hood and I deemed it better to promise if he would hunt diligently for four days, that then we would give Hepburn a letter for Mr. Franklin, a compass, inform him what course to pursue, and let them proceed together to the fort. The non-arrival of the Indians to our relief now led us to fear that some accident had happened to Mr. Franklin, and we placed no confidence in the exertions of the voyageurs that accompanied him, but we had the fullest confidence in Hepburn's returning the moment he could obtain assistance.

On the 17th I went to conduct Michel to where Vaillant's blanket was left, and after walking about three miles pointed out the hills to him at a distance, and returned to the hut, having gathered a bagful of tripe de roche *on the way. . . . Michel proposed to remain out all night, and to hunt next day on his way back. He returned in the afternoon of the 18th, having found the blanket, together with a bag containing two pistols, and some other things which had been left beside it. We had some* tripe de roche *in the evening, but Mr. Hood, from the constant griping it produced, was unable to eat more than one or two spoonfuls. He was now so weak as to be scarcely able to sit up at the fire-side, and complained that the least breeze of wind seemed to blow through his frame. He also suffered much from cold during the night. We lay close to each other, but the heat of the body was no longer sufficient to thaw the frozen rime formed by our breaths on the blankets that covered him.*

At this period we avoided as much as possible conversing upon the hopelessness of our situation, and generally endeavoured to lead the conversation towards our future prospects in life. The fact is, that with the decay of our strength, our minds decayed, and we were no longer able to bear the contemplation of the horrors that surrounded us. Each of us, if I may be allowed to judge from my own case, excused himself from so doing by a desire of not shocking the feelings of the others, for we were sensible of one another's weakness of intellect though blind to our own. Yet we were calm and resigned to our fate. . . . On the 19th Michel refused to hunt or even to assist in carrying a log of wood to the fire, which was too heavy for Hepburn's strength and mine. Mr. Hood endeavoured to point out to him the necessity and duty of exertion, and the cruelty of his quitting us without leaving something for our support; but the discourse far from producing any beneficial effect, seemed only to excite his anger, and among other expressions he made use of the following remarkable one: "It is no use hunting, there are no animals, you had better kill and eat me." At length, however, he went out, but returned very soon with a report that he had seen three deer, which he was unable to follow from having wet his foot in a small stream of water thinly covered with ice, and being consequently obliged to come to the fire. . . .

Sunday, October 20.—In the morning we again urged Michel to go a hunting that he might if possible leave us some provision, to-morrow being the day appointed for his quitting us; but he showed great unwillingness to go out and lingered about the fire under the pretence of cleaning his gun. After we had read the morning service I went about noon to gather some tripe de roche, leaving Mr. Hood sitting before the tent at the fire-side, arguing with Michel; Hepburn was employed cutting down a tree at a short distance from the tent, being desirous of accumulating a quantity of fire wood before he left us. A short time after I went out I heard the report of a gun, and about ten minutes afterwards Hepburn called to me in a voice of great alarm to come directly. When I arrived, I found poor Hood lying lifeless at the fire-side, a ball having apparently entered his forehead. I was at first horror-struck with the idea that in a fit of despondency he had hurried himself into presence of his Almighty Judge by an act of his own hand; but the conduct of Michel soon gave rise to other thoughts, and excited suspicions which were confirmed when upon examining the body I discovered that the shot had entered the back part of the head and passed out at the forehead, and that the muzzle of the gun had been applied so close as to set fire to the night-cap behind. The gun, which was of the longest kind supplied to the Indians, could not have been placed in a position to inflict such a wound, except by a second person. Upon inquiring of Michel how it happened, he replied that Mr. Hood had sent him into the tent for the short gun and that during his absence the long gun had gone off, he did not know whether by accident or not. He held the short gun in his hand at the time he was speaking to me. Hepburn afterwards informed me that previous to the report of the gun Mr. Hood and Michel were speaking to each other in an elevated angry tone; that Mr. Hood being seated at the fire-side, was hid from him by intervening willows, but that on hearing the report he

looked up and saw Michel rising up from before the tent-door, or
just behind where Mr. Hood was seated, and then going into the
tent. Thinking that the gun had been discharged for the purpose
of cleaning it, he did not go to the fire at first; and when Michel
called to him that Mr. Hood was dead, a considerable time had
elapsed. Although I dared not openly evince any suspicion that I
thought Michel guilty of the deed, yet he repeatedly protested that
he was incapable of committing such an act, kept constantly on
his guard, and carefully avoided leaving Hepburn and me together.
He was evidently afraid of permitting us to converse in private,
and whenever Hepburn spoke he inquired if he accused him of the
murder. It is to be remarked that he understood English very im-
perfectly, yet sufficiently to render it unsafe for us to speak on
the subject in his presence. We removed the body into a clump of
willows behind the tent, and, returning to the fire, read the funeral
service in addition to the evening prayers. The loss of a young
officer, of such distinguished and varied talents and application,
may be felt and duly appreciated by the eminent characters under
whose command he had served; but the calmness with which he
contemplated the probable termination of a life of uncommon
promise and the patience and fortitude with which he sustained . . .
unparalleled bodily suffering, can only be known to the companions
of his distresses. . . . Bickersteth's Scripture Help was lying open
beside the body, as if it had fallen from his hand, and it is probable
that he was reading it at the instant of his death. We passed the
night in the tent together without rest, every one being on his
guard. Next day, having determined on going to the Fort, we began
to patch and prepare our clothes for the journey. We singed the
hair off a part of the buffalo robe that belonged to Mr. Hood, and
boiled and ate it. Michel tried to persuade me to go to the woods
on the Copper-Mine River and hunt for deer instead of going to the
Fort. In the afternoon a flock of partridges coming near the tent,
he killed several which he shared with us. . . .

   . . . on the morning of the 23rd we set out, carrying with us the
remainder of the singed robe. Hepburn and Michel had each a gun,
and I carried a small pistol, which Hepburn had loaded for me. In
the course of the march Michel alarmed us much by his gestures
and conduct, was constantly muttering to himself, expressed an
unwillingness to go to the Fort, and tried to persuade me to go to
the southward to the woods, where he said he could maintain himself all the winter by killing deer. In consequence of this behaviour

and the expression of his countenance, I requested him to leave
us and to go to the southward by himself. This proposal increased
his ill-nature, he threw out some obscure hints of freeing himself
from all restraint on the morrow; and I overheard him muttering
threats against Hepburn, whom he openly accused of having told
stories against him. He also, for the first time, assumed such a tone
of superiority in addressing me as evinced that he considered us
to be completely in his power, and he gave vent to several expressions of hatred towards the white people . . . some of whom, he
said, had killed and eaten his uncle and two of his relations. In
short, taking every circumstance of his conduct into consideration,
I came to the conclusion that he would attempt to destroy us on the
first opportunity that offered, and that he had hitherto abstained
from doing so from his ignorance of the way to the Fort, but that
he would never suffer us to go thither in company with him. In
the course of the day he had several times remarked that we were
pursuing the same course that Mr. Franklin was doing when he left
him, and that by keeping towards the setting sun he could find his
way himself. Hepburn and I were not in condition to resist even
an open attack, nor could we by any device escape from him. Our
united strength was far inferior to his, and beside his gun he was
armed with two pistols, an Indian bayonet, and a knife. In the
afternoon, coming to a rock on which there was some tripe de
roche, he halted and said he would gather it while we went on, and
that he would soon overtake us. Hepburn and I were now left
together for the first time since Mr. Hood's death, and he acquainted
me with several material circumstances which he had observed of
Michel's behaviour and which confirmed me in the opinion that
there was no safety for us except in his death, and he offered to
be the instrument of it. I determined, however, as I was thoroughly
convinced of the necessity of such a dreadful act, to take the whole
responsibility upon myself; and immediately upon Michel's coming up, I put an end to his life by shooting him through the head
with a pistol. Had my own life alone been threatened, I would not
have purchased it by such a measure; but I considered myself as
intrusted also with the protection of Hepburn's, a man who, by
his humane attentions and devotedness, had so endeared himself
to me that I felt more anxiety for his safety than for my own.
Michel had gathered no tripe de roche, and it was evident to us that
he had halted for the purpose of puttng his gun in order, with the

intention of attacking us, perhaps while we were in the act of encamping.

I have dwelt in the preceding part of the narrative upon many circumstances of Michel's conduct, not for the purpose of aggravating his crime, but to put the reader in possession of the reasons that influenced me in depriving a fellow-creature of life. Up to the period of his return to the tent, his conduct had been good and respectful to the officers, and in a conversation between Captain Franklin, Mr. Hood, and myself, at Obstruction Rapid, it had been proposed to give him a reward upon our arrival at a post. His principles, however, unsupported by a belief in the divine truths of Christianity, were unable to withstand the pressure of severe distress.

Richardson and Hepburn remained where they were, stormbound, for two days, with only lichens and some singed buffalo hide to eat. On October 26 the weather cleared sufficiently to enable them to set out once more and for the next two days they made painful progress through heavy snow.

On the 29th we had clear and fine weather. We set out at sunrise, and hurried on in our anxiety to reach the house, but our progress was much impeded by the great depth of the snow in the valleys. Although every spot of ground over which we travelled today had been repeatedly trodden by us, yet we got bewildered in a small lake. . . . In the evening we saw several large herds of rein-deer, but Hepburn, who used to be considered a good marksman, was now unable to hold the gun straight, and although he got near them all his efforts proved fruitless. In passing through a small clump of pines we saw a flock of partridges, and he succeeded in killing one after firing several shots. We came in sight of the fort at dusk, and it is impossible to describe our sensations, when on attaining the eminence that overlooks it we beheld the smoke issuing from one of the chimneys. From not having met with any footsteps in the snow as we drew nigh our once cheerful residence, we had been agitated by many melancholy forebodings. Upon entering the now desolate building, we had the satisfaction of embracing Captain Franklin, but no words can convey an idea of the filth and wretchedness that met our eyes on looking around. Our own misery had stolen upon us by degrees, and we were accustomed to the contemplation of each other's emaciated figures, but the ghastly

countenances, dilated eye-balls, and sepulchral voices of Mr. Franklin
and those with him were more than we could at first bear.

Dr. Richardson and Hepburn brought to that filthy house and its
barely-alive inmates an unquenchable will to live. The three voyageurs
were too far gone to respond but the arrival of the two men was a life-
saver for Franklin. Feeble as they were, the three Englishmen took on
four priorities: to clean out the room, cut wood to keep the fire going,
hunt for food, and turn to God at regular periods each day. From the
day of Dr. Richardson's arrival they made it their practice to read
prayers and a portion of the New Testament morning and evening.
". . . the performance of these duties always afforded us the greatest
consolation, serving to reanimate our hope in the mercy of the Omni-
potent, who alone could save and deliver us."

The next seven days were marked by ever-increasing misery and
weariness. Although game was available near the house, neither
Hepburn nor the Doctor succeeded in killing anything. Peltier and
Samandré had for some days been too weak to take part in the search
for food and fuel, but on the evening of the thirty-first they roused
themselves sufficiently to mend their shirts and drawers; the activity
raised their spirits and they kept it up until one in the morning. Adam
seemed a little better and sat up with them. They even got up and
carried three or four logs across the room to the fire. Franklin was
pleasantly surprised and wondered whether they might not have more
strength than he had imagined. But by the next day, November 1, the
two were unable to eat even the tripe de roche that Dr. Richardson
brought in.

In the afternoon Peltier was so much exhausted that he sat up
with difficulty, and looked piteously; at length he slid from his
stool upon his bed, as we supposed to sleep, and in this composed
state he remained upwards of two hours without our apprehend-
ing any danger. We were then alarmed by hearing a rattling in his
throat and on the Doctor's examining him, he was found to be
speechless. He died in the course of the night. Samandré had sat up
the greater part of the day and even assisted in pounding some
bones; but on witnessing the melancholy state of Peltier, he became
very low and began to complain of cold and stiffness of the joints.
Being unable to keep up a sufficient fire to warm him, we laid him
down and covered him with several blankets. He did not, however,
appear to get better, and I deeply lament to add he also died before

daylight. We removed the bodies of the deceased into the opposite part of the house, but our united strength was inadequate to the task of interring them, or even carrying them down to the river.

Peltier had been obsessed by the conviction that if the Indians had not brought relief by November 1, it would be too late and he would not survive the day. His cheerfulness in the past and his constant desire to help and the great care he had given Adam had endeared him to all the others. Poor Samandré would have done as much if he had been able. Their deaths shocked the four survivors. Adam sank into extreme despondency and lost all the ground he had recently gained. The Doctor and Hepburn went out to collect wood but Franklin remained indoors with Adam and tried to rouse his spirits.

The Doctor and Hepburn were getting much weaker and the limbs of the latter were now greatly swelled. They came into the house frequently in the course of the day to rest themselves, and when once seated, were unable to rise without the help of one another, or of a stick. Adam was for the most part in the same low state as yesterday, but sometimes he surprised us by getting up and walking with an appearance of increased strength. His looks were now wild and ghastly, and his conversation was often incoherent.

.   .   .   .   .

I may here remark that owing to our loss of flesh, the hardness of the floor, from which we were only protected by a blanket, produced soreness over the body and especially those parts on which the weight rested in lying, yet to turn ourselves for relief was a matter of toil and difficulty. However . . . we generally enjoyed the comfort of a few hours' sleep. The dreams which for the most part . . . accompanied it were usually (though not invariably,) of a pleasant character, being very often about the enjoyments of feasting. In the day-time we fell into the practice of conversing on common and light subjects, although we sometimes discussed with seriousness and earnestness topics connected with religion. We generally avoided speaking directly of our present sufferings, or even of the prospect of relief. I observed that in proportion as our strength decayed, our minds exhibited symptoms of weakness evinced by a kind of unreasonable pettishness with each other. Each of us thought the other weaker in intellect than himself, and more in need of advice and assistance. So trifling a circumstance as a change of place, recommended by one as being warmer and more comfortable, and refused by the other from a dread of motion, frequently called forth fretful expressions which were no sooner uttered than atoned for, to be repeated perhaps in the course of a few minutes. The same thing often occurred when we endeavoured to assist each other in carrying wood to the fire; none of us were willing to receive assistance, although the task was disproportioned to our strength. On one of these occasions Hepburn was so convinced of this waywardness that he exclaimed, "Dear me, if we are spared to return to England, I wonder if we shall recover our understandings". . . .

. . . The Doctor and Hepburn went to cut wood [November 7]. They had hardly begun their labour when they were amazed at hearing the report of a musket. They could scarcely believe that there was really any one near until they heard a shout, and immediately espied three Indians close to the house. Adam and I heard the latter noise, and I was fearful that a part of the house had fallen upon one of my companions, a disaster which had in fact been thought not unlikely. My alarm was only momentary, Dr. Richardson came in to communicate the joyful intelligence that relief had arrived. He and myself immediately addressed thanksgiving to the throne of mercy for this deliverance, but poor Adam was in so low a state that he could scarcely comprehend the information. When the Indians entered, he attempted to rise but sank down again. But for this seasonable interposition of Providence his existence must have terminated in a few hours, and that of the rest probably in not many days.

The Indians had been sent by Akaitcho the moment Back had reached him two days earlier. They brought only a small supply of food in order that they might travel with all possible speed. The youngest of them rested only an hour before leaving to take word of the situation to Akaitcho. Franklin gave him a note for Back asking that more meat be sent as quickly as possible. The two Indians who remained showed kindness, but little wisdom, in letting the three Englishmen eat as much of the dried meat as they wanted. Though the Doctor kept repeating that they should eat only a little at first, yet he himself could not hold back. That night they suffered agonies of indigestion and did not sleep at all. Adam, being unable to feed himself, was given much less and consequently suffered very much less. His spirits revived hourly.

Next morning the Indians told Franklin that they would not remain in the house with the bodies of the dead men lying exposed to view; they asked him to move his party to an encampment beside the River. The day was too stormy, however, to make the move. The Doctor and Hepburn managed to drag the bodies a short distance from the house and cover them with snow. This done, the Indians agreed to remain inside.

The improved state of our apartment and the large and cheerful fires they kept up produced in us a sensation of comfort to which we had long been strangers. In the evening they brought in a pile of dried wood which was lying on the river-side, and on which we had often cast a wishful eye, being unable to drag it up the bank. The Indians set about every thing with an activity that amazed us. Indeed, contrasted with our emaciated figures and extreme debility, their frames appeared to us gigantic and their strength supernatural. These kind creatures next turned their attention to our personal appearance and prevailed upon us to shave and wash ourselves. The beards of the Doctor and Hepburn had been untouched since they left the seacoast, and become of a hideous length and peculiarly offensive to the Indians.

On November 9 one of the Indians caught four large trout. They were a blessing, especially for Franklin and the Doctor, who had suffered terribly from the unaccustomed diet of meat. The night was stormy and the wind blew in through the multitude of cracks, but the four men felt no discomfort. The food they had eaten gave them such powers of resistance that it was hard not to believe that the weather had turned milder.

Four more days passed; the Indians were by now thoroughly despondent, for no further supplies had arrived. Fearing that their companion had failed to reach Akaitcho, their helpfulness gave way to despair and they would neither hunt nor fish. That night they handed a little pounded meat to the men, walked out into the dark and did not return! Adam rather unwillingly told Franklin that they intended walking day and night back to Akaitcho's camp. They had not told Franklin of their plans because they feared he would object. Although they had gone only to seek further help for the sufferers, they had left them once again without food. The men had recovered a little of their strength but they had also recovered their appetites, and now they felt the need for food more strongly than ever. The next two days were agonizing. Adam lost hope again and would not eat his share of singed skin. The Doctor and Hepburn went back to collecting wood. Franklin found that he could now help a little by bringing it into the house.

Then, on the morning of November 15, Hepburn came in to announce that a party of Indians was approaching. The room was quickly swept and every scrap of skin carefully put out of sight, out of respect for the Indians' belief that to burn skin brought bad luck in hunting. The party consisted of three Indians, with two wives dragging the provisions. They were accompanied by Benoit, who, with Augustus, had left Fort Enterprise the previous month to get word to Akaitcho and George Back. Benoit brought excellent news of Back. He and his men had recovered to the point where they were about to leave for Fort Providence. The moment the Indians arrived, Adam recovered his spirits and started to walk around the room with surprising energy.

Preparations to leave Fort Enterprise began immediately, for it was important to move south among the reindeer before the existing supply of food was exhausted. Early next morning the whole party united in prayer and ate some breakfast, then left the house for the last time.

> Our feelings on quitting the Fort, where we had formerly enjoyed much comfort, if not happiness, and latterly experienced a degree of misery scarcely to be paralleled, may be more easily conceived than described. The Indians treated us with the utmost tenderness, gave us their snow-shoes and walked without themselves, keeping by our sides that they might lift us when we fell. . . . The Indians prepared our encampment, cooked for us, and fed us as if we had been children; evincing humanity that would have done honour to the most civilized people. . . .
>
> . . . On this day [November 26] we arrived in safety at the abode of our chief and companion, Akaitcho. We were received by the party assembled in the leader's tent with looks of compassion, and profound silence, which lasted about a quarter of an hour, and by which they meant to express their condolence for our sufferings. The conversation did not begin until we had tasted food. The Chief, Akaitcho, showed us the most friendly hospitality and all sorts of personal attention, even to cooking for us with his own hands, an office which he never performs for himself.

In the course of the day each of the Indians visited the party in turn, not merely out of curiosity but as an expression of their sympathy. This was especially significant because several of the Indian families were themselves in deep distress from the loss of three relatives who had drowned three months earlier. Each morning and evening they would bewail their loss by repeating the three names in a loud singing tone, frequently interrupting themselves by bursts of tears. One woman was so affected by her son's death that she seemed to have lost her reason and wandered among the tents all day crying his name.

On December 1 the whole party accompanied the Indians on their move toward the south. Fortunately for the Englishmen, the Indians advanced slowly. By the time they made camp that evening they had covered only four miles, but Franklin and his companions found it an exhausting day. Two days later they were joined by Solomon Belanger and another voyageur, sent from Fort Providence by Weeks. The two had brought spirits and tobacco for the Indians, and for the Englishmen, a change of clothing, a little tea and sugar, and letters from home. The letters contained the good news that Captain Parry had successfully completed his Arctic voyage. There was official word that Franklin, Back and the unfortunate Hood had received promotions; there were also letters from Back and Wentzel. Back's gave them the important news that the two fur companies had been united into a single enterprise. He also reported that the goods intended for Akaitcho and his band in reward for their services had not been shipped by the North West Company as promised. He was therefore continuing to Moose-Deer Island, where there was a supply of equipment intended for the voyageurs, which they would not now require. He intended to pick out some articles that could be given to the Indians as interim presents. The non-arrival of the goods upset the officers greatly, as they wanted very much to express to the Indians the gratitude they felt for all that they had done.

> All the Indians flocked to our encampment to learn the news and to receive the articles brought for them. Having got some spirits and tobacco, they withdrew to the tent of the Chief and passed the greater part of the night in singing. We had now the indescribable gratification of changing our linen, which we had worn ever since our departure from the sea-coast.

On December 11 Franklin and his companions finally reached Fort Providence. Weeks was still in charge and received them with great kindness.

Our sensations on being once more in a comfortable dwelling, after the series of hardships and miseries we had experienced, will be much better imagined than any language of mine can describe them. Our first act was again to return our grateful praises to the Almighty for the manifold instances of his mercy towards us. Having found here some articles which Mr. Back had sent across from Moose-Deer Island, I determined on awaiting the arrival of Akaitcho and his party [who had been travelling more slowly] in order to present these to them, and to assure them of the promised reward as soon as it could possibly be procured.

In the afternoon of the 14th Akaitcho, with his whole band, came to the Fort. . . . We discovered at the commencement of his speech to us that he had been informed that our expected supplies had not come. He spoke of this circumstance as a disappointment . . . but without attaching any blame to us. "The world goes badly," he said, "all are poor, you are poor, the traders appear to be poor, I and my party are poor likewise; and since the goods have not come in, we cannot have them. I do not regret having supplied you with provisions, for a Copper Indian can never permit white men to suffer from want of food on his lands without flying to their aid. I trust, however, that we shall, as you say, receive what is due next autumn; and at all events," he added, in a tone of good-humour, "it is the first time that the white people have been indebted to the Copper Indians." We assured him the supplies should certainly be sent to him by the autumn, if not before. He then cheerfully received the small present we made to himself; and although we could give a few things only to those who had been most active in our service, the others who, perhaps, thought themselves equally deserving, did not murmur at being left out in the distribution. Akaitcho afterwards expressed a strong desire that we should represent the character of his nation in a favourable light to our countrymen. "I know," he said, "you write down every occurrence in your books; but probably you have only noticed the bad things we have said and done, and have omitted to mention the good."

Franklin replied that he had indeed noted many good things about the Indians. He showed his further good will by having Weeks reduce their debts on his books by the amount of the provisions that they had given the party. The debts of Akaitcho and his hunters had been remitted when they first joined the expedition, so they were given credits for future purchases. Weeks was so cooperative that Franklin finally came to the conclusion that all the damage he had caused in the past must have been "actuated by the mistaken idea that he was serving the interest of his employers."

Before Franklin and Richardson left for Moose-Deer Island, Akaitcho bade them farewell with a depth of feeling seldom shown by his people, a feeling reciprocated in full measure by the white men. At Moose-Deer Island they were given another warm reception. Here too they had the joy of meeting their friend and comrade George Back, to whose courage, they well knew, they owed their lives.

Back had separated from the main party on October 4 to make all possible haste to Fort Enterprise and obtain relief for the other members of the expedition. During the five-day journey, he and his three companions had experienced privations equal to those suffered by the party in the rear, at one time being reduced to eat an old pair of leather trousers. Their disappointment on reaching the Fort had been correspondingly great, but within two days they were off again in search of the Indians. The intense suffering that marked this part of the journey reached a climax in the death of Beauparlant:

> We had not proceeded far [October 16] before Beauparlant began to complain of increasing weakness. This was so usual with us that no particular notice was taken of it, for in fact there was little difference, all being alike feeble. . . . I endeavoured to encourage him by explaining the mercy of the Supreme Being, who ever beholds with an eye of pity those that seek his aid. This passed as common discourse, when he inquired where we were to put up; St. Germain pointed to a small clump of pines near us, the only place indeed that offered for fuel. "Well," replied the poor man, "take your axe Mr. Back, and I will follow at my leisure, I shall join you by the time the encampment is made." This is a usual practice of the country, and St. Germain and myself went on towards the spot; it was five o'clock and not very cold . . . when, on leaving the ice, we saw a number of crows perched on the top of some high pines near us. St. Germain immediately said there must be some dead animal thereabouts and proceeded to search, when we saw several heads of deer half buried in the snow and ice, without eyes or tongues. . . . An expression of "Oh merciful God! we are saved," broke from us both. . . .
>
> Darkness stole on us apace and I became extremely anxious about Beauparlant; several guns were fired, to each of which he answered. We then called out, and again heard his responses though faintly,

when I told St. Germain to go and look for him, as I had not strength myself, being quite exhausted. He said that . . . if he went now he should certainly be lost. In this situation I could only hope that as Beauparlant had my blanket and every thing requisite to light a fire, he might have encamped at a little distance from us.

The night was cold and clear, but we could not sleep at all from the pains of having eaten. . . . In the morning, being much agitated for the safety of Beauparlant, I desired St. Germain to go in search of him and to return with him as quick as possible, when I would have something prepared for them to eat.

It was, however, late when he arrived, with a small bundle which Beauparlant was accustomed to carry, and with tears in his eyes, told me that he had found our poor companion dead. Dead! I could not believe him. "It is so, Sir," said St. Germain, ". . . I . . . found him stretched upon his back on a sand bank frozen to death, his limbs all extended and swelled enormously, and as hard as the ice that was near him. . . . Seeing that there was no longer life in him, I threw your covering over him and placed his snow shoes on the top of it."

I had not even thought of so serious an occurrence in our little party, and for a short time was obliged to give vent to my grief. Left with one person and both of us weak, no appearance of Belanger, a likelihood that great calamity had taken place among our other companions, and upwards of seventeen days' march from the nearest Establishment, and myself unable to carry a burden, all these things pressed heavy on me; and how to get to the Indians or to the fort I did not know; but that I might not depress St. Germain's spirits, I suppressed the feelings which these thoughts gave rise to, and made some arrangements for the journey to Fort Providence. We continued very weak.

October 18.—While we were this day occupied in scraping together the remains of some deer's meat, we observed Belanger coming round a point apparently scarcely moving. I went to meet him, and made immediate inquiries about my friends. Five, with the Captain, he said, were at the house, the rest were left near the river, unable to proceed; but he was too weak to relate the whole. He was conducted to the encampment . . . and by degrees we heard the remainder of his tragic tale, at which the interpreter could not avoid crying. He then gave me a letter from my friend the Commander, which indeed was truly afflicting. The simple story of Belanger I could hear, but when I read it in another language, mingled with the pious resignation of a good man, I could not sustain it any longer.

Although Back was himself not far from death, his inflexible determination to secure help for his friends kept him going. Exactly a month after he had left Franklin, he finally encountered Akaitcho. To his surprise Benoit and Augustus had arrived just ahead of him. The Chief received Back with the utmost sympathy and was greatly affected by his story of distress. The next morning he sent the three Indians who reached Fort Enterprise just in time to save the lives of the survivors there.

The time had come for Franklin to write the concluding paragraphs in his journal:

> I have little now to add to the melancholy detail into which I felt it proper to enter; but I cannot omit to state that the unremitting care and attentions of our kind friends, Mr. M'Vicar and Mr. M'Auley [post managers], together with the improvement of our diet, materially contributed to the restoration of our health . . . and we nearly regained our ordinary state of body before the spring. . . . The usual symptoms of spring having appeared, on the 25th of May [1822] we prepared to embark for Fort Chipewyan. Fortunately, on the following morning, a canoe arrived from that place with the whole of the stores which we required for the payment of Akaitcho and the hunters. It was extremely gratifying to us to be thus enabled, previous to our departure, to make arrangements respecting the payment of our late Indian companions; and the more so as we had recently discovered that Akaitcho and the whole of the tribe, in consequence of the death of the leader's mother, and the wife of our old guide Keskarrah, had broken and destroyed every useful article belonging to them, and that they were in the greatest distress.

Franklin and his party reached Fort Chipewyan on June 2. Here they met Wentzel and the four voyageurs who had accompanied him back from the mouth of the Coppermine River. He gave Franklin a detailed explanation of why the Indians had failed to leave supplies of meat along the Coppermine and at Fort Enterprise. It seemed that game had been so scarce as they paddled up the River that for eleven days they had themselves eaten nothing but tripe de roche. During that time an Indian, with his wife and child, had fallen behind the party and they were not seen again. A few days later most of the Indians had gone off, intending to keep a rendezvous with their families, but not one family could be located.

Akaitcho and his men reproached Wentzel bitterly for having induced them to leave their families and endure dangers and hardships. But even as they railed against him, they continued to express their sincere desire to follow Franklin's instructions and make caches of meat. Though he was convinced that none of the expedition would return, Akaitcho said, "If the Great Chief, or any of his party, should pass my tents, he or they shall be welcome to all my provisions or anything else that I may have." A serious setback was the discovery that Humpy and his party—on whom Wentzel had placed the greatest dependence for a supply of provision—were in a state of near starvation. They still wanted to help, however, and were converting old axes into ammunition. Wentzel expected to be able to send them ammunition from Fort Providence but when he got to the post, the men in charge could supply him with nothing. The final disaster was the drowning of three of the hunters in Marten Lake. In Wentzel's written report he said:

> . . . this accident was, of all others, the most fatal that could have happened—a truth which no one, who has the least knowledge of the Indian character, will deny; and as they were nearly connected by relationship to the Leader, Humpy, and . . . the three leading men of this part of the Copper Indian Tribe, it had the effect of unhinging (if I may use the expression) the minds of all these families, and finally destroying all the fond hopes I had so sanguinely conceived of their assisting the Expedition. . . .

Wentzel explained to Franklin that he *had* left a note for him, written on a plank, on his bed at Fort Enterprise. "Since it has not been found there, some Indians must have gone to the house after my departure, and destroyed it. These details, Sir, I have been induced to enter into (rather unexpectedly) in justification of myself, and hope it will be satisfactory."

At Norway House on July 4, Franklin gave all his voyageurs their discharge and sent them on their way to Montreal. All of them had orders on the Hudson's Bay Company for the amount of their wages. "We carried Augustus down to York Factory, where we arrived on the 14th of July, and were received with every mark of attention and kindness by Mr. Simpson, the Governor, Mr. M'Tavish, and, indeed, by all the officers of the United Companies. And thus terminated our long, fatiguing, and disastrous travels in North America, having journeyed by water and by land (including our navigation of the Polar Sea), five thousand five hundred and fifty miles."

On his return to England Franklin discovered that he had become something of a celebrity. The achievements of the expedition—and most of all its hardships—had caught the public interest, and Franklin found himself being recognized on the streets of London. One day an urchin called out as he passed, "That's the man who ate his boots!"

It was gratifying to be promoted to the rank of Captain and to be elected a member of the Royal Society for the contribution to the cause of geographical science. His health was steadily improving and he now settled down to the task of writing his official account of the expedition, a narrative which ran to 180,000 words and which was published in 1823. Dr. Richardson's detailed surveys of the animal life in the Arctic regions and the geological formation of the terrain were included in the book as an appendix.

But concentration on the book did not exclude matters of personal interest, and within two months of his return to England Franklin asked Miss Eleanor Porden to be his wife. He had first met her as he was about to sail under Buchan on their short-lived expedition to the North Pole. Later, back in England, he had seen more of her and had even considered proposing before he set out on his expedition to the Coppermine in 1819. She must have remained in his thoughts as he charted the Arctic coastline, for the Porden Islands appeared on the map, along with all the straits and bays named after the leaders of the nation.

Eleanor Porden had begun to keep house for her father, a well-known architect, at the age of fourteen. She took herself seriously as a poet and at sixteen wrote a poem called *The Veils*, which filled six volumes with what a modern reader would find unbearably dull verse. She was much livelier than her verse, however, and mixed with a crowd quite different from the quiet, serious and religious man she was to marry. Their differences evidently made her have doubts about the marriage, for she wrote to a former beau, "I sometimes feel as if I had in some respects made an *odd* choice." Nevertheless, the wedding took place in August 1823.

The year that followed was difficult for them both. Franklin was away a good deal attending to family matters arising from the death of his father. Moreover, he was sensitive about his wife's intellectual superiority and did not share many of her interests, while she was irritated by his religious feelings, which she considered excessive. But after the birth of a daughter in June of 1824 they drew closer together. By that time it was evident that Eleanor was suffering from an advanced case of tuberculosis and as she became steadily weaker their differences were forgotten.

It was at this time that Franklin was appointed to command his second expedition to the Arctic. Immediately he became responsible for all preparations connected with the expedition, and they filled his days. The nights he spent at home with his dying wife. Though they had married with the understanding that their private interests should never be allowed to interfere with the demands of his career, he was tormented at having to hasten the arrangements that would take him from her side. She accepted his forthcoming departure with extraordinary courage; in fact she told him that her health would probably improve when he left.

The expedition for which Franklin was preparing was to be part of the most ambitious project of its kind yet undertaken. In 1823 the Admiralty, having decided to make another attempt to discover a northern passage by sea from the Atlantic to the Pacific, appointed Captain Edward Parry to command the expedition. At the time, Parry was the most renowned Arctic explorer of his day. His expedition of 1819-20, in which he had reached Melville Island, had been acclaimed as a great accomplishment. His second expedition of 1821-23, though it had achieved no marked success, had added Fury and Hecla Strait to the map and had convinced him that a northwest passage did exist—by way of Lancaster Sound. Parry was able to persuade the Government of this fact and a third expedition was authorized.

Franklin's reaction to the Admiralty's decision was immediate and imaginative. Arctic exploration had become a passion in his life and he conceived the idea that Parry's third expedition by sea should be supplemented by an expedition overland to continue the work he himself had begun in 1819-21.

I therefore ventured to lay before His Majesty's Government a plan for an Expedition overland to the mouth of the Mackenzie River and thence, by sea, to the north-western extremity of America, with the combined object, also, of surveying the coast between the Mackenzie and Coppermine Rivers. I was well aware of the sympathy excited in the British public by the sufferings of those engaged in the former overland expedition to the mouth of the Coppermine River, and of the humane repugnance of His Majesty's Government to expose others to a like fate; but I was enabled to show satisfactorily that, in the proposed course, similar dangers were not to be apprehended, while the objects to be attained were important at once to the naval character, scientific reputation and commercial interests of Great Britain. . . . I received directions from the Right Honourable Earl Bathurst to make the necessary preparations for the equipment of the Expedition, to the command of which I was to have the honour to be nominated.

Not only did the Government accept Franklin's suggestion; it went on to expand his conception and decided that if possible he should be picked up by a ship that would enter the Arctic sea from the west through Bering Strait. For this purpose, Captain F. W. Beechey was instructed to sail HMS *Blossom* around Cape Horn and up the west coasts of South and North America, entering the Arctic sea from the west. If a rendezvous were effected, Franklin and his men were to board the *Blossom* and return to England following the same route by which the ship had come. It did not seem at all odd to the men at the Admiralty to send a naval vessel on a voyage that would last four years if such a voyage would help complete the mapping of the Arctic coast of America. Besides, the *Blossom* would visit British possessions in the Pacific and generally "show the flag."

Franklin's good friend Dr. Richardson immediately offered his services as naturalist and surgeon to the expedition, volunteering as well to lead the party that would survey the coast between the Mackenzie and Coppermine rivers. Lieutenant George Back returned from naval duty in the West Indies in time to rejoin his former companions, and E. N. Kendall, an admiralty mate, was appointed to accompany Richardson and to serve the expedition as assistant surveyor. Thomas Drummond was appointed to be assistant naturalist.

One of the many lessons that Franklin had learned from the first expedition was the importance of having supplies of food deposited beforehand along the route. He recalled with horror the desperate last-

minute searches for provision and the tragedy that had ensued. To look
after the advance food supplies he now secured the services of Peter
Dease, a chief factor of the Hudson's Bay Company. Franklin had met
him on the first expedition and had formed a high opinion of him.
Dease was also to take on all the responsibilities formerly carried by
Wentzel.

Franklin's appointment was confirmed late in 1823 and the whole
of the following year was taken up with preparations for the most
effective action possible during the brief Arctic summer of 1826. The
Hudson's Bay and North West companies having combined, their
battles were over, and Franklin received a degree of cooperation that
had been denied him before.

> As soon as I had authority from Earl Bathurst I entered into a
> correspondence with the Governor and Directors of the Hudson's
> Bay Company; and these gentlemen, taking a most lively interest in
> the objects of the Expedition, promised their utmost support to it,
> and forthwith sent injunctions to their officers in the Fur Countries
> to provide the necessary depots of provision at the places which I
> pointed out, and to give every other aid in their power. I also wrote
> to the different Chief Factors and Chief Traders of the Company, who
> resided on the route of the Expedition, explaining its objects and
> requesting their cooperation.

The supplies of pemmican requested by Franklin in the summer of
1824 could not be made available until the following spring; consequently the main body of the expedition would not attempt to reach
the Northwest earlier than that.

Experience had taught Franklin that birch-bark canoes, while well
suited for rivers, were wholly inadequate for navigating the Arctic sea.
In their place he had the Admiralty build three boats to his specifica-
tions and under his supervision. Built of mahogany and ash, their bows
and sterns were identical, and they were fitted so that they could be
steered either by a sweep-oar or a rudder. Two of them were twenty-
four feet long; the third was twenty-six feet. Together the three could
transport twenty-two men and eight tons of supplies.

Franklin had reason to remember the need for another kind of boat—
a light craft for crossing rivers and lakes in the barren lands. He therefore had one built, using as a model an ingenious design that had caught
his eye—a small boat shaped like half a walnut shell. The little vessel
that resulted was nine feet long and just over four feet wide and

appropriately called the *Walnut-Shell*. Its frame of ash was covered with waterproofed canvas. Altogether the *Walnut-Shell* weighed only eighty-five pounds and was easily taken apart and packed in six packages.

Although Franklin was "necessarily guided by their portability" in choosing astronomical instruments for the expedition, yet he did not stint himself in choosing them. Bedding, clothing, weapons, food, etc. were secured on an equally generous scale. Two suits of waterproof material were made for each man of the party by Mr. Mackintosh of Glasgow, already well established in the business of keeping people dry.

Our guns had the same bore with the fowling-pieces supplied by the Hudson's Bay Company to the Indian hunters . . . their locks were tempered to withstand the cold of winter, and a broad Indian dagger, which could also be used as a knife, was fitted to them like a bayonet. Ammunition of the best quality was provided by the Ordnance. . . . A quantity of wheaten-flour, arrowroot, macaroni, portable-soup, chocolate, essence of coffee, sugar and tea, calculated to last two years, was also supplied, made up into packages of eighty-five pounds and covered with three layers of prepared waterproof canvas. . . .

There was also an ample stock of tobacco, a small quantity of wine and spirits, marquees and tents for the men and officers, some books, writing and drawing paper, a considerable quantity of cartridge-paper to be used in preserving specimens of plants; nets, twine, fishing-lines and hooks, together with many articles to be used at winter-quarters for the service of the post and for the supply of our Indian hunters, such as cloth, blankets, shirts, coloured belts, chiefs' dresses, combs, looking-glasses, beads, tapes, gartering, knives, guns and daggers, hatchets, awls, gun-worms, flints, flint-steels, files, whip and hand saws, ice-chisels and trenching irons, the latter to break open the beaver lodges.

Before the following winter had set in, these supplies were shipped from England and delivered to Mr. Dease at Lake Athabasca by eighteen voyageurs in three large canoes. Dease himself wintered on Great Slave Lake and in the spring of 1825 proceeded to Great Bear Lake where he commenced the construction of what was to be Franklin's base camp.

Although Franklin engaged voyageurs to transport his supplies to the Northwest, he had decided that the main work of the expedition would be carried out by Englishmen and Scotsmen. In June 1824 two carpenters and some other members of the expedition sailed from England to

York Factory, taking with them the three large boats. They advanced as far as Cumberland House, where they spent the winter before continuing toward Great Bear Lake in the spring. Meantime, in the autumn of 1824 two large canoes had been deposited at Penetanguishene on Lake Huron for the use of Franklin the following spring.

By February 1825 all preparations had been completed and the time for departure was at hand. Though his wife had been responding to a new medicine, Franklin was still very worried about her. Before they parted she gave him a silk Union Jack that she had made, telling him not to hoist it until he stood for the first time on the shore of the Arctic sea. Somewhat reassured by her interest and optimism, though still with strong misgivings, he sailed for New York on the sixteenth.

When the party, consisting of Franklin, Richardson, Back, Kendall, Drummond and four Royal Marines, docked on March 15, it was well received by the civil and naval authorities. The British Consul, Mr. Buchanan, accompanied the men up the Hudson by river-boat to Albany, where the Governor of New York showed keen interest in the expedition.

The nine Englishmen were soon introduced to a variety of modes of travel. From Albany they took a coach to Niagara, sailed across Lake Ontario to York, proceeded northward to Lake Simcoe in a cart, crossed the Lake by canoe and walked nine miles to a river which they descended by canoe to Lake Huron. On April 15 they reached Penetanguishene. Franklin described this route as faster by ten days than the more usual one from Montreal up the Ottawa River. Moreover, they would have had to spend the previous winter in Montreal in order to set out from there early in the spring.

En route to Penetanguishene, Franklin had been writing frequent letters to his wife giving detailed descriptions of the people and places he saw as he travelled and recalling amusing incidents to interest her. While waiting at Penetanguishene for the voyageurs from Montreal who were to take the party west, he wrote her twice. They were his last letters to a wife who had in fact died six days after he sailed from England.

I should have rejoiced at having you by my side on our journey through New York. There were many scenes which you could have described so well and I am sure it would have given you sincere pleasure to have witnessed the industry of the American character evinced by the number of towns and villages which have sprung up within a few years. . . . I was in hopes that before we left this place

A portage on the route westward from York Factory, September 1819

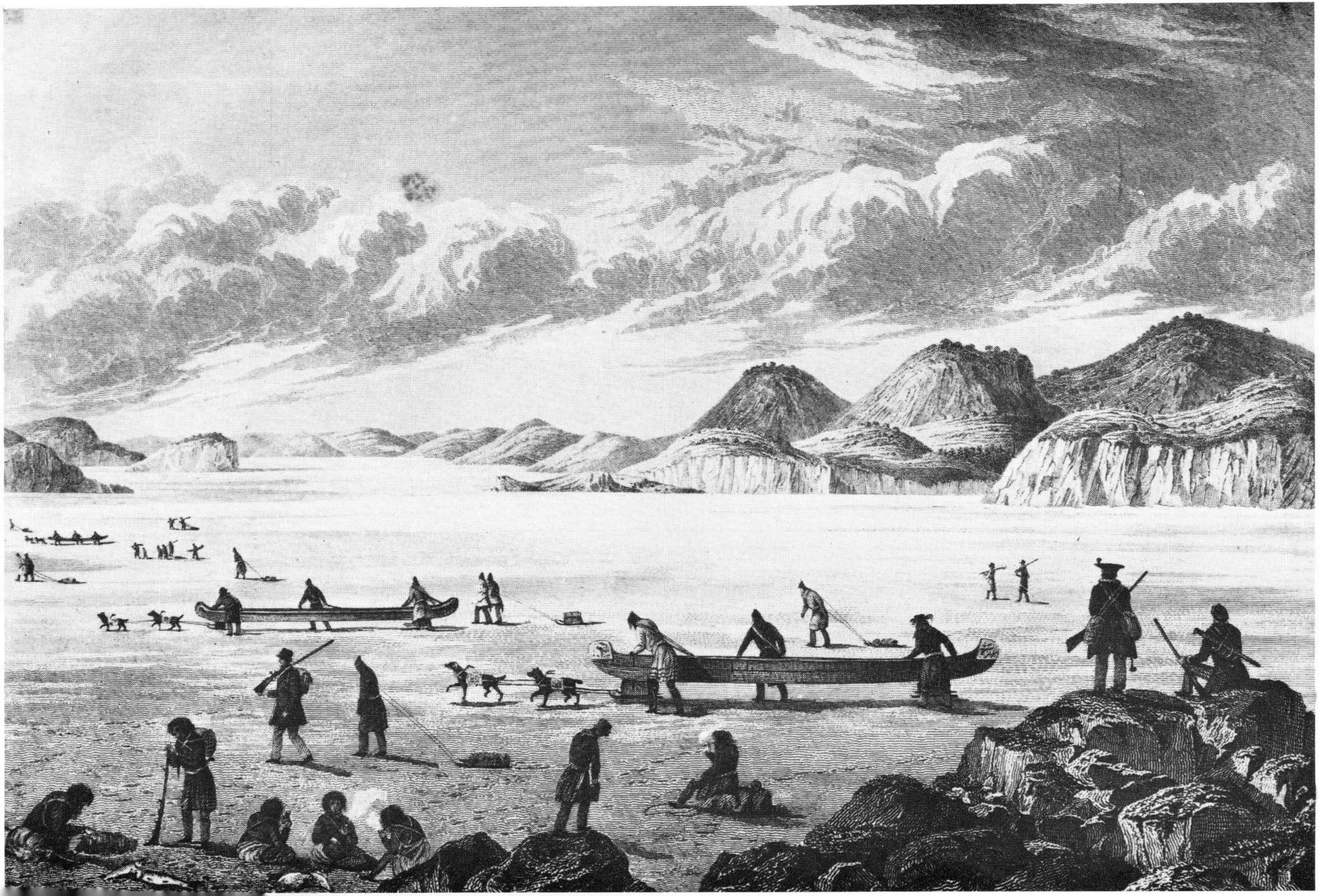

Toward the Coppermine: crossing Point Lake, June 1821

The return to Fort Providence: making camp in the Barren Lands, September 1821

Winter view of Fort Franklin, 1825

The Eskimos pillaging Franklin's boats, Pillage Point, July 1826

The Dolphin squeezed by ice, July 1826

H. M. S. *Ships Erebus and Terror*

Wintered in the Ice in

__ of May 184__ Lat. 70° 5' N Long. 98° 23' W

Having wintered in 1846–7 at Beechey Island
in Lat 74° 43' 28" N. Long 91° 39' 15" W After having
ascended Wellington Channel to Lat 77° and returned
by the West side of Cornwallis Island.

Sir John Franklin commanding the Expedition
All well

Commander.

WHOEVER finds this paper is requested to forward it to the Secretary of
the Admiralty, London, *with a note of the time and place at which it was
found*: or, if more convenient, to deliver it for that purpose to the British
Consul at the nearest Port.

QUICONQUE trouvera ce papier est prié d'y marquer le tems et lieu ou
il l'aura trouvé, et de le faire parvenir au plutot au Secretaire de l'Amirauté
Britannique à Londres.

CUALQUIERA que hallare este Papel, se le suplica de enviarlo al Secretario
del Almirantazgo, en Londrés, con una nota del tiempo y del lugar en
donde se halló.

EEN ieder die dit Papier mogt vinden, wordt hiermede verzogt, om het
zelve, ten spoedigste, te willen zenden aan den Heer Minister van de
Marine der Nederlanden in 's Gravenhage, of wel aan den Secretaris der
Britsche Admiraliteit, te London, en daar by te voegen eene Nota,
inhoudende de tyd en de plaats alwaar dit Papier is gevonden geworden.

FINDEREN af dette Papiir ombedes, naar Leilighed gives, at sende
samme til Admiralitets Secretairen i London, eller nærmeste Embedsmand
i Danmark, Norge, eller Sverrig. Tiden og Stœdit hvor dette er fundet
ønskes venskabeligt paategnet.

WER diesen Zettel findet, wird hierdurch ersucht denselben an den
Secretair des Admiralitets in London einzusenden, mit gefälliger angabe
an welchen ort und zu welcher zeit er gefundet worden ist.

Party consisting... officers and 6 men
left the Ships on Monday 24th May 1847

The Last Words from the Franklin Expedition

I should have received a letter informing me that you continued to improve. . . . I daily remember you and our dear little one in my prayers and I have no doubt that yours are offered up on my behalf. She must be growing very entertaining and I sincerely trust she will be a source of great comfort to us, especially to you in my absence. With what heartfelt pleasure shall I embrace you both on my return! Your flag is yet snug in the box and will not be displayed till we get to a more northern region. Mr. Back and the men have just arrived. . . .

Back had indeed arrived, bringing letters with sad personal news for Franklin. His letter had broken off abruptly. At the bottom of the page is written in a shaky hand, "Seven p.m. The distressing intelligence of my dear wife's death has just reached me."

It was typical of Franklin's reserve that he made no mention in his journal of his wife's death. Nor did he allow his feelings to hinder the expedition's progress. On April 23 the combined party, numbering thirty-five, set out in the *canôts de maître*. On reaching Sault Ste. Marie Franklin was told by the oldest resident that his crews had beaten by ten days the fastest time previously made by canoes coming from Montreal, and this in spite of bad ice conditions.

At Fort William the two *canôts de maître* were exchanged for four smaller canoes. Feeling the need for constant activity, Franklin pushed on ahead with Richardson, leaving Back to follow with the bulk of the supplies. Near Isle-à-la-Crosse the two Englishmen encountered several fur brigades heading for the Company port at York Factory. Officials in the canoes assured Franklin that supplies of pemmican had been deposited as requested at different posts and that his advance party, which had wintered at Cumberland House, was making good headway westward. At the Isle-à-la-Crosse post the manager reported that they were only a few hours ahead of him. The two parties joined forces in the Methy River on June 29, 1825.

> In no part of the journey was the presence of the officers more
> requisite to animate and encourage the crews, because the river itself,
> being obstructed by three impassable rapids, is usually so shallow
> through its whole course of forty miles as scarcely to admit of a
> flat-bottomed bateau floating with half its cargo, much less our boats
> which drew, when loaded, from eighteen to twenty inches. This river
> and its impediments being surmounted, the Methye Portage, ten
> miles and three quarters long, was at no great distance, which is
> always held up to the inexperienced voyager as the most laborious
> part of the journey. But whatever apprehensions the men might have
> entertained on the subject seemed to vanish on our landing among

them and Dr. Richardson and myself were received by all with cheerful, delighted countenances, and by none more warmly than by our excellent friend and former interpreter Augustus the Eskimo, and Ooligbuck, whom he had brought from Churchill as his companion.

After breakfasting with the crews Franklin inspected the boats and stores and was gratified to find everything in good shape. An hour's relaxation was given before continuing the journey. The break gave the men a chance to read the letters Franklin had brought.

It took five days to advance the forty miles up the shallow Methy River and seven more to make the portage. Here eight men were required to carry each of the two smaller boats but the larger one was hauled over the portage on a makeshift cradle. Later, Franklin regretted that he had not had cradles made for the other boats. In addition to the boats, there was of course the cargo to transport; this consisted of 116 packages, each weighing 70 to 80 pounds, together with the crew's personal luggage. Each morning it was decided how far the party would advance on the portage. The men rose at three in the morning and carried the packages to the chosen site, making as many trips as necessary. They then slept for a few hours and in the cool of the evening hauled up the boats.

Franklin's arrival in mid-July at Fort Chipewyan astonished its inmates, especially when they learned that he had only left England in February. Additional supplies, sufficient to last two years—mainly cloth, blankets, nets and twine—were picked up at the Fort. Dease had sent word from Great Bear Lake requesting more twine. The nets sent from England had a mesh too large to catch the small fish found in the Lake, so that new nets with a smaller mesh would have to be made.

Dr. Richardson left Chipewyan almost immediately for Great Slave Lake, taking with him the three boats. His crews were reduced by three Englishmen who requested discharge, feeling that they would be unable to stand up to the fatigue of the service. Even so, the boats were heavily laden, since additional supplies and pemmican had been secured at the Fort. Franklin waited at Fort Chipewyan until Back and Kendall arrived with three of the canoes obtained at Fort William. The most difficult part of the journey completed, Franklin discharged as many of the voyageurs as could be spared and supplied them with a canoe to take them home. Those who returned to Montreal were the first persons ever to travel from that place to Fort Chipewyan and back in the same season.

Four days of travel brought Franklin and his crews to the entrance to Great Slave Lake, where such a large body of Indians was waiting to welcome them that they were unable to follow the usual custom of giving a small present to each native. The loud cries that followed them as they continued to paddle gave the distinct impression that their stinginess was not appreciated! On the evening of July 29 they reached Fort Resolution on Great Slave Lake.

All the portages on the road to Bear Lake being now passed, the Canadian voyagers made a request that we would allow them to commemorate the event by a dance. It met with a ready compliance; and though they had been paddling for thirty-six out of the thirty-nine preceding hours, they kept up their favourite amusement until daylight, to the music of bagpipes, relieved occasionally by the Jews' harp.

We rejoiced to find at this post our worthy old Copper-Indian friends, Keskarrah and Humpy, the brother of Akaitcho, who had been waiting two months for the express purpose of seeing us. These excellent men showed that their gratification equalled ours by repeatedly seizing our hands and pressing them against their hearts, and exclaiming, "How much we regret that we cannot tell what we feel for you here!" Akaitcho had left the fort about two months on a hunting excursion, hoping to return, with plenty of provision for our use, by the middle of August, which was as early as he thought we should arrive. Keskarrah confirmed the melancholy report we had heard . . . that most of the hunters who had been in our service at Fort Enterprise had been treacherously murdered, with many others of the tribe, by the Dog-Ribs, with which nation we also learned the Copper-Indians had been at war since the year of our departure from them, till the last spring. The peace had been effected through the mediation of Messrs. Dease and M'Vicar, and we were gratified to find that Akaitcho and his tribe had been principally induced to make this reconciliation by a desire that no impediment might be placed in the way of our present expedition. "We have too much esteem," said Akaitcho, "for our father, and for the service in which he is about to be again engaged, to impede its success by our wars, and, therefore, they shall cease;" and on being asked by Mr. Dease whether he and some of his young men would go to hunt for the party at our winter quarters, he replied, "Our hearts will be with them, but we will not go to those parts where the bones of our murdered brethren lie, for fear our bad passions should be aroused at the sight of their graves, and that we should be tempted to renew the war by the recollection of the manner of their death. Let the Dog-Ribs who live in the neighbourhood of Bear Lake furnish them with meat, though they are our enemies." Such sentiments would do honour to any state of civilization, and show that the most refined feelings may animate the most untutored people. Happily we were now ... able to reward the friendship of these good men by allotting from our stores a liberal present to the principal persons. On the delivery of the articles to Keskarrah and Humpy, I desired them to communicate to Akaitcho and the whole tribe the necessity of their strictly adhering to the terms of peace, and assured them that I should not fail to urge the same obligations on the Dog-Ribs. A silver royal medal, such as is given to the Indian chiefs in Upper Canada, was likewise left with Mr. M'Vicar, to be presented to Akaitcho, as a further mark of our regard for his former services and present good wishes.

On the shore of Great Slave Lake Franklin's party was joined by a small group of Chipewyan Indians who said that they had supplied Dr. Richardson with dried meat only the day before at Hay River.

The chief was very importunate for rum, but I steadily adhered to the determination I had formed this time on my entering the Fur Country, of not giving spirits to any Indian. A share of our supper and tea, and some tobacco, were offered to him and accepted, though with a bad grace. The Fur Company ceased the following season to bring any rum to this quarter, and I learned that this man was one of the few natives who were highly displeased at this judicious change.

By August 2 the crews had reached the spot considered to be the commencement of the Mackenzie River, and a few days later they passed the site of the first post established in those parts by the North West Company. It had been built by Mr. Livingstone, who, with all but one of his crew, was massacred by the Eskimos on the first attempt to open up trade with them. That night Franklin's party slept at Fort Simpson, the principal fur-trading post in that area. Fortunately for Franklin, the chief factor in charge of the district was then at the post and was most helpful in arranging to have supplies of provision sent to the winter base on Great Bear Lake. Two voyageurs whom Dease had engaged to guide the party to Great Bear Lake were waiting for Franklin at the Fort. They told him that Indian hunters had already been engaged and that the necessary buildings were under construction.

Leaving Fort Simpson, the party caught a glimpse of the Rocky Mountains for the first time; on the following day Franklin described those on the east bank of the River:

We saw a chain of mountains on the eastern side of the river similar in their outline and general character to those hitherto seen only on the opposite bank. . . . In the brilliancy of the sunshine the surfaces of some of the eastern hills, which were entirely bare, appeared white as marble, and for some time we fancied them to be covered with snow. By four p.m. we reached the Rocky Island mentioned by Mackenzie where, from the river being contracted, the current flowed with great rapidity and soon brought us opposite to the remarkable hill close by the river side which that persevering traveller ascended in July, 1789. . . . It is composed of limestone, and is about four hundred feet high.

We continued a N. b. W. course for eight miles, and encamped at sunset, having travelled this day one hundred and twenty miles. A small supply of fresh deer's meat was obtained from some Dog-Rib Indians. Their canoes were made of the bark of the pine-tree, sewn at the ends and top with the fibrous parts of the root of that tree, leaving only a space for the legs of a sitter.

For some distance north of the encampment the River followed a meandering course, with numerous sandbanks and shoals to complicate the work of the crewmen. A strange phenomenon was observable at this point—bubbles of air rose continually to the surface of the water with a hissing noise "resembling the effervescence produced by pouring water on quick lime."

By August 7, 1825 the party had reached Fort Norman, only four days distant from the winter base on Great Bear Lake. Since setting out in the spring the officers and crew had travelled several thousand miles and there still remained five weeks before freeze-up. All summer Franklin had secretly hoped that it would be possible to make a preliminary trip down the Mackenzie before winter set in. Now he decided that there would be just enough time to do it. The officers and crew were accordingly divided into three parties. Franklin and Kendall, with their crew, would set off down the Mackenzie. Richardson, who had passed through Fort Norman two days earlier, was to be overtaken and asked to take a boat along the northern shore of Great Bear Lake in order to familiarize himself with some of the country he was likely to cover in the autumn of 1826 on his return journey from the mouth of the Coppermine. Back, with the men who remained, was to join forces with Dease on the site of the winter base and speed up the construction of the buildings. Once there, he was to discharge all the voyageurs who were no longer needed. They would go back to Great Slave Lake and fish for the winter and return to Montreal in the spring.

Mr. Kendall and I embarked on the 8th, at noon, taking, in addition to our crew, a voyageur, who was reported to be able to guide us through the proper channels to Fort Good Hope. . . .

A few miles above the Bear Lake River, and near its mouth, the banks of the Mackenzie contain much wood coal, which was on fire at the time we passed, as it had been observed to be by Mackenzie in his voyage to the sea. Its smell was very disagreeable. On a subsequent trial of this coal at our winter quarters we found that it emitted little heat and was unfit for the blacksmith's use. The banks likewise contain layers of a kind of unctuous mud . . . which the Indians in this neighbourhood use occasionally as food during seasons of famine, and even at other times chew as an amusement. It has a milky taste and the flavour is not disagreeable. We used it for whitening the walls of our dwellings; for which purpose it is well-adapted.

.   .   .   .   .

[August 9] The river varied from two to four miles in breadth, and its course was interrupted by several islands and sand-banks. At six p.m. we came to an open space, bounded by lofty walls of sandstone. In this expansion are found the second rapids of Mackenzie: at the first appearance they seem dangerous, but are not so. The river becomes again contracted and rushes with great force for the space of seven miles through a kind of defile, varying in breadth from four hundred to eight hundred yards, which has been appropriately named "The Ramparts" by the traders. The walls of this defile are from eighty to one hundred and fifty feet high and are composed of limestone, containing numerous shells: for a part of the way the stone is very white and in the rest it is blue. Several streams of water were running over the summits of the cliffs, which had worn the stone in some places into a turreted shape; while the heaps, over-thrown by its action at their base, resembled mounds for defence. To these appearances were occasionally added cavernous openings and other hollow parts, not unlike the arched windows or gateways of a castellated building. I could not help fancying what delight a visit to this spot would afford to any person of a romantic turn,

*especially at the time we first saw it, when the broad shadows of a
declining sun gave effect to the picture. This is a place of resort for
the Hare Indians to fish, and we were visited by a large party of men
and women of that tribe, who brought fish, berries and meat. They
were all neatly clothed in new leathern dresses, highly ornamented
with beads and porcupine quills. The paintings of animals on the
sides of our boats were very attractive to them; they scanned every
figure over and over, bursting into laughter whenever they recognised
any of the animals.*

*At eleven p.m. [August 10] we arrived at Fort Good Hope, the
lowest of the Company's establishments. . . . Our arrival at this period
of the year, at least two months earlier than that of the Company's
boats from York Factory, caused great astonishment to the few
inmates of this dreary dwelling and particularly to its master, Mr.
Charles Dease, who scarcely recovered from his surprise until we
had been seated some time in his room. But this over, he quickly put
every one in motion to prepare a meal for us, of which we stood in
much need as it was then verging on midnight and we had break-
fasted at eight in the morning. This post has been but recently
established for the convenience of the tribe of Indians whom Mackenzie calls the Quarrellers, but whom the traders throughout the
fur country name the Loucheux.*

Franklin was interested to learn from Dease that the Loucheux Indians and the Eskimos, generally at war, had recently met in friendly
fashion and were now at peace. The next morning he secured from the
store some beads and cloth as presents for the Loucheux and continued
downstream with his party. Below Trading River he and his companions were hailed by an Indian from the shore. They landed to tell
him the purpose of their visit. The Indian insisted that they must meet
his family and offered to accompany the party downstream to where
his relatives were camped. Franklin agreed to take the man and his luggage, not expecting from his poor appearance that there would be much
to carry. He was horrified when the Indian proceeded to toss load after
load of evil-smelling fish into the boat, but he could not go back on his
word. When the party drew near to the family's tents the man shouted
his news to those on shore. Baptiste, the interpreter, understood enough
of the lengthy reply to gather that many of the Indians were sick and
that two of them had died the day before. Franklin was not anxious to

walk into an epidemic, so he proceeded farther downstream before depositing the man and his repulsive baggage on shore. The party then continued an additional five miles before camping for the night.

> *At daylight [August 12] we loosened from the beach and continued with the descent of the river; winding, in our course, as numerous sandbanks rendered necessary. In a few hours we descried another collection of Indian lodges. One of the party happened to be examining his nets nearer to us than the tents; on espying the boat, he immediately desisted and paddled towards his friends with the utmost speed, bawling the whole way for them to arm. The women and children were seen hurrying up the bank to hide themselves; and by the time we had got abreast of the lodges, the whole party were in a state of defence. They stood on the beach gazing at us evidently with much distrust; and for some time no one would accept our invitations to approach. At length an adventurous youth, distinguishable among the rest by the gaiety of his dress, and the quantity of beads that were suspended around his neck, launched his canoe and paddled gently towards the boat, till he discovered Augustus, whom he knew by his countenance to be an Eskimo; then rising from his seat, he threw up his hands for joy and desired every one of the party to embark at once. The summons was instantly obeyed, and a friendly intercourse followed; each person that had a gun discharging its contents, and taking the iron heads and barbs from the arrows, to show their entire confidence. On landing to breakfast, we found that . . . Baptiste did not understand their language; consequently our communications were carried on by signs, except when they attempted to speak Eskimo, which Augustus, with difficulty, made out. He was still the centre of attraction, notwithstanding Mr. Kendall and myself were dressed in uniform and were distributing presents to them. They caressed Augustus, danced and played around him, to testify their joy at his appearance among them, and we could not help admiring the demeanour of our excellent little companion under such unusual and extravagant marks of attention. He received every burst of applause, every shake of the hand, with modesty and affability, but would not allow them to interrupt him in the preparation of our breakfast, a task which he always delighted to perform.*

Franklin was on the point of embarking when the oldest Indian approached and asked him to wait until his son arrived. The boy was very sick and shivered violently, though it was a warm day, but his

father believed that the white men could cure him. The only "remedy"
they had was some warm tea with a little brandy in it, and this they
gave to the boy. Later, they heard that he had recovered.

The expedition was now entering Eskimo country. As a precaution
the masts were taken down in case natives might see the boat at a
distance and run away. Franklin was very anxious to meet some of
them to secure information about the coastline and conditions ahead.
That night, immediately after the party had eaten supper, the fire was
extinguished and two men were placed on guard. During the day they
had passed Eskimo huts and other signs of native life with increasing
frequency as they followed the winding River, but they had not
actually seen any Eskimos.

Next day the Mackenzie opened up into a series of channels. The
water was still fresh and there was no visible sign of a tide, but the
sight of seals indicated that the sea was near. Right through the fifteenth, gales and fog made progress difficult, and on the following
morning the party could not embark until eleven, when the sun was
finally strong enough to disperse the fog.

The boat followed the shoreline of Ellice Island until it began to
trend to the southeast. "There we landed and were rejoiced at the
sea-like appearance to the northward. This point . . . forms the north-
eastern entrance to the main channel of the Mackenzie River which,
from Slave Lake to this point is 1045 miles, according to our survey."
Leaving Ellice Island, the party sailed toward another island to the
northeast which appeared blue in the distance. Near Ellice Island the
water was shallow, but as they advanced it became deeper and of a
much darker green. In the middle of the crossing a strong contrary wind
came up. For five hours the men rowed valiantly against it, until they
were drenched by spray and totally exhausted from their labours. As a
last resort, the sails were set and double reefed. The boat showed an
encouraging seaworthiness, and after an hour of tacking into the wind
they reached the shelter of the island. Here, to their intense joy, the
water was discovered to be decidedly salty.

*The sun was setting as the boat touched the beach, and we hastened
to the most elevated part of the island about two hundred and fifty
feet high, to look around; and never was a prospect more gratifying
than that which lay open to us. The Rocky Mountains were seen
from S.W. to W.½N.; and from the latter point, round by the north,
the sea appeared in all its majesty, entirely free from ice and without*

any visible obstruction to its navigation. Many seals and black and white whales were sporting on its waves; and the whole scene was calculated to excite in our minds the most flattering expectations as to our own success and that of our friends in the Hecla and the Fury. There were two groups of islands at no great distance; to the one bearing south-east I had the pleasure of affixing the name of my excellent friend and companion Mr. Kendall, and to that bearing north-east the name of Pelly was given, as a tribute justly due to the Governor of the Hudson-Bay Company. . . . A similar feeling towards my much-esteemed friend Mr. Garry, the Deputy Governor of the Company, prompted me to appropriate his name to the island on which we stood. . . .

. . . the men had pitched the tent on the beach, and I caused the silk union-flag to be hoisted, which my deeply-lamented wife had made and presented to me as a parting gift, under the express injunction that it was not to be unfurled before the Expedition reached the sea. I will not attempt to describe my emotions as it expanded to the breeze—however natural and, for the moment, irresistible, I felt that it was my duty to suppress them, and that I had no right by an indulgence of my own sorrows to cloud the animated countenances of my companions. Joining, therefore, with the best grace that I could command in the general excitement, I endeavoured to return, with corresponding cheerfulness, their warm congratulations on having thus planted the British flag on this remote island of the Polar Sea.

Some spirits which had been saved for the occasion were issued to the men; and with three fervent cheers they drank to the health of our beloved monarch, and to the continued success of our enterprise. Mr. Kendall and I had also reserved a little of our brandy in order to celebrate this interesting event; but Baptiste, in his delight of beholding the sea, had set before us some salt water, which having been mixed with the brandy before the mistake was discovered, we were reluctantly obliged to forego the intended draught and to use it in the more classical form of a libation poured on the ground.

Baptiste, on discovering that he had actually reached the ocean, stuck his feathers in his hat and exultingly exclaimed, "Now that I am one of the Gens de la mer, you shall see how active I will be and how I will crow over the Gens du nord," the name by which the Athabasca voyagers are designated. . . .

Garry Island is about five miles long by two broad, and seems to be

a mass of frozen mud. . . . The vegetable productions were grasses,
a few mosses and some shrubs, the latter in flower. Four foxes were
the only land animals we saw. . . .

. . . I wrote for Captain Parry an account of our progress, with such
information as he might require in case he wished to communicate
either with the Company's Post at Fort Good Hope or our party, and
deposited my letter, with many others I had in charge for himself
and the officers of the ships, under a pole erected for the purpose, on
which we left a blue and red flag flying to attract his attention.
Another statement of our proceedings was encased in a water-proof
box and committed to the sea a mile to the northward of the island.
The wind blew strong off the land at the time and there was a gale
from the northwest the next day, so that there is every chance of the
letter having made good way to the eastward.

Next day, August 17, the men embarked at two p.m. and reached the
eastern point of Ellice Island by seven. Here they encamped, well
pleased with the way the boat had behaved in the face of a strong wind
and high seas. The visit to Garry Island had shown Franklin that once a
boat got beyond the mouth of the Mackenzie there was no visible
obstacle to its proceeding eastward along the coast. Hoping to find out
if the way was also open to the west, he attempted to sail across to the
coastline west of the river mouth. However, a strong northwest gale
forced the crew to turn instead to the entrance of the River before they
had been able to make much headway. They had difficulty in finding the
right channel connecting with the main stream, and at one point had
to drag the boat half a mile over a sand bar.

The weather during the next few days became increasingly cold as
the party returned up river to their winter base. On August 21 the
temperature dropped to thirty-seven degrees and the next day a thick
fog changed to snow and sleet. On the twenty-third as they were
rounding one of the bends in the River they suddenly came upon a
party of Indians who had not seen them on the way to the sea.

Our appearance, therefore, created great alarm; the women and
children were instantly despatched to the woods and the men came
down to the beach with their guns and arrows prepared and knives
drawn; but the explanation that Baptiste gave soon allayed their
fears. They were indeed objects of pity; all their property had been
destroyed to testify their grief at the death of some of their relations,
and the bodies of several were still sore from the deep gashes they had

inflicted on themselves in their demonstrations of sorrow. We
distributed such useful articles among them as we had remaining,
but the supply was not at all equal to their necessities. Several of
them attempted to follow us in their canoes by poling, which they
dexterously perform by pushing at the same time with a pole or
paddle in each hand; the boat, however, was towed faster than they
could ascend the stream, and they were soon far behind.

When Franklin and his crew reached Fort Good Hope late in the day
they were welcomed with extra warmth, the Indians having previously
reported that the whole party had been massacred by the Eskimos. Had
they been delayed a week longer, the story would probably have spread
throughout the north country. Franklin left five bags of pemmican and
other superfluous stores at the post to lighten the boat and to await
their return the next year.

For the next four days a contrary wind blew so strongly that it was
impossible to paddle against it, and the crew had to resort to tracking.
The men remained in good spirits although three of them had dysentry,
which weakened them considerably.

[August 29] The weather was extremely sultry throughout this
day; at two p.m. the thermometer stood in the shade at 66°, and at
76° when exposed to the sun. The refraction of the atmosphere,
which we had often remarked to be unusually great since we had
entered the Mackenzie, was this day particularly powerful. The
mountains were distorted into the most extraordinary shapes, and
the banks of the river which we knew to be only from thirty to sixty
feet high, appeared to have such an elevation that it would have been
impossible for us to recognise the land. The air became cooler in the
evening and the atmosphere less refractive. Soon after sunset the
objects appeared in their proper form, and we enjoyed the prospect
of the delightful mountain scenery that distinguishes this rapid.

On September 1 they left the muddy waters of the Mackenzie and
entered the clear stream that flowed from Great Bear Lake. Here they
met a voyageur and two Indians who had been sent by Dease to get
some white mud for use on the new buildings. Some difficult rapids had
to be surmounted before the winter base was reached. In the middle of
one of these rapids the tow-line broke and the boat was driven against
a boulder some distance from shore. There she lay broadside to the
heavy pressure of the current. The strongest man in the party, Gustavus

Aird, succeeded in wading out toward the boat without being swept off
his feet. When he was at last close enough, he caught a line thrown to
him from the boat. Once ashore, the boat was found to be badly
damaged, with part of the keel gone altogether. The carpenter made
temporary repairs but from there to the post one of the men had to
bail continually.

Franklin's party reached the base on the evening of September 5.
Dr. Richardson had already returned from his trip along the northern
reaches of Great Bear Lake, so for the first time all the members of the
expedition were assembled together. They were in a happy frame of
mind as they compared notes and congratulated themselves on the
prospect of being comfortably settled in their winter quarters before
the severe winter commenced.*

*During the spring and summer of 1825 the following distances were travelled
by members of the Franklin Expedition:

New York to Penetanguishene	760 miles
Penetanguishene to Fort William	656
Fort William to Cumberland House	1018
Cumberland House to Great Bear River	1589
Great Bear River to, and back from, Garry Island	1206
Great Bear River to Fort Franklin	91
Dr. Richardson's excursion	483
Distance travelled	5803
Number of miles surveyed	2593

The officers had done me the honour, previous to my arrival, of giving the name of Franklin to the fort, which I felt a grateful pleasure in retaining at their desire, though I had intended naming it Fort Reliance." The site chosen by Dease for the building of Fort Franklin was near the remains of a long-abandoned North West Company post. The trees in the immediate area having been cut down by the former residents for fuel, timber for the new buildings had to be brought some distance on rafts, and this involved considerable trouble and delay. The site had been chosen largely because there was plenty of fish in that part of the Lake.

We found . . . on our arrival, all the buildings in a habitable state but wanting many internal arrangements to fit them for a comfortable winter residence. They were disposed so as to form three sides of a square, the officers' house being in the centre, those for the men on the right, with a house for the interpreter's family and the store on the left. A blacksmith's shop and meat store were added and the whole was inclosed by the stockading of the original fort, which we found highly serviceable in screening from us the snow-drift and wintry blasts. The officers' dwelling measured forty-four feet by twenty-four and contained a hall and four apartments, beside a kitchen. That of the men was thirty-six feet by twenty-three and was divided into three rooms. These buildings were placed on a dry sandy bank, about eighty yards from the lake and twenty-five feet above it.

The establishment consisted of fifty-one people: five officers, including Dease; nineteen British seamen and marines; nine voyageurs; two Eskimos; Beaulieu and four Chipewyan hunters; three women, six children and one Indian boy. There were also several Indians who were infirm and needed temporary support. It was too large a party to be maintained in one place, so two additional houses were built, one four miles from the Fort and the other seven miles distant. About twenty people were sent to live in these houses, having first been provided with the necessary gear for fishing.

From fifteen to twenty nets were kept in constant use near the Fort under the direction of an experienced fisherman and two assistants. The catch was generally a fish called "Herring Salmon of Bear Lake," but sometimes there were trout, tittameg and carp as well. The four Dog-Rib Indians taken on to hunt reindeer turned out to be poor hunters who contributed very little fresh meat. The two Eskimos then tried their hand at hunting, but since they had no experience operating in wooded country they were little more successful.

Next to the procurement of food, the most important consideration was to keep the men occupied. Some brought in the catches of fish and kept the nets in good repair; others cut wood or brought it in from the woods and split it. Two of the best travellers were kept busy almost all the time carrying letters to and from the posts in the Mackenzie River and Slave Lake areas. As the days grew shorter it became more important to provide something to do during the long evenings. A school established by the officers met three times a week with most of the Scots and Englishmen in attendance. Instruction was given in reading, writing and arithmetic, and good progress was made by the men. Sunday was always a day of rest and the whole party, with the exception of two or three of the voyageurs, made a practice of attending divine service morning and evening. If there was nothing planned for the evening and the men felt like it, the hall was at their disposal to play any game they chose. On such occasions the officers always joined them. Everyone helped pass the time as agreeably as possible, awaiting the arrival of spring when they could return to the purpose of the expedition.

The officers found employment in making and registering the thermometrical, magnetical and atmospherical observations, which were hourly noted from eight a.m. to midnight; and in addition to the duties which they had in common, each had a peculiar department allotted to him.

Lieutenant Back had the superintendence of the men; and the accurate drawings which he finished during the winter from sketches taken on the voyage afford ample proof of his diligence and skill. Dr. Richardson, beside the duties of medical officer, which, from the numerous applications made by the natives, were not inconsiderable, devoted his attention to natural history, as well as to a series of observations on the force of the sun's radiation. Mr. Kendall constructed all the charts after the data had been recalculated by myself; he also made several drawings; and he undertook an interesting series of observations on the velocity of sound. . . .

The chimney of the last of the buildings being completed this morning [September 23], the flag-staff erected, and all the men assembled, we commemorated these events by the festivities usual on the opening of a new establishment in this country. The first part of the ceremony was to salute the flag; the men having drawn themselves up in line, and the women and children and all the Indians resident at the fort being disposed in groups by their side, a deputation came to solicit the presence of the officers. When we appeared, we found our guns ornamented with blue ribbons and we were requested to advance and fire at a piece of money which was fastened to the flag-staff. The men then fired two volleys and gave three hearty cheers, after which Wilson the piper struck up a lively tune, and placing himself at the head of his companions, marched with them round to the entrance of the hall, where they drank to His Majesty's health and to the success of the Expedition. In the evening the hall was opened for a dance, which was attended by the whole party, dressed in their gayest attire. The dancing was kept up with spirit to the music of the violin and bag-pipes, until daylight.

These entertainments over, Beaulieu and the hunters were despatched to the chase, and they soon added two moose-deer to our store.

With the approach of the long northern winter the men were supplied with fur caps, leather mittens, trousers and the rest of their warm clothing. The boats were laid up in a sheltered place and screened as much as possible by a strong fence made of boughs. The coming of cold weather produced clear, fine days, a welcome contrast to the wet, unsettled weather of late autumn. As ice formed on the lake and the nets were reset underneath, the fishing improved and the daily catch ranged from 400 to 500. Except for what was needed for immediate consumption, the fish were hung up to freeze. A snowstorm on October 25 put an end to the skating and games the men had enjoyed on the clear ice the preceding week. Nevertheless, everyone was glad when the snow was deep enough to allow winter travel. Four men were sent out with sledges to bring in from the woods fifteen reindeer shot and stored by the hunters earlier in the season. From then on two dog sledges were used to bring in the wood, instead of the men having to haul it.

When Franklin heard that the Hudson's Bay Company intended sending their annual despatch from the Mackenzie River area to York Factory at the end of November, he sent a packet of letters to Fort Norman to be included with it. He also sent a sledge to bring Thomas Mathews to Fort Franklin. Mathews, the master carpenter on the expedition, had broken his leg months before at Cumberland House and had been away from the main party ever since. When he arrived on November 18, he was still too weak to walk more than a short distance.

On November 28 the principal leader of the Dog-Ribs and a large party of his tribe arrived at the Fort. It was usual for Indians to make their first visit to an establishment an occasion of considerable formality, but this time the visitors showed an unusual degree of caution. Their distrust, it was soon learned, had originated in a trifling occurrence at the close of the house-warming festivities on September 23. Some of the voyageurs having asked Dease if the Highlanders came from the same country as the rest of the English party, he answered that they were natives of mountainous lands, or *Montagnards*. Unfortunately, this name was also used by the voyageurs to designate the Dog-Ribs, and the Highlanders considered it an insult when applied to them. A scuffle ensued, and order was restored only when the officers sent the noisiest men to bed. Next morning when the true meaning of the word Montagnard was explained to the Highlanders, the usual harmony was restored among the men and they all went back to work. But during the fight an unlucky Dog-Rib had been attracted to the scene by hearing the name Montagnard being bandied about, and having thrust his head into the crowd, he had received a hearty blow. This confirmed all his fears and he fled to spread the report among his people that the white men intended to destroy the Indians. Though the story was not fully believed, it produced the vague distrust shown by the Indians when they approached the Fort that morning. Only when Franklin had explained the incident to them was their confidence restored.

Later that day an old man belonging to the Hudson's Bay establishment at Fort Norman arrived with his wife and reported that the supply of food at that post had failed. The men at the Fort were glad to share their means with the aged couple, who were very weak from lack of food.

By December the brief period of daylight made hunting impossible for the Indians, so many of them came to Bear Lake to fish. Franklin

reported that they put very little effort into the operation and consequently caught practically nothing. They apparently preferred to beg,
while their women and children lived off the refuse from the fish eaten
at the Fort. Franklin supplied them with nets and other fishing equipment, but they made little use of them, and on several nights actually
came over and stole the fish from Franklin's nets. Every year, the
traders reported, some of these Indians died of starvation, although
with such quantities of fish in the country, they could easily have
caught and stored a sufficient quantity to last throughout the year.
Because of the recurring famines, self imposed though they sometimes
were, the women of the tribe often destroyed their baby girls. That
winter two of the women at the fort were pregnant and let it be known
that they intended to follow this course. One actually did destroy her
baby after she left the Fort although Dease had threatened her with
severe punishment. "Infanticide is mentioned by Hearne as a common
crime among the northern Indians, but this was the first instance that
came under our notice, and I understand it is now very rare among
the Chipewyan tribes;—an improvement in their normal character
which may be fairly attributed to the influence of the traders resident
among them."

On December 18 a party of nineteen Indians arrived with sledges of
dried meat and furs. Amidst the confusion of unpacking, a melancholy
scene took place that aroused the deep sympathy of the Englishmen.
The wife of one of the Dog-Rib hunters brought in her only child, a girl,
for medical advice. As she entered the room it was evident that the
hand of death was upon the child. Dr. Richardson happened to be out
but all the remedies the officers could think of were applied, and when
he returned, other means were tried. But in vain. "So gentle was its last
sigh that the mother was not at first aware of its death, and continued
to press the child against her bosom. As soon, however, as she perceived
that life had fled she cast herself on the floor in agony, heightened by
the consciousness of having delayed in seeking relief until too late, and
by apprehension of the anger of her husband, who was dotingly
attached to the child." The Indians showed their sympathy by their
silence, standing with pity on their faces. At dawn the next day the
poor creature, although nearly exhausted from having cried the whole
night through, carried the body across the lake to be buried.

Two voyageurs arrived at the Fort on the twentieth with letters from
Fort Good Hope and some good news from a band of Loucheux Indians:
the Loucheux had encountered some Eskimos who had found the

presents left in their huts by Franklin on his brief run down the Mackenzie in August. The Eskimos sent word that they would welcome a return of the white men to their lands.

Christmas was coming, and everyone joined in the preparations. The house was replastered with mud, and all the rooms were whitewashed and repainted. Mathews brightened the main hall with decorations made from cut paper and trinkets. On Christmas Eve the wives and children of the Indian hunters were invited to share in a game of snap-dragon, which was a complete novelty to them. Once they had recovered from their surprise, they showed immense enjoyment in the game.* "When the candles were extinguished the blue flame of the burning spirits shone on the rude features of our native companions, in whose countenances were portrayed the eager desire of possessing the fruit and the fear of the penalty."

Christmas Day fell on a Sunday and the whole party was treated to the finest fare that the stores could supply. Next evening a dance was given with sixty people present including the Indians, who sat and watched. Such a small hall could seldom have been filled with such a variety of characters or confusion of tongues—Englishmen, Highlanders (mostly talking and shouting in Gaelic), French-speaking voyageurs, Eskimos, Chipewyan, Dog-Rib and Hare Indians, Cree women and children. Between the dances there was boisterous singing in English, Gaelic and French.

Late in January, 1826, the Englishmen received a packet of letters that had left England the previous June. In addition, there were piles of newspapers and periodicals. These were spread out on a table and examined with great care and pleasure. "Could any of our friends have dropped in upon us, in the evening, they would have found us discussing the events of the by-gone year with all the earnestness and interest which we could have shown had they been the occurrences of the day, and depended upon our decision." This valuable mail had nearly been lost en route to the men. An Indian guide had agreed to accompany the voyageurs carrying the packet from York Factory to Cumberland House. Along the way he decided that the packet must contain valuables and one day stole the canoe and its contents and crossed to the other side of the river. The unfortunate voyageurs had no way of pursuing him, nor food, nor guns, nor even the means of making a fire. After walking many days and suffering great hardships, they managed to reach the nearest post. The post manager immediately sent search

*The game of snap-dragon required the players to snatch raisins out of a bowl of burning spirits and eat them while they were still alight.

parties after the thief, but he was never found. They did find the packet, however, torn open and the letters left scattered over the ground. Franklin expressed his appreciation to the voyageurs by giving them a reward.

Throughout January the catch of fish steadily diminished until the daily ration had to be reduced to three or four small herrings per man, with nothing at all for the dogs. Besides giving very little nourishment, the herring caused some of the men to have severe diarrhea. By early February Franklin was forced to send three sledges to Fort Norman for some of the pemmican, arrowroot and portable soup stored there in the autumn. He hated to draw upon these supplies, which had been intended for use along the Arctic coast in the coming summer, but there seemed no alternative. At the same time, he wrote to Governor Simpson requesting that supplies of meat be stored along the route to York Factory for the expedition's use during the summer of 1827, since Richardson's party, at least, would be returning to England that way.

When word reached the Fort that the tracks of a moose had been seen about twelve miles away, Beaulieu, who was the best hunter, set out immediately with two other hunters. The three found the track and had followed it for four days when Beaulieu sprained his ankle. They knew that the moose was near at hand and believed that it would soon give in, as its footprints in the snow were stained with blood. But Beaulieu could continue no farther and returned to the Fort, accompanied by his companions. Following a good night's sleep one of the hunters set out again and after two days' fast travel drew near the wounded animal. ". . . the moose, on receiving a shot, made a rush at him, striking furiously with its fore feet. He had but just enough time to shelter himself behind a tree, upon which the animal spent its efforts, until his gun was again ready." The second shot found its mark and the moose fell to the ground.

Several days later Beaulieu and two men went out in one direction to hunt, while the Dog-Rib hunters went out in another. Both parties succeeded in killing moose, but the Dog-Ribs made up for their starvation diet by consuming nearly all their meat on the spot. Inevitably, they became so violently ill that they could not move. But about that time there was a turning point in the food situation. The fishing improved and occasionally some deer were killed. With adequate meals the men began to regain their strength, and so did the dogs.

The conduct of the men during this period of scarcity was beyond all praise and the following anecdote is worthy of record as displaying

*the excellent feeling of a British seaman and as speaking the senti-
ments of the whole party. Talking to Robert Spinks as to the difference of his present food from that to which he had been accustomed
on board ship, I said I was glad the necessity was over of keeping
them on short allowance. "Why Sir," said Spinks, "we never minded
about the short allowance but were fearful of having to use the
pemmican intended for next summer. We only care about the next
voyage and shall be glad when spring comes that we may set off;
besides, at the worst time we could always spare a fish for each of
our dogs." During the time of greatest shortage the three dogs under
Spinks' charge were in better condition than any of the others. . . .*

The improvement in fishing made possible a party, which Dr.
Richardson described in a typically cheerful letter to his sister in
Scotland:

*Last Tuesday the lady of Peter Warren Dease, Esq., chief trader of
the Hudson's Bay Company, resident at Fort Franklin, was safely
delivered of a daughter. A party of friends met to celebrate the event.
They sat down in the grand hall of the Fort to a sumptuous enter-
tainment comprising all the luxuries of the season. At the head of the
table there was a large dish of white fish excellently boiled; at the
bottom, a dish of equal magnitude of white fish, roasted; and on each
side a tureen of white fish soup. Owing to the mice having eaten the
flour, no bread was sported on this joyous occasion, but the place of
that unattainable luxury and of vegetables of every description was
amply supplied by a bottle of delicious bird-peppers.* The travels of
this bottle might furnish an interesting article.*

In his journal Franklin noted the first hint of spring:

*We observed with pleasure on March 7 that the sun had sufficient
power to soften the snow in exposed places . . . but the return of
strong winds from the NWN brought back severe weather. On the
11th there was a violent gust of wind which in its passage over
the lake gathered up the snow in a column similar to that of a
waterspout.*

> .   .   .   .   .

*The Chipewyan hunters who had been absent since Christmas
returned to us with their families [March 21] and brought with them*

---

*The sister to whom Richardson was writing had sent him the bottle of peppers.

a Dog-Rib girl, about twelve years old, who had been deserted by her tribe. When they found her she was in the last stage of weakness, from famine, sitting by the expiring embers of a fire and but for their timely appearance death must soon have ended her sufferings. They fed and clothed her and waited until she gained strength to accompany them. The wretches who had abandoned the poor creature were on their way to a fishing station which they knew to be very productive, and not above a day's march distant. She was unable to keep the pace at which they chose to proceed, and having no near relation but an aged aunt, who could not assist her, they left her at an encampment without any food. The hunters met this party of Indians about a month afterwards, when they were living in abundance. The girl by that time had perfectly recovered her strength, and they desired that she should be restored to them, but the hunters firmly resisted their importunity and one of them adopted her as his own child. . . . When the Indians came to the fort I took the first opportunity of their being assembled in the hall to send for the hunters and their wives and to reward them by a substantial present of clothing and ammunition. I also gave to them some . . . steel instruments . . . which they were desired to preserve and show to other Indians as a testimony of our approbation of their humanity. A present was also bestowed upon the girl, and then the Dog-Ribs were addressed as to their unfeeling conduct towards her. They listened quietly and merely stated her weakness as the cause. There is little doubt but that the transactions of this day were canvassed afterwards and it is to be hoped that the knowledge of our sentiments . . . may induce a discontinuance of their inhuman practices.

The men who had conveyed the last packet from Fort Franklin to Fort Simpson returned with news that some Chipewyans had seen indications that there were white people on the coast east of the Coppermine River. The Chipewyans said that in the autumn they had found some saws and axes and a store of meat on the borders of a river near the sea. There was snow on the ground, they said, and in it were footsteps that appeared to be recent. The officers concluded from the story that Captain Parry had laid up his ships in the vicinity of Bathurst Inlet and had sent hunting parties up the river to add to his stock of food. Franklin immediately dispatched two men with letters to Mr. McVicar at Slave Lake, asking that the matter be thoroughly investigated and that all information be forwarded to the Admiralty. He also begged McVicar to send a party of Indians to the spot and take with them a letter which he wrote to Captain Parry. In the letter he suggested that Parry employ the Indians as hunters or perhaps have them carry his letters to the nearest post for conveyance to England. The idea that the ships might be on the northern coast with good prospects of success and the expectation that Richardson's detachment would meet them in the summer gave the officers a lot to talk about for several days.

On April 10 Richardson and Kendall left Fort Franklin with an Indian guide and a voyageur who was to drive a dog sledge carrying provisions. They went to complete the survey of Great Bear Lake which Richardson had begun the preceding autumn. It was a hot day as they set out. The thermometer registered ninety degrees in the sun, and everyone was delighted at the prospect of a complete thaw. In order to waste no time the rest of the party cleared the snow from a piece of ground and laid the keel for the new boat that was to be built. At the same time, every available sledge was sent to Fort Norman to bring back the supply of charcoal needed for the construction of the boat.

Next day the water was dripping from the roofs, and the flies came to life indoors. For six days this mild weather continued, but even then no ground showed through the snow. When the men returned from Fort Norman with the charcoal they reported that the season was more advanced there than it was at Fort Franklin.

Thirty Hare Indians arrived on the nineteenth with their winter's catch of furs for the Hudson's Bay Company and with enough dried meat to supply the needs of the expedition until it set out for the Arctic.

> The party consisted mostly of young lads who, very good-naturedly, sang and danced for our amusement all the evening. They likewise gave us specimens of the dances in use among the Loucheux, which were more graceful than their own. The tune they sung to the Medicine-dance of the Loucheux struck me as being soft and pretty. The ludicrous attitudes and grotesque figures of the dancers as they wheeled in a circle, shaking their knives and feathers which they held between their fingers, were happily sketched by Lieut. Back.

The appearance of swans on May 7 was considered a sure sign of the approach of spring. Next day a goose was seen, the day after two ducks and the day after that several gulls. The snow was rapidly diminishing and preparations were begun for the summer voyages. The seamen repaired the coverings and sails of the boats and refitted the rigging. Everyone was given something to do. By the end of the month the carpenters had finished building the new boat. The *Reliance*, as she was called, was similar in design to the expedition's largest boat, the *Lion*, but the carpenters had had to show great ingenuity in constructing her from the limited materials available. She was made of fir with birch timbers, and fastened with iron nails instead of copper. All the spare axes and ice-chisels had had to be cut up to provide enough nails. Strips of waterproof canvas soaked in rubber varnish to fill in between the seams were used as a substitute for tar. Resin from pine trees, which the crew boiled and mixed with grease, was a good substitute for paint. After the new boat was finished the boats brought from England were given a good overhaul.

Preparations for the voyage along the Arctic coast were well in hand by the beginning of June. Franklin instructed Dease to be fully prepared for the return of Dr. Richardson's party to the Fort in the autumn, and to have enough meat available to meet the needs of his party as well, should he be unable to rendezvous with Beechey and return with him to England by way of the Pacific. Dease was to keep the Fort in operation and well provisioned until the spring of 1828.

Beaulieu and four voyageurs were instructed to leave Fort Franklin on August 6, 1826, with a bateau and proceed to the Dease River. They were to wait there until September twentieth. If Dr. Richardson had not appeared by then they were to return to the Fort in canoes, leaving the bateau and provisions for his eventual use. Dease was to make sure that Beaulieu left on time.

Fourteen men were picked to accompany Franklin and Back in the two larger boats, the *Lion* and the *Reliance*. They were all naval seamen or marines except for two voyageurs and Augustus. Dr. Richardson took ten men, including Ooligbuck, in the *Dolphin* and the *Union*.

Spare blankets and everything that could be useful for the voyage, or as presents for the Eskimos, which our stores could furnish, were divided between the eastern and western parties, and put up in bales of a size convenient for stowage. This interesting day was closed by the consumption of a small quantity of rum, reserved for the occasion, followed by a merry dance in which all joined with great glee, in their working dresses. On the following Sunday the officers and men assembled at Divine Service, dressed in their new uniforms. . . . The guns were cleaned the next day and stowed in arms chests which had been made to fit the boats. A strong breeze occurred on the 21st [June], which removed the ice from the front of the house and opened a passage to Bear Lake River. The men were sent with the boats and

*stores to the river in the evening and were heartily cheered on
quitting the beach. The officers remained to pack up the charts,
drawings and other documents which were to be left at the fort. . . .
We quitted the house at half past ten on Tuesday morning leaving
Coté, the fisherman, in charge until Mr. Dease should return from
Fort Norman. This worthy old man, sharing the enthusiasm that
animated the whole party, would not allow us to depart without
giving his hearty, though solitary cheer, which we returned in full
chorus.*

Heavy drift ice in the Great Bear River held the boats up for a whole
day, but on the morning of the twenty-fourth they were able to
continue. The junction with the Mackenzie was reached at eight o'clock
that evening. Fort Norman, where more supplies awaited them, lay
upstream and the current was so strong that the men had to resort to
tracking. This continued throughout the night. It was a fatiguing
business, for the ground along the bank was so soft that the men
hauling the ropes were up to their knees in mud. The party halted for a
meal at the spot where Alexander Mackenzie saw flame rising from the
bank in 1789. It was still on fire, the smoke issuing from several springs.
Dr. Richardson took some specimens of the coal with him.

*We reached Fort Norman at noon on the 25th. On the following
morning the provision and stores which had been left at this place
were examined and found to be in excellent order, except the powder
in one of the magazines. . . . I had ordered a supply of iron-work,
knives and beads for the sea voyage from Fort Simpson; they had
arrived some days before us and with our stock thus augmented we
were well furnished with presents for the natives. The packages being
finished on the 27th, the boats received their respective ladings and
we were rejoiced to find that each stowed her cargo well, and with
her crew embarked, floated as buoyantly as . . . anticipated. The
heavy stores however were afterwards removed into the bateau that
was to be taken to the mouth of the river, manned by Canadian
voyagers, to prevent the smaller boats from receiving injury in
passing over the shoals.*

At Fort Norman Franklin received letters which dashed his hopes
that Captain Parry might be wintering on the northern coast. Apparently the Indians had only seen some pieces of wood, recently cut, and
a deer killed by an arrow, both most probably the work of Eskimos.

The voyage down the Mackenzie was in general uneventful. Fewer

Indians were encountered than the previous autumn, for the water was now too high for fishing. There were, however, many more mosquitoes. These Franklin described as a "ceaseless torment." At Fort Good Hope the whole expedition was welcomed by a discharge of muskets set off by a large party of Loucheux who had been at the Fort for some time. The post manager informed Franklin that a large number of Loucheux had recently met an equally large party of Eskimos by appointment for the purpose of buying their furs. During the process of bargaining a violent quarrel had broken out, though fortunately it did not lead to bloodshed. Franklin could secure no satisfactory impression of the Eskimos' movements except that they had arrived in sixty canoes and were supposed to have gone downstream by the eastern channel to fish.

Having learned that he would probably run into more Eskimos than he had expected, Franklin picked up an additional supply of presents at the Fort and exchanged two guns that were defective. He also asked the company traders to have as much meat as possible stored during the summer months, to be available in the event of his return along the Mackenzie. Letters to England occupied the greater part of the night, and Franklin was glad to be able to tell the Colonial Secretary that the expedition was well equipped against every need. They set off from Fort Good Hope at five a.m. on July 2.

Next day the expedition reached a point in the River where one channel branched eastward and the other westward, and the two parties prepared to separate. "We were joined by an elderly Loucheux who gave us a better account of the eastern and western channels than we had hitherto obtained. The west branch, he said, would take us to the sea and flowed the whole way at no great distance from the mountains. The eastern channel was a good channel and passed close to the hills on that side."

The clothing, and articles for presents, had already been divided; now the provisions were allotted in proportionate amounts. Twenty-six bags of pemmican and two of grease (to be used if necessary for making additional pemmican) were set aside for Richardson's party in the *Dolphin* and *Union*, together with a supply of arrowroot, macaroni, flour and portable soup sufficient for eighty days. The *Lion* and *Reliance* received thirty-two bags of pemmican and two of grease, with a proportionate amount of other provisions. "Provided no accident occurred, neither party could be in absolute want for the whole summer, because at two-thirds allowance the pemmican could be made to last one hundred days; and we had reason to expect to meet with deer occasionally."

Franklin was sorry that he could not supply Richardson's party with a chronometer, but the mainsprings of two of the three in his possession had been broken. However, he gave Kendall an excellent watch that he had borrowed from Dease. With it he would be able to calculate his party's longitudinal position by lunar distances. Franklin had a high opinion of Kendall's ability as a marine surveyor and was confident that he would make an accurate survey of the coast between the Mackenzie and the Coppermine.

As the parties entertained for each other sentiments of true friendship and regard, it can easily be imagined that the evening preceding our separation was spent in the most cordial and cheerful manner. We felt that we were only separating to be employed on services of equal interest and we looked forward with delight to our next meeting, when after a successful termination we might recount the incidents of our respective voyages. The best supper our means afforded was provided and a bowl of punch crowned the parting feast.

By six on the morning of July fourth the boats were loaded and ready. As the two parties prepared to separate Franklin was struck by the difference between his present well-equipped expedition and the situation on the first disastrous journey. Then, he and his crew had faced their sea voyage with frail birch-bark canoes and a scanty supply of food. This time they had excellent boats and enough food to last three months. At Dr. Richardson's request, the western party embarked first. The Doctor and his companions gave three hearty cheers as the two boats moved down the river and out of sight. For a while Augustus' countenance was downcast as he contemplated the long separation from Ooligbuck, but by evening he was his usual cheerful self again.

The western branches of the Mackenzie were shallow and winding and seldom more than a quarter of a mile wide. An occasional glimpse of the Rocky Mountains afforded the travellers a welcome relief from the generally uninteresting shoreline. They landed at what appeared to be the site of an Eskimo encampment and Franklin left presents of an ice-chisel, a kettle and a knife. Soon afterwards the two boats entered a more westerly channel and passed some lop-sticks, pine trees stripped of their lower branches. These were evidently Eskimo landmarks. Farther along there were some deserted huts and beside them a pile of chips and some driftwood that had recently been gathered and split. Next day heavy rain delayed the boats' progress and fog forced the crews to camp at 8 p.m. It was a cold night and in the morning the temperature registered thirty-six degrees.

On the seventh the party reached a stretch of shallow water, where the channel joined the open sea. To get through, the crews of the two boats had to unload half the cargoes, make the crossing, unload what they had retained and return for the rest of the cargo. They had just completed this tiresome operation and were stowing the cargo in their boats again when they saw at the mouth of the River an island dotted with tents, and among the tents numerous Eskimos walking about.

Hasty preparations were begun to make contact with the natives. A selection of articles for presents and trade was picked out, the rest of the cargo was covered up and every man was directed to keep his gun ready for immediate use. Franklin had told Back earlier of his intention to make contact with the Eskimos by personally landing among them, accompanied only by Augustus, and he now instructed Back to keep the boats afloat with the crews ready to support him in case the natives should prove hostile. But on no account was Back to fire unless he was convinced that the safety of the expedition could be secured in no other way. Franklin knew that on some earlier occasions Europeans meeting natives for the first time had mistaken noise and violent gestures for active hostility, and needless loss of life had resulted. Now he made it very clear to his men that they were not to fire unless one of the officers gave the order. They were also told to leave all trading to the officers.

With ensigns flying the two boats headed for the island. The officers made signs to the Eskimos to come out and visit them, and immediately three canoes put out from shore, followed by so many boats that the water between the white men and the shore was soon completely covered. The men approached in their kayaks, the women and children in umiaks. The officers tried counting their numbers but got only as far as seventy-three kayaks and five umiaks when they lost track. The first three kayaks, paddled by elderly men, approached cautiously until Augustus assured them that the white men came as friends. He told them in detail the reasons for coming and said that if a navigable channel for big ships could be found, there would be a very profitable trade for them in the future. This pleased the old men and they repeated the news to their countrymen, who threw up their hands and gave a deafening shout of applause.

Soon there were between 250 and 300 natives surrounding the two boats, eagerly trying to sell their bows, arrows and spears to the visitors. Franklin tried to make himself heard above the tumult to get information about the coast, but in vain. The natives were by now so noisy and demanding that he ordered the boats taken farther out to sea. Thus far they seemed basically friendly, in spite of their eagerness to obtain some of the fascinating articles that lay in the boats; and when Augustus told them that the boats were to be moved, they actually helped to drag the *Lion* into deep water. But the tide was ebbing rapidly, and soon both boats were solidly grounded.

Just then an unfortunate thing happened. One of the *Lion*'s oars upset a kayak, and its owner was plunged into the water with his head in the mud. Some of the crewmen hurried to his rescue and hauled him into the boat, while his kayak was righted and emptied of water. Augustus saw him shivering from cold and wrapped him in his own greatcoat. The man's initial anger soon subsided and he was almost calm when he spotted some of the many articles that were under cover in the boat. Immediately he began asking for everything he saw and became very annoyed when his demands were refused. He shouted to his companions that there were inexhaustible riches in the *Lion*, and several of them tried to get into both boats. They pressed so closely that Franklin accepted the offer of two chiefs, who said that if they were allowed to enter the boats themselves they would keep the others out. For a time they were able to keep their word and the crews took advantage of the respite to try to float the boats. The *Reliance* got clear but the *Lion* was immovable. Just then one of the *Lion*'s crew saw that the man who had been upset had a pistol under his shirt. He was about to take it from him when Franklin interrupted, thinking that perhaps the man had bought it from the Loucheux Indians. Actually the Eskimo had stolen the pistol from Back, and when he realized that he had been spotted he leaped from the boat, taking Augustus' greatcoat with him.

Now the tide was so low that the younger men were able to wade in crowds around the boats and they began trying to steal everything within reach. Franklin told the crews to try to keep them off. Then, speaking through Augustus, he told the two chiefs that if they would go ashore and persuade their companions to accompany them, the white men would return later from the great ship that they expected to meet nearby, with a much more abundant supply of goods. The chiefs seemed well satisfied and passed this proposal on to their companions. When some of them began to withdraw, Franklin thought they had accepted his offer, but as it turned out they only retired to plan another attack. In a moment they returned, shouting some words that Augustus could not make out. When some of them took hold of the *Reliance* and began hauling her closer to shore, their intentions became obvious. Back asked the chief who was still with him to stop his men, but at first the chief's only reply was to point to the beach and repeat the word "teyma" with a good-natured smile. Then he shouted something to the men surrounding the boat and they began throwing their long knives and arrows into the boat, taking care, however, that the handles and feathered ends were turned toward the crew, as an indication of their peaceful intentions. Now other Eskimos began dragging the *Lion* after the *Reliance*.

Two of the most powerful men, jumping on board at the same time, seized me by the wrists and forced me to sit between them; and as I shook them loose two or three times, a third Eskimo took his station in front to catch my arm whenever I attempted to lift my gun or the broad dagger which hung by my side. The whole way to the shore they kept repeating the word teyma, *beating gently on my left breast with their hands and pressing mine against their breasts. As we neared the beach two umiaks, full of women, arrived and the* teymas *and vociferation were redoubled. The* Reliance *was first brought to the shore, and the* Lion *close to her a few seconds afterwards. The three men who held me now leaped ashore, and those who had remained in their canoes taking them out of the water, carried them to a little distance. A numerous party now drawing their knives and stripping themselves to the waist, ran to the* Reliance *and having first hauled her as far up as they could, began a regular pillage, handing the articles to the women who, ranged in a row behind, quickly conveyed them out of sight. Lieutenant Back and his crew strenuously but good-humouredly resisted the attack and rescued many things from their grasp, but they were overpowered by numbers and had even some difficulty in preserving their arms.*

One Eskimo was so bold as to snatch the knife belonging to one of the seamen and cut the buttons from his coat, while three others surrounded Back with their daggers raised and demanded everything that took their fancy, especially the anchor buttons on his waistcoat. A young chief rushed to Back's aid and tried to persuade his countrymen to desist. By sitting on Back's knee he managed to save a number of articles from being taken!

So far the *Lion* had only been set upon by a few natives, and her crew had managed to prevent anything of importance from being stolen by beating the natives on the head with the butt ends of their muskets. When Franklin saw what was happening to the *Reliance* he went with Augustus to try to end the tumult. The bold little interpreter rushed in among the crowd on shore and harangued them until he had almost lost his voice. In a matter of minutes Franklin was called back to the *Lion*, for it too had now been surrounded by Eskimos. They brandished their knives in a most furious manner and tried to seize everything movable. The main object was to prevent the loss of arms, oars or masts, or anything else essential for the continuance of the voyage. Duncan, one of the seamen, rescued the box containing the astronomical instruments three times, then made it fast to his leg with a cord, vowing that if they took it they would have to take him as well.

Throughout this unequal contest the self-control of the men was as conspicuous as the unconcern of the Eskimos when hit heavy blows with the butts of the muskets. Finally, several natives, angered at being foiled so often, jumped on board and tried to take the daggers and shot-belts from the men. Three men tried to disarm Franklin. Seeing his commander's need, Back sent over the young chief who had protected him, and before long Franklin's antagonists had been driven out of the boat. Now the crew were on the point of being overpowered in the fore part of the boat and he hastened to their aid, fortunately arriving in time to stop George Wilson from discharging his musket into the body of an Eskimo. The native had struck at him with a knife and cut through his coat and waistcoat. No sooner was the bow cleared of one set of marauders than another party commenced operations in the stern. They were after Franklin's gun again and the crew of the *Lion* seemed about to be overrun when the whole body of natives suddenly fled and hid themselves behind driftwood on the beach. The *Reliance* had been refloated and Back had wisely decided that the moment had come for more active interference: he had ordered his men to level their muskets at the natives; this had produced the sudden panic. The *Lion* was soon refloated as well and both boats pulled farther offshore, while the Eskimos, recovering from their fright, prepared to follow. Franklin told Augustus to make it clear to them that he would shoot the first man who came within musket range. The announcement had the desired effect.

It was 8 p.m., and the men had been doing battle for several hours. They were relieved to discover that the only important articles carried off were the mess canteens and kettles, a tent, a bale containing blankets and shoes, and some sails. All the other articles taken could be spared. Ironically, most had been intended as *gifts* for the Eskimos. On the map Franklin labelled the spot where the struggle had taken place "Pillage Point."

I cannot sufficiently praise the fortitude and obedience of both the boats' crews in abstaining from the use of their arms. In the first instance I had been influenced by the desire of preventing unnecessary bloodshed, and afterwards, when the critical situation of my party might well have warranted me in employing more decided means for their defence, I still endeavoured to temporize, being convinced that as long as the boats lay aground and we were beset by such numbers, armed with long knives, bows, arrows and spears, we could not use fire-arms to advantage. The howling of the women

and the clamour of the men proved the high excitement to which
they had wrought themselves; and I am still of the opinion that,
mingled as we were with them, the first blood we had shed would
have been instantly revenged by the sacrifice of all our lives.

Though the conduct of the Eskimos had been alarming, several of
them had shown themselves to be friendly and Franklin was very
anxious to develop an understanding with them. He was still in the dark
about the state of the ice ahead of him and was anxious to make a
second contact with them. But he was not prepared to let them surround
the boats again. They had to be made to realize that the forbearance of
the white men had been due to their good will, not to their lack of
power.

Toward nightfall the boats went aground again and the party was
held up for five hours. Some of the Eskimos walked along the beach
calling out to Augustus to come ashore and talk with them. Rather
reluctantly Franklin let him go. Though about forty natives had congregated by the time he reached the shore, he showed absolutely no fear
in what he said to them:

Your conduct has been very bad, and unlike that of all other
Eskimos. Some of you even stole from me, your countryman, but that
I do not mind. I only regret that you should have treated in this
violent manner the white people who came solely to do you kindness.
My tribe were in the same unhappy state in which you now are,
before the white people came to Churchill, but at present they are
supplied with every thing they need, and you see that I am well
clothed; I get all that I want and am very comfortable. You cannot
expect after the transaction of this day that these people will ever
bring goods to your country again, unless you show your contrition
by returning the stolen goods. The white people love the Eskimos and
wish to show them the same kindness that they bestow upon the
Indians; do not deceive yourselves and suppose that they are afraid
of you; I tell you they are not, and that it was entirely owing to their
humanity that many of you were not killed today; for they have all
guns, with which they can destroy you either when near or at a
distance. I also have a gun, and can assure you that if a white man
had fallen I would have been the first to have revenged his death.

Augustus had shown great courage. While he spoke forty armed men
surrounded him, but the shouts and applause when he finished indicated

his audience's approval. Later, he told Franklin that they had told him they were very sorry for their behaviour. Their excuse was that they had never seen a white man before and could not resist the temptation to steal when they saw such wonderful things in the boats. They promised never to act in such a way again and said they wanted to become friends of the white men and receive presents, as Augustus' tribe had done. To test their sincerity Franklin told Augustus to ask them to return the large kettle and the tent. This they did. They then asked Augustus to join them in a dance, and for about an hour he danced and sang with all his might in the middle of men armed with knives, bows and arrows. Augustus said afterwards that the words of the song and the nature of the dances were exactly the same as those used in his own country when a friendly meeting took place with strangers.

Exhausted from the previous day's action, the crews of both boats slept in until eleven a.m. Just as they had finished repairing the sails and the rigging damaged the day before, the whole body of Eskimos came paddling toward them. The two boats were immediately launched through the surf and pulled into deep water. A man in the leading kayak held up a kettle, shouting that he wanted to return it. Franklin decided that one kettle was not worth the risk of being surrounded again and had Augustus call to the Eskimos to turn back. When they continued to advance he had a gun fired across the bow of the leading kayak. This stopped them immediately and caused them to retreat.

I have been minute in my details of our proceedings with these Eskimos for the purpose of elucidating the character of the people we had to deal with; and I feel the account would be incomplete without the mention in this place of some communications made to us in the month of August following, which fully explained the motives of their conduct. We learned that up to the time that the kayak was upset, the Eskimos were actuated by the most friendly feelings towards us, but that the fellow whom we had treated so kindly after the accident, discovering what the boats contained, proposed to the younger men to pillage them. This suggestion was buzzed about and led to the conference which the old men held together when I desired them to go away, in which the robbery was decided upon and a pretty general wish was expressed that it should be attended with the total massacre of our party. Providentially a few suggested the impropriety of including Augustus; and for a reason which could scarcely have been imagined. "If we kill him," said they,

"no more white people will visit our lands and we shall lose the
opportunity of getting another supply of their valuable goods; but if
we spare him he can be sent back with a story which we shall invent
to induce another party of white people to come among us." This
argument prevailed at the time; but after the interviews with
Augustus at the dance, they retired to their island, where they were
so much inflamed by the sight of the valuable articles which they had
obtained, that they all without exception regretted that they had
allowed us to escape. While in this frame of mind the smoke of our
fire being discovered, a consultation was immediately held and a very
artful plan laid for the destruction of the party, including Augustus,
whom they conceived to be so firmly attached to us that it was in
vain to attempt to win him to their cause. They expected to find us
on shore; but to provide against the boats getting away if we should
have embarked, they caused some kettles to be fastened conspicu-
ously to the leading kayak, in order to induce us to stop. The kayaks
were then to be placed in such a position as to hamper the boats, and
their owners were to keep us in play until the whole party had come
up, when the attack was to commence. Through the blessings of
Providence their scheme was frustrated.

Franklin and his men were greatly relieved to be free of the Eskimos.
The two boats set sail and proceeded along the Arctic coast in a west-
north-west direction until eleven p.m., when they landed on a low-lying
island whose shoreline was covered with driftwood. Having made
further repairs to the sails and hulls, they took advantage of a favourable wind and continued for another twelve miles, keeping about two
miles offshore. Progress was halted at that point by ice which stretched
solidly from the shoreline out to sea as far as they could follow it. To
find an opening in the ice that would allow them to return to the shore
it was necessary to go back several miles, at which point the shoreline
rose in a series of cliffs from 60 to 250 feet high. From the top of the
cliffs they could see a level plain, with many small lakes, extending
westward to a line of hills; beyond the hills lay the Rocky Mountains.
The plain was covered with grass and there were many plants in flower.
Franklin named the nearest range of mountains after Dr. Richardson.

Franklin and Back took observations for longitude and turned in at
about eight a.m., but they had barely fallen asleep when the guard
called out that three Eskimos were approaching. The unexpected sight
of so many strangers terrified the natives, and they were on the point of
discharging their arrows when Augustus managed to reassure them that

the white men had come as friends. When the three had been presented with gifts their fears rapidly disappeared; they became absolutely overjoyed as Augustus told them of all the good things that the white men could bring. In typically generous fashion they returned to the camp to bring back the rest of their party.

But Franklin was not taking any more chances. He prepared for their return by having a line drawn along the beach 150 yards away from the tent and twice that distance from the boats. When the whole party arrived—twenty-two in all—they were stopped at this line and told that no one would receive presents if he crossed it. The Eskimos readily agreed to the condition and gave Franklin and Back hearty handshakes. Presents of beads, fish hooks, awls and various trinkets were distributed and soon everyone felt completely at ease.

Franklin was on the point of questioning his visitors about the coast and when it was likely to be clear of ice when Augustus interrupted to ask if he might put on his best clothes and his medals. This was the work of a few minutes, but when he returned the natives were so delighted with his appearance and his numerous ornaments that they could think of nothing else for the next half hour. One of them, taking hold of his coat, asked, "What kind of animal do these skins which you and the chiefs wear belong to? We have none such in our country." The anchor buttons also excited their admiration.

At length Franklin managed to get their attention and ask his questions. A strong offshore wind sometimes shifted the ice away from the coast, they told him, but farther to the west the ice often adhered to the land all summer. When it did break away, it was carried only a short distance out to sea and then brought back again by the next strong on-shore wind. One of the natives added, "If there be channels in these parts, they are unsafe for boats as the ice is continually tossing about. We wonder therefore that you are not provided with sledges and dogs, as our men are, to travel along the land when these interruptions occur."

Next morning the Eskimos paid a second visit, this time with their women and children—forty-eight persons in all. As before, they seated themselves in a semi-circle, the men in front and the women behind. Presents were given to those who had not received any the day before and Franklin purchased several pairs of sealskin boots, and some deer-skin, cut and twisted to be used for cords. The crews were much amused to see how the Eskimos used some of the presents: some of the men danced about with a large codfish hook dangling from their nose; others struck an awl through their nose. The women immediately decorated their dresses with earrings, thimbles and whatever other trinkets they were given. Most of those in the party were elderly, though very active and in excellent health. Except for the young people, they were all suffering from sore eyes caused by the glare of ice and snow. Two of the old men were nearly blind.

Franklin noted in his journal that some of the natives had long beards, and hair on their upper lip. A few had a circular spot on the crown, cut like the tonsure of a Roman Catholic priest. Every man had pieces of bone or shell inserted through the septum of the nose, and round pieces of ivory projected from each side of the underlip. The latter ornaments were valued so highly that their owners would not sell them. Those who were too poor to use beads or ivory had used bone. The perforations had been made when they were boys of about fifteen. One parent proudly pointed to his son and announced that he would be ready the next year for the operation. He was a good-looking boy, and it seemed to Franklin quite unlikely that his appearance would be much improved by the insertion of bone or ivory, which had the effect on his elders of depressing the lower lip and keeping the mouth open.

The men in the party wore a jacket made of reindeer skin, and a small hood. Their trousers were of the same material and their boots were of sealskin. Their bows and arrows were very neatly made. The arrows were tipped with bone or iron and they had fishing spears tipped with bone. They also had nets and lines for fishing. All were armed with knives. Though they had heard from the Loucheux Indians of the destructive power of guns, they still did not possess any. The women were dressed in the same way as the men, but with wider trousers and wider hoods for carrying their children. As ornaments they wore strips of different coloured skins, and round the top of their hair they had a band of wolf's hair fastened to stand erect. Their hair was tastefully piled on top of the head and tied by strings of beads or cords of white deerskin. The women were from four-and-a-half to four-and-three-quarters feet in height and most of them were fat. Some of the younger ones were pretty and so were the children. Back sketched one lady, much to her delight. The men whom he sketched were less demonstrative but no less pleased.

Franklin and Back now asked questions about the animals in the region, sometimes using sketches to make themselves understood. They concluded that the walrus was not found that far west along the coast, since when Back drew a sketch of one, none of them recognized it. But they immediately recognized his sketches of seal and reindeer. They told the officers that the polar bear was seldom seen and then only in autumn. There were also very few brown bears, they said, though Franklin had seen them frequently along the coast east of the Copper-mine River. A few white whales had already been seen and the natives said that there would be many more later in the season.

When Augustus described to them the behaviour of the Eskimos encountered earlier, they were distressed but not surprised, for they had themselves been attacked by them in the past. As a token of friendship they promised to escort the white men past their common enemies if they were still on the coast when the return passage was made.

Next morning an east wind moved the ice a little offshore and the party was able to embark. But when they had advanced only a mile and a half they were faced with ice solidly adhering to the shore. The view from the top of a nearby hill was of an unbroken field of ice stretching westward. Close at hand were a group of Eskimo houses. Constructed of drift timber, with the roots of the trees upwards, they contained from two to three rooms besides a cellar for their stores. There were generally north and south entrances, both so low that anyone going in had to crawl through. A hole at the top let the smoke out and this, like the doorways, could be filled in with a block of snow. When the holes had been covered with snow and when lamps or fires were burning within, such dwellings were extremely warm, though rather uncomfortable by the white man's standards.

Progress continued to be slow in the days that followed. Ice was an almost constant obstacle and there was frequently fog, as well as strong winds and heavy rain. From time to time the party encountered other groups of Eskimos. On one of these occasions Franklin had the greatest difficulty persuading Augustus to give a message to some Eskimo women to the effect that he wanted to meet their husbands. They were what the Eskimos called "old wives" and Augustus felt it beneath his dignity to speak to them. On Herschel Island they met natives who possessed various articles made by white men, though not of British make. Franklin concluded that they had come from Russian traders. The natives told him that Herschel Island was much frequented by Eskimos at that time of year because the deer congregated there and fishing was excellent. The island was composed of black earth and covered with grass. Franklin decided that the strait between it and the mainland was the only place he had seen since quitting the Mackenzie where a ship could find shelter, and even in this channel there were many shoals.

Franklin's journal entry for July 19 recorded what was a fairly typical day in the journey westward along the Arctic coast:

The boats were launched at 3 a.m. in fine calm weather and we set off in high spirits, but after pulling three miles we perceived the channel of open water becoming narrow and the pieces of ice heavier than anything we had before seen. Some of them being aground in three fathoms [eighteen feet] of water. At six a.m. after having gained five and a half miles we were stopped by the ice which adhered to the reef and was unbroken to seaward. Imagining we saw water at some distance beyond this barrier we were induced to drag the boats across the reef and launch them into the channel on the inside, in the hope of reaching it. This proved to be a bay at the head of which we arrived in a short time. It was then discovered that fog hanging over the ice had been mistaken for water. The boats were therefore reconveyed across the reef, the tents pitched and we had to draw largely on our nearly exhausted stock of patience as we contemplated the dreary view of this closely-packed icy field.

Four days later the crews succeeded in advancing ten miles, and the day after they gained a further two and three-quarter miles, but for the next two days they were unable to move. During that time, the only signs of life were a grey wolf, some seals and some ducks. Franklin observed in his journal, "More tedious hours than those passed by us in the present situation cannot well be imagined." After the astronomical observations had been obtained and worked out, the survey brought up to date, a sketch made of the encampment, and specimens of the plants and stones in the vicinity collected, there was literally nothing to do. Anxiety at the advanced period of the season gave the men little inclination to read and still less composure to invent amusements. Even if there had been no mosquitoes, the ground was too swampy to allow the pleasure of a walk. They often talked of visiting the Rocky Mountains, but this would have taken two days and they did not dare leave the boats that long in case the ice, in its fickle movements, should open up even for a short time.

On July 27 Franklin reached what he estimated to be the boundary between British and Russian territory. He marked the occasion by hoisting the Union Jack and depositing a tin box in which were a silver medal and an account of the progress made until then by his party. Even though he was now in Russian territory, he continued to name bays, points, etc. after his friends in the navy or leaders of state, but when he came to a really significant mountain range he called it the Romanzoff Range in honour of Count Romanzoff, Chancellor of the Russian Empire.

The two British-built boats stood up magnificently to extremely rough treatment in the trip along the coast. Though they were damaged a number of times they were never put out of commission by the sometimes heavy blows against reefs or ice. More than once they shipped a lot of water in high seas but they never swamped, and the sails proved to be invaluable.

The party's worst experience took place on an island that Franklin named "Foggy Island." Here the men were held up for seven days by almost continuous fog. About midnight on August 7 the carpenter finished making repairs to one of the boats, and the crews were on the point of setting out when a very thick fog moved in and continued to envelop everything until eleven next morning. The storm raged all that day but the fog cleared for about two hours, allowing the men to see that large masses of ice were being tossed about in the rough surf. The hunters went off after deer and Augustus succeeded in making a kill. During the chase they discovered that they were on an island separated from the mainland by a channel that could be crossed at low tide. After sunset the squalls became still more violent and the fog so thick that nothing could be seen beyond forty yards.

The gale continued through the tenth and the fog was thicker than ever and heavily laden with moisture. In the eerie world which it created the men were unable to recognize even the most familiar objects: the hunters fired several times at what they thought were deer, but the "deer" took wing and turned out to be cranes or geese. Next morning the fog lifted enough to reveal a point about three and a half miles away. The party hastily embarked, but before the boats could be dragged into deep water the fog had enveloped them again. Even so, Franklin decided to try to make the point, steering by compass, since the wind was favourable. They had to alter course slightly to avoid shoals but the boats finally arrived at the place where the point should have been, according to their reckoning. Here the crews rested on their oars and waited for the fog to lift, but they waited in vain and in the end they had to return to the island. The men were wet through from hauling the boats over the flats and had only begun to get their clothes dry when the fog lifted and again they pushed off. Once more the fog came down before they had advanced many miles and once more they had to return to the island. They had covered seven miles that day, the men having spent two hours in the ice-cold water hauling the boats through mud—and all to no purpose. The temperature of the water was forty degrees, and by evening the men's legs were very much swollen and inflamed. Franklin decided there was no point in trying again until the weather had really cleared.

"Fog is of all others the most hazardous state of the atmosphere for navigation in an icy sea, especially when it is accompanied by strong breezes, but particularly so for boats where the shore is unapproachable." As he made this observation in his journal, Franklin also noted that the present expedition had run into a great deal more fog than his party had done during the same period in 1821. On the course east of the Coppermine he had been held up only three times by fog, whereas now he and his companions hardly passed a day without encountering it. He concluded that the difference must be due to the greater amount of ice along the coast to the west and to the low and swampy character of the land. The coast east of the Coppermine River was high and dry and there was much less ice.

On Sunday, August 13, the men assembled for divine service and then amused themselves as best they could in their tents, though everything was saturated with moisture. Finally, on the fifteenth, the fog dispersed, but the gale from the northeast made it impossible to launch the boats through the surf. It was not until the following day that they escaped from what Franklin called "this detestable island."

August 16] *The period had now arrived when it was incumbent on me to consider whether the prospect of attaining the object of the voyage was sufficiently encouraging to warrant the exposure of the party to the daily increasing risk, by continuing on. We were now only halfway from the Mackenzie River to Icy Cape; and the chance of reaching the latter depended on the nature of the coast that was yet to be explored, and the portion of the summer which yet remained for our operations. I knew, from the descriptions of Cook and Burney, that the shore about Icy Cape resembled what we had already passed . . . while the general trending of the coast from the Mackenzie to the west-north-west, combined with the information that we had collected from the Eskimos, led me to conclude that no material change would be found in the intermediate portion. . . .*

While a hope remained of reaching Behring Straits, I looked upon the hazard to which we had, on several occasions, been exposed, of shipwreck on the flats or on the ice, as inseparable from a voyage of the nature of that which we had undertaken; and if such an accident had occurred, I should have hoped, with a sufficient portion of the summer before me, to conduct my party in safety back to the Mackenzie. But the loss of the boats when we should have been so far advanced, and at the end of the season, would have been fatal. The deer hasten from the coast as soon as the snow falls, no Eskimo had been lately seen, nor any winter houses, to denote that this part of the coast was much frequented; and if we did meet them in adverse circumstances we could not, with safety, trust to their assistance for a supply of provision.

Till our tedious detention at Foggy Island we had had no doubt of ultimate success; and it was with no ordinary pain that I could now bring myself even to think of relinquishing the great object of my ambition, and of disappointing the flattering confidence that had been reposed in my exertions. But I had higher duties to perform than the gratification of my own feeling, and a mature consideration of all the above matters forced me to the conclusion that we had reached that point beyond which perseverance would be rashness and our best efforts must be fruitless.

The whole party accepted Franklin's decision as cheerfully as they would have accepted an order to continue. Their spirit was all the more creditable, since many of them had swollen and inflamed legs from having waded so frequently in ice-cold water. Later, writing in his journal, Franklin commented that no one familiar with the resolute temperament of the British sailor would have been surprised at their complete readiness to proceed, but he felt it his business to judge their capability of doing so, and this was an additional factor in the decision he reached.

Could I have known . . . that a party from the Blossom had been at the distance of only one hundred and sixty miles from me, no difficulties, dangers, or circumstances should have prevailed on me to return; but taking into account the uncertainty of all voyages in a sea obstructed by ice, I had no right to expect that the Blossom had advanced beyond Kotzebue Inlet, or that any party from her had doubled Icy Cape. It is useless now to speculate on the probable result of a proceeding which did not take place; but I may observe that, had we gone forward as soon as the weather permitted, namely on the 18th, it is scarcely possible that any change of circumstances could have enabled us to overtake the Blossom's barge.

Franklin discovered later that the Blossom's barge had turned back on August 25.

Captain Beechey had sailed from England on May 19, 1825, with instructions to be available for a possible rendezvous with Franklin and his party along the coast of what is now Alaska by July of 1826. He arrived at Kotzebue Sound on time and proceeded as far northeastward as Icy Cape. (This was the farthest point reached by Captain Cook in 1778.) As he proceeded, Beechey left a series of prearranged signals and messages for Franklin along the coast. During this part of the journey he and his men encountered numerous groups of Eskimos, most of whom were friendly. The *Blossom* then returned to the appointed rendezvous, while a party in a barge was sent forward in hopes of making contact with Franklin. The barge reached the most northerly point of North America, which its crew named Point Barrow (after the Secretary of the Admiralty, Sir John Barrow), before turning back. The barge encountered adverse gales, currents and ice but somehow survived to reach the *Blossom*.

Turning his back on the icy waters, Beechey sailed his ship to the southwest and followed the coast as far as San Francisco. Then, heading out into the Pacific, he and his crew passed the winter visiting the Sandwich Islands, Wake, Formosa, Canton and Macao. Beechey had not given up his mission, and the next summer he sailed through Bering Strait once again in hopes of finding Franklin. The barge again advanced farther than the mother ship, but this time she got only as far as Icy Cape before weather conditions forced her to turn back. As she battled her way through stormy seas toward the waiting ship, her luck ran out and she was wrecked. Miraculously, the whole crew was picked up by the *Blossom* and the ship set out on the long voyage home.

On August 17, 1826 Franklin took a last look along the coast to the west; the most distant point visible to his eye he named Beechey Point. Then, putting from his mind thoughts of what might have been, he turned his attention to the arduous return voyage to the Mackenzie River.

The two crews landed again on Foggy Island, perhaps just in time to save their lives: violent squalls and raging seas would have made further advance extremely hazardous. On shore the men enjoyed the first good fire and warm meal in many days. On the highest part of the island fronting the sea they erected a pile of driftwood. On it a red signal flag was left flying, and underneath Franklin deposited in a tin case a letter to Captain Parry giving an account of their proceedings. On the chance that an accident might befall his party Franklin wrote a similar letter to the Admiralty in London. This one he left unsealed, wrapped in bark, and addressed to the Russian fur traders, in hopes that the Eskimos would carry it to them. An ice chisel, a knife, a file and an axe were hung on the post for the Eskimos. In digging a hole to erect the necessary posts the men found that the ground was frozen at a depth of sixteen inches.

Franklin made a special point of stopping at the site of a former camp to look for a gun and some ammunition, left behind by mistake. He was much disturbed to find that it had already been taken by Eskimos; they had no experience with firearms and could easily hurt themselves. Besides, he wanted to prevent the introduction of firearms among the

Eskimos. A few days later he encountered some natives who told him that they had seen the gun and that it had been taken farther to the east.

The return voyage to the Mackenzie was a story of gales, ice, reefs and constant discomfort. A fierce storm on August 26 brought the party close to death.

The gale increased with rapidity; in less than ten minutes the sea was white with foam, and such waves were raised as I have never before been exposed to in a boat. The spray and sea broke over us incessantly, and it was with difficulty that we could keep free by baling. Our little vessels went through the water with great velocity under a close-reefed sail, hoisted about three feet up the main-mast, and proved themselves to be very buoyant. Their small size, however, and the nature of their construction, necessarily adapted for the navigation of shallow rivers, unfitting them for withstanding the sea then running, we were in imminent danger of foundering. I therefore resolved on making for the shore as the only means of saving the party, although I was aware that in so doing I incurred the hazard of staving the boats, there being few places on this part of the coast where there was sufficient beach under the broken cliffs. The wind blowing along the land, we could not venture on exposing the boat's side to the sea by hauling directly in, but edging away with the wind on the quarter, we most providentially took the ground in a favour-able spot. The boats were instantly filled with the surf, but they were unloaded and dragged up without having sustained any material damage. Impressed with a sense of gratitude for the signal deliverance we had experienced on this and other occasions, we assembled in the evening to offer up praise and thanksgiving to the Almighty.

Next day the surf was still too heavy for the boats to embark. The men took the opportunity to dry their bedding, clothing and pemmican and to put their guns in proper order. A party of Eskimos visiting from a nearby encampment said they had watched the two boats land the night before and were astonished that the whole party had not been drowned. That night Augustus slept in the Eskimos' tents, while their women cheerfully sewed soles of heavier sealskins to the men's moccasins to make them more comfortable when walking over rocky ground.

The Eskimos told Augustus that each year they travelled east to purchase furs from the natives at the mouth of the Mackenzie, then returned immediately to the west, hauling the furs overland to the Russian establishments which were situated in the interior. Each time, they ran the risk of being attacked by large parties of Mountain Indians; and in fact the Indians often overcame them and took their furs. During this conversation Franklin thought he recognized one of the Eskimos as having been in the party that had attacked them at the mouth of the Mackenzie. The man admitted he had been there but showed a friendly spirit and told Franklin the story of their plan to kill his whole party. He said that his former companions had gone farther to the east but some might have remained to keep a look-out for the white men. They might be avoided, he explained, by entering the River by a more westerly branch than the one they had used on the outward journey.

Franklin and his companions continued along the coast until on August 28 they could see Garry Island off to the northeast. Shortly after, a gale kept them on shore for twenty-four hours. During this wait they were visited by a large party of Eskimos. The visitors told Franklin that they had seen Dr. Richardson's party get clear of the Mackenzie after having to escape from Eskimos who had tried to drag his boats on shore. Naturally, this worried Franklin considerably.

> Our visitors left us about two p.m. but shortly afterwards we heard loud cries and on looking round saw two young Eskimos running in breathless haste to announce that a large party of Indians had come down from the mountains with the express purpose of attacking the boats and killing every man of the party. They desired us to embark instantly as the only means of escape; for the Indians, they said, were already at the tents within our view, and when they left them they were on the point of spreading round us to commence the onset. . . . As soon as Spinks returned, who had gone to shoot, we shoved off; and never were men more delighted than our two Eskimo friends seemed to be at our escape; and especially at that of Augustus, to save whom, they asserted more than once, was their principal motive in coming to us.

As they proceeded, Augustus told Franklin more of what he had learned in those brief moments from the two Eskimos. Seven Mountain Indians had gone to Herschel Island to trade with the Eskimos and there they had been shown the different articles received from the white men. When the seven had returned to their tribe with the news, a hurried meeting was held. The men of the tribe decided that these intruders would ruin their trade and that they must be tracked down and destroyed.

Leaving their women and children behind in order to travel faster, they had set out. Their plan was to wait for the white men at the mouth of the Mackenzie, where there were shoals. While Franklin's crews were hauling the boats over the flats, some of them would approach and offer assistance. They believed that they would be mistaken for Loucheux Indians, who were friendly, and that their offer would be accepted. While pretending to help, they would knock holes in the boats. Then the rest of their party would emerge from hiding and rush down to kill the crews.

The two young men who had brought word of the plan to Franklin had been urged to do so by an old Eskimo who had been given a knife and other presents the day before. When he had heard of the Indians' plans he had called the two men aside and said, "These white men have been kind to us and they are few in number. Why should we suffer them to be killed? You are active young men, run and tell them to depart instantly."

On August 31 the crews reached what appeared to be the mouth of the Mackenzie River, but the series of channels was very confusing and it was not until September 4 that they arrived at Point Separation, where they had parted company with Dr. Richardson two months earlier. There they found the different articles that they had left on the way down river. The kettle was of special value because the Eskimos had robbed them of all but one. Franklin searched for some message from Richardson, but there was nothing. On the chance that the Doctor might still be on his way he deposited a letter and a bag of pemmican where they could easily be found.

As he left the Arctic coast behind him and headed up river, Franklin was more convinced than ever that a navigable northwest passage *did* exist. But he noted in his journal, ". . . we traced the coast westward from the mouth of the Mackenzie 374 miles without having found one harbour in which a ship could find shelter."

The ascent of the Mackenzie was made without incident. During this part of the journey they met several bands of Indians, among them the chief of the Loucheux. He seemed anxious to tell Franklin something but was unable to make himself understood. Later, Franklin discovered what he had been trying to say: apparently during the summer a chief had been murdered along the sea coast, and somehow his death had developed into a rumour that Franklin had died.

Arriving at Fort Franklin on September 21 the party was given a warm welcome. "The eastern detachment had arrived on the 1st of September after a most successful voyage; and Dr. Richardson being anxious to extend his geological researches as far as the season would permit, had gone in a canoe to the Great Slave Lake, having previously sent a report of his proceedings to meet me at Fort Good Hope, in case of our being obliged to return by the Mackenzie; but the bearer of them had passed us without being seen." Kendall, left in charge of the Fort by Richardson, had also written an account of his journey and Franklin stayed up all the first night studying it and then writing an account of the achievements of both expeditions. By morning the completed report was ready to be taken by special messenger on the first leg of the long journey to the office of the Colonial Secretary in London.

The distance travelled in the three months of our absence from Fort Franklin amounted to 2048 statute miles of which 610 were through parts not previously discovered. The eastern detachment had travelled a distance of 1980 miles, including the coastal voyage of 863 miles. Altogether they had explored 1015 miles of previously unknown territory, including 433 miles overland.

Richardson had evidently experienced much better weather on his coastal voyage than Franklin. Whereas Franklin ran into fog on twenty-six of the fifty-three days spent on the Arctic sea, Richardson encountered it only a few times and then it generally cleared within a few hours. He had had to navigate his boats through some heavy floe ice and on one occasion the *Dolphin* was dangerously squeezed. Yet he had never been held up by ice barriers. His progress had varied from a few miles a day to as many as thirty-nine.

So many bays, straits and rivers had already been named after the great men of the day that Richardson was able to include a wide variety of friends and acquaintances on the map that he and his party were drawing. He also showed his appreciation of his two little boats when he named an important strait the "Dolphin and Union Strait." But most generous recognition seems to have gone to the Victualling Board. The names of its chairman, commissioner and secretary were all permanently attached to some frozen extremity of the Canadian north, probably in gratitude for the excellence of the arrowroot, portable soup and essence of coffee!

Richardson's account (which Franklin later published in his own journal) began on July 4 after he had parted company with Franklin at Point Separation. Three days later he and his crew encountered a large party of Eskimos. Their manner was friendly and trading began without delay, with beads, fire-steels, flints, files, knives, hatchets and kettles bartered for fish, axes, spears and arrows. These Eskimos showed much greater curiosity about the construction of the boats than the Indians had done. It was the first time they had seen a rudder and they admired it particularly. The sight of Ooligbuck lighting his pipe excited them greatly, and they shouted "ookah, ookah" (fire, fire) when they saw smoke coming from his mouth. They quickly understood the purpose of Richardson's pocket telescope, referring to it as "eetee-yawgah" (far-eyes). Combs were in great demand in their trading. Richardson noted that they possessed some wooden ones that they had made themselves. "The females, as they passed in their umiaks, bestowed on us some glances that could scarcely be misunderstood—their manners in this respect differing widely from those of the Indian women who have a modest and even shy demeanour. Some of the young girls had a considerable share of beauty and seemed to have spared no pains in ornamenting their persons."

As they proceeded along the coast Richardson and his companions came upon a number of other Eskimo encampments. Each time the natives embarked bag and baggage and followed the white men. The larger their numbers, the bolder they were: they would try to push their kayaks alongside the two boats and steal everything within reach, showing great cunning in their manner of approach. Richardson was against showing his guns, for he hoped to win their good will if he could; and in fact they did show considerable friendliness, pointing out the deepest channels to follow and inviting the party ashore to cook breakfast and sleep with their wives. The crewmen regretted that neither invitation was accepted!

Later that day, July 7, the Dolphin grounded on a sandbank and one of the natives tried to come aboard. Between his kayak and the boat there were three other kayaks. At a signal from him, the men aboard these kayaks laid their broad paddles across their gunwales, turning them into a sort of runway. The man then ran across this runway and leaped into the stern seat of the Dolphin. But in a moment he was tumbled out again.

Richardson then decided to buy nothing more from the Eskimos except their bows, and these only as a means of disarming them before they got worked up. (These bows were made of spruce, strengthened by cords made of sinews of reindeer, and were far superior to the Indian bows.) The idea was a good one, but it came too late; the natives were already in an excited state. In his journal Richardson described the scene that followed:

> Mr. Kendall, seeing that he would almost immediately be surrounded by a force too great to permit his men to act, called to me that he should be obliged to fire. Fully aware of the necessity of prompt measures I answered that he was at liberty to fire, if necessary. Upon which, snatching up his fowling piece, he presented it at three of the most daring, who had hold of the sweep-oar, and his crew who were now in the water endeavouring to shove the boat off and struggling with the natives, jumped on board and seized their muskets. The crew of the Dolphin likewise displayed their arms and stood ready, but I ordered that no individual should fire until called upon by name. . . . Happily, however, there was no occasion to fire at all; the contests of the Eskimos with the Indians had taught them to dread firearms, and on the sudden sight of every man armed with a musket, they fled to the shore. . . . I do not believe that the natives had matured a plan of attack, but the stranding of a boat on their own shore was too great a temptation to be resisted. . . . It is probable that the Eskimos were doubtful as to the sex of some of our party until they saw them prepare for battle. None but women row in their umiaks and they had asked Ooligbuck if all the white women had beards. . . .
>
> In about an hour after leaving Point Encounter (so named to mark the encounter with the natives) we observed ten kayaks coming towards us from a cluster of islands; they soon overtook us but kept at a reasonable distance and no longer gave us any trouble by coming alongside. We wished to show that we had no desire to hurt them, notwithstanding their past conduct, and therefore began again to trade with them, yet we were naturally anxious that they should leave us before we encamped. . . . Our wishes were seconded by a fresh breeze of wind springing up and enabling us to set our sails, by which the crews enjoyed a rest after fourteen hours' labour at the oars. . . . Ooligbuck was not of much use as an interpreter in our intercourse with these people, for he spoke no English; but his presence answered the important purpose of showing that the white people were on terms of friendship with the distant tribes of Eskimos. As a boatman he was of the greatest service, being strongly attached to us, possessing an excellent temper and labouring cheerfully at his oar. . . . We could not ascertain the number of people we saw in the

course of the day . . . but we passed at least 30 tents. . . . Four grown
people is perhaps the average number of the inhabitants of each tent.
A short time before the attack on the Union I counted forty kayaks
round the two boats.

Weather conditions along the coast east of the Mackenzie were often
severe. One night the *Union* broke from her moorings in a gale and
began to drive toward the lee shore. Kendall and one of the seamen had
been sleeping on board and they managed to keep her off the rocks until
some men in the *Dolphin* reached them and threw a line. The boats
were rowed back to the beach and hauled up well above the water. The
men turned in, soaking wet, but they were barely asleep when the tent
pegs were torn out by the force of the wind and the tent fell in on them.
When morning came, a good fire dried both their clothes and provisions.

Eskimo winter huts were frequently seen along the coast. These rows
of drift-trees, "planted" in the sand with their roots uppermost, assumed
very curious forms when viewed through a hazy atmosphere. Sometimes they resembled a crowd of people; at other times the men fancied
they were not unlike the spires of a town just appearing above the
horizon.

Richardson sat up the whole of one night to watch the motion of the
tide, perhaps not such a hardship considering that they set off again at
three a.m.! In his journey along the coast he noted forty species of
plants in flower, one of them similar to a plant often seen on sandy
parts of the British coast. Others resembled plants that grew in the
Scottish hills.

On the morning of July 18 the party encountered another band of
Eskimos. As usual the natives' first reactions were hostile, but when
they discovered that there was trading to be done they became very
eager. The situation was greatly helped when the men made a barricade
of the masts and spare oars eighteen inches above the gunwhale of the
boats. The barricade kept the natives from stealing, and in the event of
a quarrel it could supply protection against arrows if the men threw
blankets or sails over it. When a light breeze sprang up the party set
sail and with the help of the oars advanced at the rate of four miles an
hour. Eleven kayaks continued alongside the boats, as well as three
umiaks, each one rowed by two women and steered by a third. The
Eskimo craft were faster than the *Dolphin* and *Union*. In his journal,
Richardson described the women in the Eskimo party:

The females, unlike those of the Indian tribes, had much handsomer

features than the men; and one young woman of the party would
have been deemed pretty even in Europe. Our presents seemed to
render them perfectly happy and they danced with such ecstasy in
their slender boats as to incur more than once great hazard of being
upset. . . . They gave us many pressing invitations to pass the night at
their tents, in which they were joined by the men; and to excite our
liberality the mothers drew their children out of their wide boots,
where they were accustomed to carry them naked, and holding them
up begged beads for them.

For a time the white men responded quite generously to their requests,
but they were anxious to be free of the natives by breakfast time and
finally told them that they had run out of presents. At this, the Eskimos
took their leave.

The last party of Eskimos had been as inquisitive as the others in
wanting to know the names of the strangers. They also tried to teach
the white men their names. They had seen Indians, they said, and had
heard that white people existed, but they had never seen any before.
When Richardson gave one of them a little reindeer meat in exchange
for fish they all wanted to know how it had been killed. Ooligbuck
showed them his gun and Richardson gave him permission to fire, after
the natives had been warned not to be alarmed by the noise. Even so,
the report astonished them, and an echo from some ice nearby made
them think that the ball had struck the shore about a mile away.

Richardson's journal entry for July 19 described the country they
were passing:

The coast consists of precipitous banks. . . . They gradually increase
in altitude from Cape Bathurst, and near our encampment their
height exceeded 250 feet. The shale was in a state of ignition in many
places and the hot sulphurous airs from the land were strongly
contrasted with the cold sea breezes with which, in the morning,
they alternated. The combustion had proceeded to a considerable
extent on the point where we landed at noon. Much alum had formed
and the baked clays of yellow, brown, white and red colours caused
the place to resemble a brick-field or a pottery. . . . The interior of the
country, as seen from the top of the cliffs, appeared to be nearly level
and to abound in small lakes. The soil was clayey and from the recent
thaw, wet and soft. Tufts of the beautiful phlox, before mentioned,
were scattered over these otherwise unsightly wastes and, notwith-
standing the scanty vegetation, reindeer were numerous. Some of the

young ones, to whom man was doubtless a novel object, came
trotting up to gratify their curiosity and were suffered to depart
unmolested.

Next day Richardson and his men passed cliffs 600 feet in height.
They were now half way between Point Separation and the Coppermine
River and had every reason to be satisfied with their progress.

After following the coastline of an extensive bay for three days,
Richardson named it after his commanding officer. Later, back in
England, he wrote:

> *In bestowing the name of Franklin on this remarkable bay I paid*
> *an appropriate compliment to the officer under whose orders and by*
> *whose arrangements the delineation of all that is known of the*
> *northern coast of the American Continent has been effected; with*
> *the exception of the parts in the vicinity of Icy Cape discovered by*
> *Captain Beechey. It would not be proper, nor is it my intention, to*
> *descant on the professional merits of my superior officer; but after*
> *having served under Captain Franklin for nearly seven years in two*
> *successive voyages of discovery, I trust I may be allowed to say that*
> *however high his brother officers may rate his courage and talents,*
> *either in the ordinary line of his professional duty, or in the field of*
> *discovery, the hold he acquires on the affections of those under his*
> *command, by a continued series of the most conciliating attentions*
> *to their feelings, and a uniform and unremitting regard to their best*
> *interests, is no less conspicuous. I feel that the sentiments of my*
> *friends and companions, Captain Back and Lieutenant Kendall, are*
> *in unison with my own, when I affirm that gratitude and attachment*
> *to our late [former] commanding officer will animate our breasts to*
> *the latest period of our lives.*

The two weeks following the discovery of Franklin Bay were marked
by no major crises. On the whole, the weather was favourable, with
only occasional fog and gale winds, though ice was a recurring problem.
Because the weather remained fairly constant, the party was able to
follow a comparatively regular schedule. Usually they set out between
two and four in the morning, halted briefly for meals and continued
until early evening. Like Franklin, Richardson was constantly on the
look-out for safe harbours and good landing places for ships. More often
than not he was disappointed. "There are many well sheltered coves in
the vicinity of Cape Parry and among the Booth Islands but the bottom

is rocky, and numerous reefs render the navigation unsafe for a ship."
But if Cape Parry offered little of practical value, it at least provided
spectacular scenery. "The eastern side of Cape Parry exhibits a succession of limestone cliffs . . . and we passed many excavations ornamented
by graceful, slender pillars and exhibiting so perfect a similarity to the
pure Gothic arch, that had Nature made such displays in the Old World
there would be but one opinion as to the origin of that style of
architecture."

When on August 7 the party entered George IV's Coronation Gulf
it had succeeded in linking up Richardson's discoveries with those of
Franklin on his earlier expedition. This gave Richardson the honour of
having completed a portion of the Northwest Passage. The achievement
carried with it a reward of £5000 established by His Majesty's Order-
in-Council. Unfortunately the order was framed without any expectation that the discovery would come from west to east or that it would
be made in vessels as small as the *Dolphin* and *Union*. Consequently no
claim could be made to the reward.

Having arrived at his destination Richardson took stock of what he
had seen and learned about "his" portion of the Arctic coast. The most
important question was whether ships could safely make such a
passage. During their coastal voyage, he and his companions had not
seen the tide rise more than twenty-two inches, and in some places it
was not more than eight or nine inches. The velocity of the ebb and
flow varied from one to three miles an hour. They had seen no ice that
would have held up a ship and there were four places among the islands
where a vessel could find shelter. There were, however, many sunken
rocks all along the coast. The abundance of driftwood meant that a
sufficient supply of fuel could easily be collected for a ship, and
wherever the party had landed on the main shore they had found
streams or small lakes of fresh water. Richardson noted that if the
course of events should ever bring a steam vessel to the Arctic coast her
crew would be able to obtain firewood for her daily consumption
between Cape Bathurst and the Mackenzie River, while west of the
Mackenzie they would find a supply of pitch coal of excellent quality.
But it appeared to Richardson that floating ice would always be a
problem. It seemed to him that the heat of summer was almost always
sufficient to break up the ice but not powerful enough to dissolve it
entirely. Hence, loose ice was constantly being driven about by the
wind and becoming firmly packed in the narrow straits.

Along the coast he and his companions had noticed about 170
flowering plants. There were a number of shrubby plants like the

juniper, willow and dwarf birch, while a few clumps of white spruce and some straggling black spruce and canoe birches grew in sheltered places on the banks of rivers at a distance of twenty to thirty miles from the sea.

The party had done well to complete the sea voyage so early in the season. Richardson and Kendall were especially pleased that the men were still in good health and eager to start the laborious march across the barren lands. They all knew that the comparative comfort and ease of the voyage had been due largely to Franklin's foresight in arranging for adequate supplies of food and other necessities. Their awareness of this made them hope all the more that he and his party had been equally fortunate in their voyage west of the Mackenzie. Another source of gratification was the accuracy with which Kendall had been able to reckon their position, working solely from lunar observations. These observations had been made as often as possible, and as it turned out, his reckoning at the mouth of the Coppermine River differed only two and a half miles from Franklin's observations in 1821. Considering that the party had travelled 902 miles from Point Separation to the mouth of the Coppermine, this was accuracy indeed!

Richardson knew that it would be quite impracticable to take the *Dolphin* and *Union* up the Coppermine above Bloody Fall. The two boats were accordingly drawn up on shore out of reach of high water, to be left behind. The remainder of the articles brought as presents for the Eskimos were packed in boxes and placed in tents beside the boats. The tents were securely pitched, and a Union Jack was hoisted to attract the attention of the natives. The presents left in the tents would be a regular windfall for the party discovering them. And perhaps the Eskimos would learn to use the tents for their summer journeys. Richardson had the surplus gunpowder thrown into the river to safeguard the natives from the possibility of an accident if they found it.

On August 10 packages of food, astronomical instruments, charts, specimens of plants and rocks, guns and ammunition, were divided equally among the members of the party. Shortly after they set out, Richardson had their collapsible boat, the *Walnut-Shell*, put together, and an attempt was made to tow it upstream. But the tiny craft had been designed to cross rivers and lakes and proved itself quite unsuitable for towing. Richardson knew that there would be no rivers to cross on the overland route to Fort Franklin, so he decided to leave the boat behind, together with half a bag of arrowroot and five muskets, which he now concluded were also unnecessary. This reduced the load by fifteen pounds per man. After that "the march was resumed with alacrity. . . ."

The journey across country to Fort Franklin was completed in twenty-one days. On the evening of the fifth day the party had eaten supper and most of the men were asleep when someone saw three Indians approaching. Richardson threw some moss on the fire and tied the flag of St. George to the end of a gun to show who they were. Two of the Indians approached slowly and suspiciously, after first hiding the boy who was with them. Richardson walked out to meet them, unarmed. One of them had his bow and arrow ready in his hands and the other his gun. But as soon as they recognized the white men by their clothing they shouted for joy, shook hands warmly and called the boy out of hiding. They had met the white men the previous winter when they brought furs and provisions to Fort Franklin. Now Richardson learned from them, mostly by sign language, that they had been hunting in that area for some time in hopes of meeting the party. They gave the white men all the meat they had collected and said they would accompany them to Bear Lake. Meanwhile, they sent word to all the Indians in the area, telling of the party's return.

The gift of meat, and the hunting that continued to supply more as they advanced, was sufficient to keep everyone in good health, but the men suffered considerably from the cold and from sore feet. The rendezvous with Beaulieu on Great Bear Lake took place, as planned in the spring, although Beaulieu was a few days late. On September 1, seventy-one days after they had left, the men in the eastern detachment of the expedition triumphantly entered Fort Franklin to receive a warm welcome from Dease.

Having brought the Narrative of the proceedings of the Eastern Detachment to a conclusion [Richardson wrote], the pleasing duty remains of expressing my gratitude to the party for their cheerful and obedient conduct. Not a murmur of discontent was heard throughout the voyage and every individual engaged with alacrity in the laborious tasks he was called up to perform. . . . Our good-natured and faithful Eskimo friend, Ooligbuck, carried with him to his native lands the warmest wishes and esteem of the whole party.

On his return from the western coastal voyage on September 21 Franklin had found that the food situation at Fort Franklin was highly unsatisfactory. The hunters attached to the expedition, members of the Dog-Rib tribe, had failed to lay up a good supply of meat, as promised. Those living at the Fort were existing on the daily catch of fish but it was barely enough to keep them going. Five men were immediately sent to a fishing ground that had been very productive the year before.

> Our anxiety was in some measure relieved on the 28th of September by the arrival of Beaulieu and some hunters from the north side of Bear Lake with a supply of dried meat. The term of Boileau's [sic] engagement being now expired, he was desirous of quitting our service; and though he was our best hunter, Mr. Dease advised me to comply with his request, as he had collected a number of useless followers whom we must have fed during the short days. He accordingly took his departure, accompanied by seventeen persons, which was a very important relief to our daily issue of provision. I supplied them with ammunition from the store to enable them to hunt on their way to Marten Lake, where they intended to fish until the return of spring.

The routine of the previous winter was resumed. Franklin, Back and Kendall were busy completing their maps, drawings and journals, which Franklin was to take with him to England. He planned to proceed on the ice to Fort Chipewyan as soon as the material was in order and there arrange for provisions for the rest of the party on its journey east in the spring. From Fort Chipewyan Franklin intended to return to England by the earliest conveyance. Meantime, at Fort Franklin hunting and fishing continued and as usual the officers had to deal with problems of human behaviour:

By the return of our men from Fort Norman we learned that one of
our Dog-Rib hunters had murdered a man of his tribe, in the autumn,
near the mouth of the Bear Lake River. The culprit being at the house,
we enquired into the truth of the report, which was found correct;
and he was in consequence instantly discharged from our service. His
victim had been a man of notoriously loose habits, and in this
instance had carried off the hunter's wife and child, while he was in
pursuit of deer at a great distance from the Fort. The husband
pursued the guilty pair the moment he discovered their flight and, on
overtaking them, instantly shot the seducer; but the woman escaped
a similar fate by having the presence of mind to turn aside the muzzle
of the gun while in the act of being discharged. She was not, however,
to escape punishment; her husband struck her senseless with the
stock of his gun and would have completed her destruction but for
the cries and entreaties of their only child.

A week before Franklin's departure in February 1827 the temperature
descended to fifty-eight degrees below zero, the coldest weather he had
ever experienced in the north. The cold spell was followed by windy
but milder weather, which brought the reindeer closer to the Fort. In a
single day seven were killed. Franklin was relieved that he could leave
his men without having to worry about the food situation.

When the travel arrangements had been completed, the charts,
drawings, journals and provisions were distributed between a cariole
and three sledges. The dogs were in too weak a condition to draw such
a heavy load, so two Indians were engaged to carry part of it. Augustus
and two Dog-Ribs left two days before Franklin, with instructions to
join him along the route.

At ten a.m. [February 20] I quitted the fort accompanied by five of
our men and the two Indians, the latter drawing each sixty pounds
of pemmican on their sledges. Captain Back, the officers, and men
assembled to give us a farewell salute of three hearty cheers, which
served to renew my regret at leaving a society whose members had
endeared themselves to me by unremitting attention to their duties
and the greatest personal kindness.

On the second evening out of Fort Franklin the two Indians deserted
the party, taking the pemmican with them. A gale was blowing,
completely obliterating their tracks in the snow. Franklin decided that
rather than lose several days searching for the deserters, he and his

companions should continue on their journey, making do with shorter rations. They reached Fort Simpson on March 8. Their Indian guide had never approached the Fort by land; once before he had come to the area by following the Mackenzie River, but that had been many years before the Fort was actually built. Yet he led them directly to it. His course was governed by his recollection of a certain mountain that he remembered having noticed from the River. Franklin's party passed within two miles of the mountain, but on his other visit the guide had been no closer than eighteen miles. Considering how different its outline must have appeared at the two distances, Franklin could hardly imagine anyone but an Indian recognizing its distinguishing points, especially since it was not a separate mountain but one of several in a line of hills.

The dogs were completely tired, so Franklin remained a week at Fort Simpson to allow them to recoup their strength. During that time he examined all the accounts which the Hudson's Bay Company presented for goods supplied to the expedition and made provision for the outward journey of Captain Back and his party. Arrangements were also made for the Company to buy any stores still unused when the rest of the expedition was ready to leave Fort Franklin.

"While I was there [Fort Simpson] an Indian woman committed suicide by hanging herself in a fit of jealousy at an encampment near the Fort. I had thought that suicide was extremely rare among the Northern Indians but I subsequently learned that it was not so uncommon as I had imagined."

Leaving Fort Simpson on March 15 Franklin and his party followed the course of the Mackenzie, and on the twenty-first arrived at the expansion of the River called Little Lake.

> . . . there we had the pleasure of meeting two voyageurs on their way to Bear Lake with a packet of letters from England. . . . though the night was piercingly cold I spent the greater part of it most agreeably scanning the contents of the box by the unsteady light of a blazing fire. After breakfast next morning I dispatched the packet to its destination under the charge of McLeay, one of the men who had accompanied me from Bear Lake, and retained one of the voyageurs in his stead.

The party arrived at Fort Resolution on March 26. There Franklin learned that Dr. Richardson had left the Fort in December to join Mr. Drummond, the assistant botanist, on the Saskatchewan River in order to take advantage of the earlier spring there to collect plants.

By April 12 Franklin was at Fort Chipewyan. There he found Mr. Stewart, the Chief Factor of the Department, surrounded by a large number of Indians. As soon as the Indians had exchanged their furs, they left the Fort to seek their living in the woods by fishing and hunting, instead of lying about in idleness for four or five weeks as had been their custom. This change was due to the fact that the Hudson's Bay Company had stopped bringing spirits into the north country, and to some other regulations respecting trade with the natives. The new plan offered supplies of clothing and other necessities to those Indians who were most active in collecting furs, and the Indians responded with increased exertion. Franklin noted that some other excellent regulations had also been introduced by the Company. One directive had to do with growing vegetables at all posts where the soil was sufficiently fertile. Even at a post as far north as Chipewyan the men were frequently supplied with potatoes and barley at their meals. Another directive said that Sunday should be properly observed, with divine service read at every post. "Feeling a deep interest in the welfare of this country, in which I have spent a large portion of the past seven years, I have much pleasure in recording these improvements."

We reached Cumberland House on the 18th June where I had the happiness of meeting Dr. Richardson after a separation of eleven months. I learnt from him that during our absence in the north Mr. Drummond, the Assistant Botanist, had been indefatigable in collecting specimens of Natural History, having been sent for that purpose to the Rocky Mountains at the head of the Athabasca River, in the course of which service he had been exposed to very great privations. To his perseverance and industry, science is indebted for the knowledge of several new and rare quadrupeds, birds, and plants.

Between June 1825 and April 1827 Drummond had collected, largely on his own, 1500 species of plants, 150 birds, 50 quadrupeds and a very large number of insects. He had not continued north with the rest of the expedition in the summer of 1825. Instead, he had separated from the others at Cumberland House and from there he had worked his way west. During that first summer he had accompanied a brigade of company traders the 260 odd miles from Cumberland House to Carlton House and then moved on to Edmonton, arriving there in late September. He was determined to base himself in the Rocky Mountains, so the Company supplied him with horses and a hunter to accompany him. But the hunter "loitered so much on the way that the snow became

too deep to admit of our proceeding to our destination." Drummond
pitched his tent while his hunter went on to secure provision.

> *I remained alone for the rest of the winter [he wrote], except when
> my man occasionally visited me with meat; and I found the time
> hang very heavy as I had no books and nothing could be done in the
> way of collecting specimens of Natural History. I took however a
> walk every day in the woods to give me some practice in the use of
> snow shoes. The winter was very severe and much snow fell in the
> month of March, when it averaged six feet in depth.*

Spring finally arrived, but his hunter refused to accompany him into
the mountains as he had earlier agreed to do, and he could not secure
another until August. His objective was the Columbia River but he had
not gone far when a message from Franklin caught up with him, telling
him to rejoin the other members of the Expedition the following spring
in time to proceed with them to York Factory. "The few mosses that I
gleaned in this excursion were so fine that I could not but deeply regret
that I was unable to pass a season or two in that interesting region."

At Norway House on June 24 Franklin said goodbye to Augustus.

> *The tears which he shed on parting, so unusual to one of his race,
> showed the strength of his feelings and I have no doubt they
> proceeded from a sincere affection, an affection which I can venture
> to say was mutually felt by every individual. He learned with great
> regret that there was no immediate prospect of our meeting again
> and he expressed a very strong desire to be informed if another
> Expedition should be sent to any of the northern parts of America,
> either by land or by sea; and repeatedly assured me that he and
> Ooligbuck would be ready at any time to quit their families and their
> country to accompany any of their present officers wherever the
> Expedition might be ordered.**

For Franklin and Richardson the long journey home involved a round
of social visits in Montreal and New York. They finally reached Liver-
pool on September 26 after an absence from England of two years,
seven and a half months. Back, Kendall and Drummond arrived at

---

*"I have pleasure in mentioning that, by permission of Government, the pay
that was due to Augustus and Ooligbuck has been delivered to the Directors
of the Hudson's Bay Company, who have undertaken to distribute it to them
annually, in the way best suited to their wants."

Portsmouth two weeks later with the rest of the party. Franklin was distressed to hear from Back that two of his men had died while en route from Great Bear Lake to York Factory. One had died of consumption; the other, Gustavus Aird, was drowned when he jumped into the water while trying to save his boat from going over a waterfall.

Until this account reached me I had believed that our expedition would have ended without a single casualty. I felt the loss of these men all the more deeply because of their outstanding conduct, which I had observed and admired countless times when they were my companions in the Lion *during our voyage along the coast.*

. . . . .

On my arrival in London on September 29th, accompanied by Dr. Richardson, I had the honour of laying the charts and drawings before His Royal Highness the Lord High Admiral and Mr. Secretary Huskisson; and from the latter I received directions to publish this account of our proceedings.

Franklin concluded his report with an analysis of the best methods to be followed in opening up a northwest passage. His belief in the practicability of the route had been considerably strengthened by the information he had obtained on his second expedition. His final paragraph reveals the deep feelings that would one day take him on his last adventure:

Arctic discovery has been fostered principally by Great Britain; and it is a subject of just pride that it has been prosecuted by her from motives as disinterested as they are enlightened; not from any prospect of immediate benefit to herself but from a steady view to the acquirement of useful knowledge and the extension of the bounds of science. Each succeeding attempt has added a step towards the completion of northern geography; and the contribution to natural history and science have excited a general interest throughout the civilised world. It is, moreover, pleasing to reflect that the loss of life which has occurred in the prosecution of these discoveries does not exceed the average number of deaths in the same population at home under circumstances the most favourable. And it is sincerely to be hoped that Great Britain will not relax her efforts until the question of a north west passage has been satisfactorily set at rest, or at least until those portions of the northern shores of America,

which are yet unknown, be laid down in our maps; and which, with
the exception of a small space on the Asiatic continent . . . are the
only intervals waiting to complete the outline of Europe, Asia and
America.

The journals covering the two expeditions filled 836 large pages. In
addition, there were appendices at the back of both books that filled
425 pages. These included topographical and geological notices and
meteorological tables, as well as data on solar radiation, velocity of
sound, magnetic variations, and the Aurora Borealis. There were also a
zoological appendix and notes on fishes and a list of 663 plants.

This accumulation of data represented a remarkable work output on
the part of the officers, whose research was often carried out under very
difficult conditions. Its volume is especially impressive when we recall
that numerous records were lost during the first expedition. It answers
Stefansson's criticism of the slowness of these expeditions compared to
the speed shown by Hearne and Mackenzie—who left practically no
scientific records.

Franklin was now forty-one, acclaimed as one of the greatest explorers of his age. Although he was extremely active socially and very busy preparing his journals for publication, the death of his wife had left a gap in his personal life. His friends were therefore delighted when he announced that he was about to remarry. At the time of their wedding, in 1828, Jane Griffin was thirty-seven, a beautiful and talented young woman with a wealth of experience behind her. Her father was an inveterate traveller and she had accompanied him everywhere. At twenty-four she had seen 600 galley slaves in their chains in the port of Toulon. In Rome she had seen the Pope and most of his cardinals ready to fly before the advancing armies of Prince Murat, one of Napoleon's great generals. Everywhere she went she wrote detailed impressions of people, cities and events in her diary. (Her visit to Florence alone filled ninety-five pages.) At home in London, a book society which met in her father's house every month had as one of its members Benjamin Disraeli.

The first mention of Franklin appeared in her diary in March 1818, when she and some of her friends went aboard his ship, the *Trent*, before his departure on the short-lived attempt to reach the North Pole. At the time she seemed more interested in the way the hull of the ship had been strengthened and in an Eskimo kayak than in Franklin himself. However, she got to know him and his first wife after their marriage; her diary noted that she and her sister called on the Franklins with gifts before he left on his 1825 expedition. She gave him a silver pencil case engraved with his crest, and a pair of fur gloves. Franklin called the gloves the most sensible present he had received.

Following his return to England in 1827 Franklin had called on the Griffins on his first day in London, but they were out of town. A month later Jane Griffin noted in her diary, "Captain Franklin called. . . . He told Father that he had called a Cape in the Arctic by his name and asked him if we would come and see his child and his Arctic drawings at his house." The visit took place the very next day. A later entry noted that Franklin had made a present to the family of some reindeer tongues and three pairs of shoes made by Indian women. As an explorer Franklin had a considerable edge over city dwellers in the originality of his gifts!

Franklin and Jane Griffin became engaged in 1828 just before the Griffins left for another visit to Russia. When Franklin joined them in that country, he was received with honour by the great men of science and navigation and had an audience with the Dowager Empress. On their departure, an admiral who had been their guide on many occasions gave Franklin a copy of his books and maps with the inscription, "From Admiral K to Captain F as a small token of his respect for that celebrated navigator and explorer, to whom science is so greatly indebted."

There were no doubts in Jane Griffin's mind about her future life with Franklin. Shortly before their marriage she wrote to him: "I should rejoice to see with you the same things for the first time, to help or be helped in every little difficulty, to become acquainted together with the same people, to be objects of the same hospitality and kindness."

They were married during one of Franklin's spells of inactive service, which were frequent in the peacetime navy, and for the next two years they occupied their leisure with a great deal of travelling. During that time the King honoured Franklin with a Knighthood, and Oxford conferred on him the degree of Doctor of Common Law. Finally, in May 1830, he was given command of the twenty-six gun corvette *Rainbow*, stationed in the Mediterranean. But even "active" service in the navy was not very exacting and Lady Franklin was able to spend much of the winter of 1831-32 with her husband in Corfu. Franklin's command of the *Rainbow* ended in December 1833 but it was nearly a year before his wife rejoined him in England; she was travelling in areas seldom visited by Englishwomen in those days—Alexandria, Cairo, Jaffa, Jerusalem, Cyprus and Constantinople.

Another period of hated idleness ended for Franklin when he accepted a post in the colonial service as Governor of Van Diemen's Land. He landed at its capital, Hobart Town, with Lady Franklin in January 1837. The island colony (which was soon to be renamed Tasmania) had originally been settled by convicts transported from Britain, but there had since been a considerable influx of free settlers. The dual character of its society inevitably created problems and Franklin's predecessor had left under a barrage of abuse because he had not passed out favours as generously as some felt was their due. Though the cruelty and injustices that had marked the earlier colonial era were coming to an end by 1837, much remained to be done. The Franklins responded eagerly to the challenge. Concluding that the most pressing need on the island was better education, they decided to establish a college. Franklin wrote to Dr. Thomas Arnold, the famous headmaster of Rugby, and asked for help in finding the right man to organize and operate the proposed college. Arnold sent out the Reverend Philip Gell, who did excellent work there for seven years and later married Franklin's daughter.

During the years 1839-43 Sir James Ross, who was in command of an important expedition to the Antarctic, established his base at Hobart Town. His ships, the *Erebus* and *Terror*, were later to take Franklin on his final expedition to the Arctic, while his second-in-command, Captain Crozier, was to fill the same post under Franklin in 1845. It was well that no one could foretell the future on the night the officers gave a dance aboard the *Erebus*. Everyone enjoyed the balmy night under the southern stars, especially Sir John Franklin, who was the guest of honour.

Franklin envied Ross and his men and spent as much time as he could in their company. Philip Gell wrote that his delight at their presence and his interest in their experiences had the effect of making them twice the men they had been before and nerved them for their important work ahead. He would sit up all night with the young officers in their observatory, taking his turn at the instruments, reading Shakespeare to them, joking and telling them stories of the sea.

Ross formed a high opinion of Franklin's administration of Tasmania. He wrote, "Under his wise and judicious government the revenue has been so greatly increased that the debts have been liquidated and a super-abundant income produced, though the country was deeply in debt when he arrived."

Both the Governor and his wife had too much energy to keep indefinitely at routine work. They became curious about an abandoned harbour on the west coast of the Island. It was difficult to approach by sea and practically impossible to reach by land. Escaping convicts who had tried to get there overland had generally died of starvation. The Franklins decided that they would try to visit the place. Their party would travel across country to the half-way mark, where a ship was engaged to wait for them until a specified date. Once aboard ship, they would travel the rest of the way by sea. But the fine weather gave way to torrential rains and the Franklins with their convict helpers had to sit it out in a cave for a week. Then they were faced by a river in flood. The river seemed impassable but two members of the party, both convicts, showed great courage by crossing on a raft. They managed to get word to the ship just as it was about to set sail. Meantime, as anxiety mounted in Hobart Town for the Franklins' safety, a rescue party was sent out to find them. When no word came either from Franklin or the rescue party, a second party was sent out to find the first. This it succeeded in doing, reaching the original searchers when they were on the verge of starvation. After the Franklins had visited the harbour they returned home, apologetic about the uproar they had caused but rejuvenated by their adventures.

Franklin's right-hand man in the administration of the Island was its Colonial Secretary, an able, engaging and ambitious man named Montague. It seemed a routine matter when Montague publicly recommended the dismissal of a district officer for neglect of duty, and Franklin accepted his recommendation and acted on it. But when the Governor looked into the records he decided that his Colonial Secretary had been wrong in his conclusions and reinstated the district officer. Montague was livid. He had always resented any check on his authority and in effect he now went on strike—keeping away from his office and refusing to attend to his work. Franklin was too patient for a while, then he abruptly dismissed Montague. He had weakened his case by waiting so long and Lord Stanley, the Colonial Secretary in London, found his written explanations less convincing than the personal protests made by Montague—who had sailed for London immediately after he was dismissed. Stanley appointed Montague to a better position. He then sent word to Franklin that he was dismissed from his post as Governor of Tasmania. The same ship brought Franklin's successor to the Island!

The Franklins must have gained some comfort from the affection and sorrow expressed by the massed crowds who saw them leave Hobart Town in 1843, but even so the recall was a bitter pill. Their final act before leaving was to give £500 toward the erection of the college, together with 400 acres of land for its permanent site. The museum already built by Lady Franklin on the land became part of the college.

Franklin spent the next two years trying to clear his name. His old Arctic friends stood with him to a man, but Stanley was the type who, having made up his mind, simply did not hear what others had to say.

Finally, in desperation and deep frustration, Franklin started writing a "Narrative" which would have made public all the facts of the case. The narrative was about to be printed for private distribution and would undoubtedly have created a stir in the land, but suddenly it ceased to have importance. Franklin was again a national hero, for the Government had appointed him to command the greatest expedition ever formed to discover once and for all a northwest passage.

O fficial interest in Arctic exploration had been dormant for many years, but in 1844 Sir John Barrow urged upon the First Lord of the Admiralty the value of sending one more expedition to complete the search for a northwest passage. He effectively demolished those of little vision who were opposed to his views:

The utilitarians were at all times ready to ask "to what good?" But Queen Elizabeth and her Ministers with their enlightened minds sought for "knowledge," the result of which, they needed not to be told, was power. Observe what followed: the knowledge gained by the Arctic voyagers was not thrown away. Sir Humphrey Gilbert by his grant of the Island of Newfoundland, made his voyage thither in which he nobly perished, but his knowledge did not perish with him, on the contrary it laid the foundation of the valuable cod industry, which still exists. Davis by the discovery of the strait that bears his name, opened the way to the whale fishing, still carried on; and Frobisher pointed out the strait which conducted Hudson to the bay that bears his name, and which gave rise to the establishment of the Hudson's Bay Company, whose concerns are . . . carried on across the whole continent of America and to the very shores of the Polar Sea.

Lastly, the discovery of Baffin, which pointed out, among others, the great opening of Lancaster on the Western coast of that bay which bears his name, has in our time been found to lead into the Polar Sea through which the North-West Passage from the Atlantic to the Pacific will one day be accomplished, and for the execution of which we are now contending, and which if left to be performed by some other power, England by her neglect of it after having opened *the East and West doors should be laughed at by all the world for having hesitated to cross the threshold.**

In 1845 the Admiralty decided to do as Sir John Barrow urged and send an expedition that would attempt to complete the search for a northwest passage. It was to be the best equipped expedition of any that had left the shores of England. Sir James Ross, who had already been to the Arctic and the Antarctic, refused the honour of the command, having promised his bride not to go on any more voyages of exploration. Franklin was next in line for the appointment and both Ross and Parry backed him in his claim for the appointment. Parry told the First Lord of the Admiralty, "He is a fitter man than any I know and if you don't let him go, the man will die of disappointment." Franklin had good reason to desire the appointment: his treatment by the Colonial Office had sickened him of that career and it was natural for him to turn again to his real profession. He had explored and mapped more of the Arctic coast than any other man, and now he believed that he could complete the mapping of the area, since, as a result of recent discoveries, there remained only some 300 miles to be charted between Back's Great Fish River† and the waters connecting with Hudson Bay.

These recent discoveries had been made by two chief factors of the Hudson's Bay Company, Peter Dease and Thomas Simpson. Dease had been in charge of providing food supplies for Franklin's second expedition. Simpson was a young cousin of Sir George Simpson, Governor of the Hudson's Bay territories and was—like Dease—a man of action. In 1836 he left Fort Garry and walked 1377 miles in sixty-two days to join Dease at Fort Chipewyan. From there the two men set out in June 1837 with a small party and three boats. After descending the Mackenzie River to the sea they proceeded westward beyond the farthest point attained by Franklin, ultimately reaching Point Barrow. In so doing they had established a link with the survey made by Captain Beechey when, on board the *Blossom*, he had entered the Arctic sea through Bering Strait.

Dease and Simpson returned from Point Barrow the way they had

*Quoted in *Sir John Franklin's Last Arctic Expedition*, R. J. Cyriax (London, Methuen & Company, Limited, 1939).

†Franklin's former companion George Back had explored this River when in 1833 he was sent by the Government to search for the then-missing John Ross expedition.

come and wintered at Fort Confidence on Great Bear Lake. During the summer of 1838 they descended the Coppermine River and proceeded eastward along the coast. Ice prevented their crossing Bathurst Inlet direct, so they had to make the circuit of 140 miles. On Bank's Peninsula they discovered several pieces of pure copper, and according to their report the adjacent islands ". . . had the appearance of being strongly impregnated with this metal." Three miles short of Point Turnagain they were held in the ice for twenty-two days. During that time Simpson set out with five voyageurs and two Indians and proceeded a further hundred miles eastward on foot.

The men returned to Fort Confidence for the winter but the following summer they descended the Coppermine River again. Aided by better weather, they were able to get as far as the mouth of Back's River on the second attempt. Dease and Simpson had now linked together the discoveries of Beechey, Franklin and Back. Dease Strait had been opened up; Victoria Land and King William Land (later discovered to be islands) were now known, as well as Simpson Strait.

The Hudson's Bay Company had stated on many occasions that its interest in exploration was purely scientific, although it was naturally hoped that any discoveries would lead to an increase in the fur trade. Company-sponsored explorers had performed a valuable service to Britain by bringing into her orbit areas that might otherwise have been taken by Russia. In his history of the Hudson's Bay Company, E. E. Rich commented on the skills of these explorers:

The Company might justly be proud. . . . The ability to live off the country, depending on a gun, a trap and a fishing net, allowed the Hudson's Bay men to preserve their pemmican for emergencies, to lighten their loads and to travel without the cumbersome equipment that other expeditions required. The techniques and the hardihood of the traders-turned-explorers was exemplified in the voyages of Dr. John Rae. . . . Twice during his career Rae walked 1000 miles within two months and he had the reputation of being able to walk a hundred miles in two days. . . . Thomas Simpson's capacity to cover a steady twenty miles a day on foot along the Arctic shore greatly enlarged the range of the Dease-Simpson expedition.*

The Admiralty had misgivings about appointing a man of fifty-nine

*Hudson's Bay Company, 1763-1870, E. E. Rich (London, Hudson's Bay Record Society, 1959)

years to command its greatest Arctic expedition, but Franklin had great prestige, as well as the backing of influential men. John Richardson agreed to give Franklin a clean bill of health, although he had not examined him professionally for several years. He wrote, "I should have no hesitation in signing a certificate stating that I believe your constitution to be perfectly sound and your bodily strength sufficient for all calls that might be made upon it in conducting a squadron even through an icy sea."

On February 7, 1845 the Admiralty officially notified Franklin that he had been appointed to the command. He was given instructions to sail through Lancaster Sound and Barrow Strait as far west as Cape Walker, then southward and westward "towards Bering Strait in as straight a line as is permitted by ice or any unknown land." Should a permanent obstruction be found to the southwest of Cape Walker, Franklin was to consider following an alternative route northward between Cornwallis Island and North Devon Island if the channel between them should prove to be open. The Admiralty also advised Franklin, "Although the principal object of the expedition is to sail from the Atlantic Ocean to the Pacific, the position of any land which may be discovered is to be carefully noted and every opportunity is to be seized of making observations in natural history."

The two ships commissioned, the *Erebus* (370 tons) and the *Terror* (340 tons), were to be the first sailing ships in Arctic waters equipped with auxiliary screws and engines. The engines were two dismantled railway steam engines, each one of twenty horsepower. Captain Fitzjames, Commander of the *Erebus*, watching their arrival from his cabin, wrote his wife, "Our engine has come alongside. It came drawn by ten coal black horses and weighs fifteen tons." The *Erebus* had a complement of sixty-seven officers and men, while the *Terror* had sixty-two. Captain Crozier, who commanded the *Terror*, was to be second-in-command on the expedition. The 129 officers and men chosen represented the cream of the Royal Navy. Sufficient supplies were carried to last more than three years. One well-known authority on Franklin later observed, "No Arctic Expedition has ever been so lavishly equipped."

Franklin said that no one should worry if they did not return for two years. The young officers told their best girls to write them via Russia. Everyone had high hopes of success when in June 1845 the two ships sailed from England. A supply ship accompanied them as far as the Whalefish Islands off the coast of Greenland. There she discharged her cargo aboard the two vessels and set her course for England, carrying with her a packet of letters from Franklin and his party to their families and friends. They were to be the last words the world would receive from the men.

One such letter was from Lieutenant James Fairholme, a twenty-four-year-old junior officer aboard the *Erebus*. Fairholme wrote his family:

. . . I will now tell you something about the ship and expedition, having given an outline of our voyage up to this time. When I last wrote, I told you how comfortable we all were in this ship, and since then everything has tended to make us still more so. We now all know each other probably as well as we ever shall, and I really think there could hardly have been selected a set more likely to get on well together. Sir John is a new man since we left. He has quite recovered from his severe cold, looks 10 years younger and takes part in everything that goes on with as much interest as if he had not grown older since his last Expedition. We are all delighted to find how decided he is in all that he resolves on, and he has such experience and judgement that we all look on his decisions with the greatest respect. I never felt that the Captain was so much my companion with anyone I have sailed with before. He has certainly made a friend of every person on board and I believe not a thing he has said or done has given rise to the slightest complaint. . . . Sir John still continues to receive three of us at dinner every day and to dine with us on Sunday, and instead of the formal parties which both these are in most ships, one really looks forward with the greatest pleasure to meeting him. . . . Sir John is very fond . . . of all scientific observations and encourages it much among us all. Indeed he makes all take an equal share in the navigation of the ship and determining positions, etc. By this means I have learnt much on these subjects which, in the common run of the service, would perhaps never have come in my way. Soon after leaving the Orkneys, Sir John sent for us all into his cabin and read to us such portions of his orders as were not private, particularly as to observing everything, and collecting specimens; also his authority from the Admiralty for claiming all them, all our logs, journals and everything connected with the expedition.

·   ·   ·   ·   ·

You will wonder what sort of climate we have here under these snowy mountains and among icebergs. Well! At present I must admit that my feet are rather cold, but today we have had most lovely

*weather, the sun shining for twenty hours and upwards and the
mean temperature at about thirty-eight°....*

*Our appetites are enormous in this sharp weather.... Fortnum and
Mason* have done their part well and we find all their stores of the
best description. Our mess is very comfortable.*

·   ·   ·   ·   ·

*There are two important members of the Expedition who I must
not forget to mention, viz: Neptune and Jacko. Old Nep has lost much
of his unwieldiness since we left and now runs up and down our step
ladders with ease. He is the most lovable dog I ever knew and is a very
general favourite. I often give him an extra kiss on William's account
[Fairholme's brother] and he seems to know that it comes from a
friend! The Monkey continues to be the annoyance and pest of the
whole ship and yet not a person in her would hurt him for the world.
He is a dreadful thief but such a very amusing one that his robberies
bring very little sympathy for the unfortunate losers! The Doctor
declares that Jacko is in a rapid consumption and he has certainly a
very bad cough, but the only other symptom I can see of it, is the
rapid consumption of everything eatable that he can lay his paws on!*

·   ·   ·   ·   ·

*We have got a Catalogue made out of all the books, public and
private, that are on board (and the Terror is doing the same) and we
find that there is scarcely a book we can think of as being required
that is not in the list. We shall supply each other with these lists, and
thus when a book is wanted the Librarian will at once know which
ship and what cabin it is in.†*

*I fear there has been a great loss among our livestock, as by the
last accounts only 5 or 6 of the 18 bullocks were alive. Our provisions,
however, are of such excellent quality, and [the] government have
been so liberal in the ships' supplies that this does not so much
matter. Besides, the supply of fish meat which we have had for some
days, has been a good substitute for fresh meat.*

·   ·   ·   ·   ·

*It is curious how few wants we find. There is scarcely anything that
would be of use that has been neglected and I really do not think that,
if I could be in London for an hour or two, I would want to get*

*Still famous in London as a shop for quality products
†The *Erebus* had a library of 1700 books, the *Terror* 1200.

*anything! I am delighted with my watch and pray tell Elizabeth [Fairholme's sister] that the chains she made for me are invaluable.**

Franklin's last letter to his wife ended with these words:

I trust that I have not omitted any point that you wished to be informed upon. If so, exercise your own excellent judgement if it relates to any of our own personal matters. This also I particularly wish you to do with regard to my dear Eleanor and Gell [his daughter and son-in-law]. . . . They will both prove blessings and comforts to you and to me. I have written to each of my dearest friends to comfort and assist you with their best counsel. To the Almighty I commit you and dear Eleanor. . . . Again, that God may bless and support you both is and will be the constant prayer of your most affectionate husband.

Two years passed and a few people began to worry. But Sir James Ross said that there was no need for anxiety, and the words of so respected an explorer were sufficient to dispel most fears. One who disagreed with Ross's opinion was Dr. King, an able explorer who had succeeded in making himself highly unpopular with the authorities. King wrote repeatedly to the Admiralty urging that a relief expedition be dispatched immediately down the Great Fish River, but his letters were not even acknowledged. Having been down the River in 1833 with Captain Back, he was convinced that Franklin would be somewhere in the area of the river mouth if anything had gone wrong on the expedition. If his letters had been heeded, most of Franklin's men might have been saved.

Lady Franklin, meanwhile, had been continuing her travels—to Madeira, the West Indies, the United States. Returning home in 1847 she began to suspect trouble, and once aroused, embarked on an epic fight for the rescue of her husband and his men, and their records, a struggle that was to continue without letup for thirteen years. She began by writing to Lord Palmerston, the Prime Minister and to Louis Napoleon, Emperor of France, to the Czar of Russia and the President of the United States, asking all of them to send ships for the rescue of the Franklin Expedition.

The British Government took a modest step that year by instructing the Hudson's Bay Company to send ample supplies of food and clothing to their northern posts. Company officials were also asked to warn the Indians to be on the look-out for men coming from the north. A reward

*From a copy of the letter in the Public Archives of Canada, Ottawa.

was offered to the northern whalers for any information. When in 1848 there were still no signs, the Government became alarmed and dispatched three expeditions to the Arctic. Sir James Ross commanded two ships that approached from the east. Two ships were sent round Cape Horn and up the west coast of America, with instructions to proceed as far east as possible along the Arctic coast beyond Bering Strait. Sir John Richardson and Dr. Rae proceeded overland down the Mackenzie River to cover the Arctic coast eastward to the Coppermine.

The period of most intensive search began in 1850 when the Government offered a reward of £20,000, to which Lady Franklin added £3000 of her own money. By autumn, 15 ships and 500 men were in the Arctic. But they had been instructed to search the northern waters, not the coastal regions farther south as Dr. King had urged. Two of the six expeditions were naval operations, a third was subsidized by the Government, and the other three were privately organized and financed. Of these three, one was sent by Lady Franklin, aided by a gift of £1700 from the people of Tasmania. Another was equipped by the Hudson's Bay Company, supported by public subscriptions and placed under the command of the aging Sir John Ross. A third was financed by the wealthy American Henry Grinnell of New York.

Lady Franklin was to spend most of her personal fortune in financing expeditions to the Arctic. Eventually she even moved from her home into rented rooms. Her courage caught the imagination of many people in other countries, including Grinnell. He became an active ally in the search and paid for the cost of outfitting ships in order to have his country participate. He wrote to Lady Franklin, "I shall purchase two small schooners of about seventy tons each and put them in order as soon as possible, taking my chance of procuring officers and men. I intend that they shall sail about May 1st." The ships Grinnell bought were actually larger than planned, 140 tons and 90 tons. So that they would sail under naval discipline and leadership he turned them over to the United States Navy. It required an act of Congress for the Navy to accept his offer, but interest in the mystery of Franklin's disappearance was so great that the bill was quickly passed. When the two ships sailed on May 23, 1850 they received an enthusiastic public sendoff. Before sailing, the officers and men had shown their magnanimous spirit by signing a bond stating that in no circumstances would they claim the £20,000 reward offered by the British Government for the rescue of the missing men.

Never before or since have the Arctic wastes seen such a variety of ships. Some wintered close together, some were separated by as much as twenty miles, others were still farther away. Occasionally the various crews signalled to each other by means of rockets. Someone made an ingenious attempt to communicate with Franklin, on the chance that he was somewhere near, by means of balloons, each trailing a long line prepared so that it would burn slowly when ignited. Pieces of coloured paper were attached at intervals to the line. On these were written the location of the rescue ships and the intended routes to be followed the next summer. As each balloon was released, the end of the line was ignited, the plan being that the pieces of paper would drop to the ground when the fire reached them. Several of these papers were actually picked up the following spring as far as fifty miles away from the ship. Sir John Ross optimistically took two brace of carrier pigeons with him as a means of keeping in touch with London. He let each one go at intervals through the long winter night with messages attached. In addition to his own official messages, he allowed word to be sent by a few of the younger men to their wives or sweethearts. One pigeon actually made the 3000 miles home, but sad to say, the messages had dropped from his leg!

During the summer of 1851 the site of Franklin's first winter base was discovered on Beechey Island.* One of the officers described what was found:

> The ruins and traces that they left behind all attest to the cheerful fashion [in which] the crews spent the first winter. The observatory with its double embankment of earth and stones, its neat finish and the lavish expenditure of labour in pavement and pathway. The shooting gallery under the cliff, the seats formed of stones, the remains of pleasant picnics in the form of empty bottles and meat tins strewed about, the elaborate cairn on the north point of Beechey, a pyramid of eight feet high and at least six feet long on each side of the base, constructed of old meat tins filled with gravel—all tell the same tale of manful anxiety for physical employment to distract the mind from suffering and solitude. There were not wanting traces at Cape Riley to show how earnestly the naturalists laboured to collect specimens. . . . There is more than one site still visible of tents in which the magnetical observations were obtained.

There were also the remains of a garden, with borders of lichen and moss, and with poppies and anemonies that still showed life. Near some tubs that must have been used for washing was a pair of cashmere

*A tiny island off the southwest coast of Devon Island

gloves, evidently laid out to dry and held down by two small stones. The graves of three of the seamen were found, "scrupulously neat, as in an English churchyard."

Lady Franklin's small ship, the *Prince Albert*, returned to England before freeze-up to report the discoveries on Beechey Island, while the other ships wintered in Barrow Strait. When the *Prince Albert* returned to the Arctic in the summer of 1852 aboard her as one of the crew was John Hepburn, Franklin's companion on his first expedition down the Coppermine. Ever since 1822 the two had kept in touch, Franklin having twice helped the seaman to secure suitable work. Hepburn's second post was in Tasmania, but he had given it up and returned to England in order to help in the search for his old friend and leader.

Also on board was a young French midshipman, Joseph René Bellot. Having learned that a Frenchman was taking part in the search, the Empress Josephine wrote to Lady Franklin:

It is above all as a woman and a wife that I am glad to see France associated with England in these generous expeditions which are trying to find your husband. His private virtues must equal his ability and courage since he has inspired in you such an admirable devotion. I hope that Heaven will grant you the success that your love as a wife deserves and on that day, Madame, there will be one who will actively share in the joy of the wife of Captain Franklin, it will be the wife of the Emperor Napoleon.

The search for Franklin was carried on overland as well as by ship. In 1851 Dr. Rae and two companions had travelled east from the Coppermine along the coastline. Farther north he had made a sledge journey of over 1000 miles, inspecting every corner along the shore of Wollaston Land (Victoria Island). But after eight months of continuous travel the small party returned with nothing to report, having travelled 5380 miles.

The final year of active government participation in the search was 1852. Five ships set out under the command of Sir Edward Belcher. In addition, Lady Franklin sent out the *Isabel*. The Belcher expedition had the dual aim of searching for Franklin and for two missing ships, the *Enterprise* and *Investigator*, unheard from since 1850, when they had sailed through Bering Strait into the Arctic sea.

The captains of the *Enterprise* and *Investigator*, Collinson and McClure, had been instructed to operate closely together, but they had become separated during a storm. Collinson, who was senior officer of the expedition, eventually brought the *Enterprise* back to England, after having penetrated the Arctic as far east as Cambridge Bay. But McClure had sailed the *Investigator* farther north. She was beset in ice off the northeast coast of Banks Island in 1851. The following year McClure sledged across the strait to Winter Harbour on Melville Island, vainly seeking help. In February 1853 he abandoned ship and was making a desperate bid to lead his men to safety when they were found by members of the Belcher expedition. The combined crews endured another Arctic winter, the fourth for McClure, aboard Belcher's ships.

The next summer only one of Belcher's ships worked free of ice. When two other Royal Navy search ships came into the area, Belcher decided to load his and McClure's men on board, and the three un-trapped vessels sailed for England. Six ships were left abandoned in the ice. Ironically, in the months that followed, one of them, the *Resolute*, drifted eastward with the ice flow. The following summer, 1855, she was sighted by an American whaler 1000 miles east of where she had been abandoned. The whaler's captain put a skeleton crew aboard her and sailed her to an American port. A group of Americans who had been following the search for Franklin with the greatest sympathy purchased the *Resolute* from her new owners and in December 1856 sailed her back to England and presented her to Queen Victoria as a gift of the American people.*

By crossing the ice to Melville Island McClure and his men had become the first to complete the Northwest Passage from west to east. Though the passage was permanently blocked by ice, they were awarded the £10,000 promised by the Government for its discovery. The drama of M'Clure's achievements and providential rescue brought him fame and placed M'Clure Strait on the map, though he had lost his ship. In contrast, Collinson was soon a forgotten man, though he had brought his ship back to England after coming very close to the object of all the expeditions.

Meanwhile, Dr. Rae had been continuing his search overland. On a survey of the west coast of Boothia in 1854 he encountered a party of Eskimos who told him that a group of white men had perished for want of food at some distance farther west. Rae gained considerable informa-tion from the Eskimos, which he put together in the following report:

---

*When the *Resolute* was scrapped Queen Victoria had a desk made from her timbers and presented it to the President of the United States as a token of her appreciation. During President Kennedy's occupancy of the White House, this was his favourite desk.

In the spring four winters past* a party of white men amounting to about forty were seen dragging a boat with them by some Eskimos who were killing seal near the north shore of King William Land. . . . None of the party could speak the Eskimo language intelligibly but by signs the natives were made to understand that the white men's ship or ships had been crushed by ice and that they were now going where they expected to find deer to shoot. From the appearance of the men, all of whom looked thin, and with exception of an officer were hauling on the drag-ropes of the sledges, they were supposed to be short of provisions and they purchased a small seal from the natives. At a later date the same season, but previously to the breaking up of the ice, the bodies of some thirty persons were discovered on the continent and five on an island near it, about a long day's journey to the north west of a large stream that can be no other than Back's Great Fish River, as its description and that of the low shore in the neighbourhood of Point Ogle and Montreal Island agree exactly with that of Sir George Back. Some of the bodies had been buried . . . some were in a tent or tents; others under the boat which had been turned over to form a shelter and several were scattered about in different directions. Of those found on the island one was supposed to have been an officer as he had a telescope strapped over his shoulders and his double-barrelled gun lay beneath him.

Rae bought from the Eskimos as many articles taken from these men as they would sell him. These included silver spoons and forks with the crests of some of the officers engraved on them. A round silver plate was engraved "Sir John Franklin."

When it received this evidence, the Government decided that it had fully carried out its responsibilities and that no further expeditions should be sent at public expense. Between 1848 and 1854 the sum of £760,000 (about the equivalent of 4,000,000 dollars) had been expended, a huge sum in those days. But Lady Franklin refused to accept this decision as right or final and spent the next two years trying to convince the Prime Minister and others in authority that the search should be continued. She insisted that no second-hand account from the natives should be accepted as the final word, that the search should be continued until some of the bodies and the records of the expedition had been found. She visited every seaport and fishing town of the

---

*This would have been the spring of 1850, but it was later discovered the Eskimos were wrong in their estimate of time.

English north country, travelling long distances to search out and question veteran seamen as to their opinion of her husband's fate.

When it became obvious that the Government would not change its mind and continue the search Lady Franklin purchased the *Fox*, a luxury yacht of 177 tons. The *Fox's* interior was ripped out and her hull strengthened to withstand the ice. Captain McClintock, an outstanding participant in earlier searching expeditions, agreed to take command, and in July 1857, less than three months after Lady Franklin had bought it, the *Fox*, with a crew of twenty-seven, sailed for the Arctic. This miracle of speed was due to the desire of everyone to help. The shipbuilders worked day and night on the structural alterations. Captain McClintock was flooded with requests from men wishing to join the crew. As his second-in-command he chose Lieutenant Hobson, whose father, the Governor of New Zealand, had been a great friend of the Franklins. His sailing master was James Young, a senior captain of merchant ships accustomed to command vessels twelve times the size of the *Fox*. Young volunteered to serve in any capacity. Not only would he accept no pay; he also gave £500 of his own money toward Lady Franklin's costs.

It was essential to have in the party a man who knew the Eskimos and could talk to them. The man considered best qualified was a Dane, Carl Petersen, so McClintock wrote and asked him to join the *Fox*. Petersen had just rejoined his family in Copenhagen after a year's absence in the Arctic, but within a week of receiving McClintock's letter he was aboard the *Fox*. The Admiralty granted leave of absence to several officers and men to enable them to join the expedition, and turned a blind eye while McClintock was supplied with the best of equipment and stores—clothing, arms and food. On the eve of his departure Lady Franklin wrote to McClintock:

> You have kindly invited me to give you "Instructions," but I cannot bring myself to feel that it would be right in any way to influence your judgement in the conduct of your noble undertaking. Indeed I have no temptation to do so since it appears that your views are almost identical with those which I have independently formed. . . . But had this been otherwise I trust you would have found me ready to prove the implicit confidence I place in you by yielding my views to your more enlightened judgement. I know that your whole heart is in the cause, even as my own is. As to the objects of the Expedition and their relative importance I am sure you know that the rescue of any possible survivors of the Erebus and Terror would be to me as it

would to you the noblest result of your efforts. . . . Next to it in
importance is the recovery of the unspeakably precious documents of
the expedition, public and private, and the personal relics of my dear
husband and his companions. Lastly, I trust it may be in your powers
to confirm directly or inferentially the claims of my husband's
expedition to . . . the earliest discovery of the Passage which, if Dr.
Rae's report be true, these martyrs in a noble cause achieved at their
last extremity. . . .

   I am sure that you will do all that man can do for the attainment
of all these objects, my only fear is that you will spend yourselves
too much in the effort, and you must therefore let me tell you how
much dearer to me even than them is the preservation of the valuable
lives of the little band of heroes who are your companions and
followers.

McClintock viewed the chances of success with realism, but certainly
not with pessimism: "The less the means, the more arduous is the
achievement. The greater the risk, for the Fox is launched into turbulent
seas from which every other vessel has long been withdrawn, the more
glorious will be the success—and the more honourable even the defeat
if again defeat awaits us."

On his first journey to the Arctic in 1848 McClintock had come to
realize that long journeys over the ice were impossible for men loaded
with heavy equipment. Before long this conviction had come to be
shared by others. In 1848 men had been able to remain away from their
ships for a maximum of forty days; by 1851 they could be away for
eighty days and travel over 800 miles. Later still, journeys were made
lasting 100 days and covering 1400 miles. By 1858-59 the crew of the
Fox was able to attain a much faster pace, one party covering 420 miles
in twenty-five days. But nothing came easily to the crew of the Fox.
Before entering Lancaster Sound the small vessel was caught in heavy
ice and carried 1200 miles off-shore in a southerly direction. It would
be hard to find better proof of the spirit of the twenty-six men who
survived the winter than the fact that with scarcely room to turn
around they were in top form eight months later when the ship finally
got free of ice.

The Fox reached Beechey Island in the summer of 1858. Dr. Rae's
encounter with the natives four years earlier had determined that the
obvious area for the search would be much farther south, but before
turning southward McClintock erected a monument, a memorial to
Franklin and his men sent out earlier by Lady Franklin. By late Septem-

To the memory of
FRANKLIN
CROZIER, FITZJAMES
and all their
gallant brother officers and faithful
companions who have suffered and perished
in the cause of science and
the service of their country
this tablet
is erected near the spot where
they passed their first Arctic
winter, and whence they issued
forth, to conquer difficulties or
to die
to commemorate the grief of their
admiring countrymen and friends
and the anguish, subdued by faith,
of her who has lost, in the heroic
leader of the expedition, the most
devoted and affectionate of
husbands

"And so He bringeth them unto the
Haven where they would be"
1855

ber the party aboard the *Fox* had established the winter base at the eastern outlet of Bellot Strait. From there, small sledging parties under McClintock, Hobson and Young began the series of journeys that was to bring them final success.

On February 13, 1859 McClintock set out on a trip down the west coast of Boothia Peninsula. Near Cape Victoria his small party encountered about forty-five Eskimos, and through Petersen he learned that they possessed relics of the Franklin expedition. Silver spoons, a medal, buttons and other articles that had belonged to the dead men were purchased. One Eskimo said he had been told of a ship that had sunk off the west coast of King William Island, but the people on board were said to have landed safely. McClintock then returned to the *Fox*. He had travelled 425 miles in twenty-five days and added 120 miles of previously unknown coastline to the map.

Early in April he set out with Hobson on a second journey. McClintock was to search the east coast of King William Island; Hobson, the west. A few days later a third party under Young left the *Fox* and headed west to explore Prince of Wales Island. The doctor and five crewmen were left in charge of the ship.

On King William Island McClintock encountered some of the Eskimos he had met earlier near Cape Victoria. Now they said that *two* ships had been seen. One of them had sunk and nothing had been recovered, but the other had been forced up on the ice. Many articles and a great deal of wood had been taken from her. One Eskimo reported that the body of a man had been seen on board the ship. The Eskimo said that he must have been a very big man and that he had long teeth. Farther down the coast McClintock met a party of natives who had actually visited the wrecked ship. From them he bought six pieces of silver plate bearing the crests of Franklin, Crozier and others, as well as bows and arrows made of English wood and some buttons taken from uniforms. The Eskimos said that there had been many books on the ship but that all had been destroyed by the weather long before. One old woman said that many of the white men had dropped and died as they walked; some of them were buried and some were not.

A few days later walking along a gravel ridge near the beach, McClintock found the skeleton of a young crewman face down in the snow. Remnants of his clothing and a few personal possessions were still visible, but a thorough search of the area yielded no clue to the fate of any others on the lost expedition. Leaving the site, McClintock advanced up the west coast of the island, following the route taken by Hobson's party several days before.

It proved to be the correct route. A few miles up the coast he found a
note from Hobson reporting that six days before, at Victory Point, his
party had found the final record of the Franklin expedition. The record
was written on the standard Admiralty report form and carried the
usual request that it be forwarded to the Admiralty in London. The first
message read:

> 28 May, 1847. H.M. Ships Erebus and Terror wintered in ice in Lat.
> 70°5'N, Long. 98°23'W.
> Having wintered in 1846-47* at Beechey Island in Lat. 74°43'28"N,
> Long. 91°39'15"W after having ascended Wellington Channel to Lat.
> 77° and returned by the west side of Cornwallis Island.

> Sir John Franklin commanding the expedition. All well.

> Party consisting of two officers and six men left the ships on Monday,
> 24th May 1847.
> > Gm Gore, Lieut.
> > Chas F. Des Vœux, Mate.

Everything had changed when a second message was written round the
margin of the paper a year later:

> April 25, 1848. H.M. Ships Terror and Erebus were deserted on the
> 22nd April, 5 leagues NNW of this, having been beset since 12
> September, 1846. The officers and crew consisting of 105 souls under
> command of Captain F. R. M. Crozier, landed here.
> Sir John Franklin died on the 11th June, 1847 and the total loss by
> deaths in the expedition has been to this date 9 officers and 15 men.
> > F. R. M. Crozier   James FitzJames
> > Captain & Senior Officer   Captain H.M.S. Erebus
> and start on tomorrow 26th for Back's Fish River.†

In these few words, Franklin's officers had told the story of the
achievement, stalemate and final disaster of the expedition. To have
sailed 150 miles up Wellington Channel that first summer and to have
circled Cornwallis Island marked a magnificent beginning. Even at the
end of May 1847, Lieutenant Gore had every reason to write "All Well,"

---

*This was pointed out by McClintock as an error. The party was known to
have spent the winter of 1845-46 on Beechey Island.
†See picture section for a photograph of the original document.

for the ships, although icebound, were within 100 miles of known waters and the completion of the Northwest Passage. But a year later, when they still remained prisoner in the ice, Crozier and FitzJames prepared for final tragedy.

By now McClintock was running short of food and it became essential to make all speed back to the *Fox*. On May 30, while en route to the waiting ship, he and his men came upon another relic of the expedition —a large boat containing quantities of clothing and the skeletons of two men. The boat also contained an amazing assortment of unnecessary articles. McClintock was astonished and dismayed at the collection, taken at such cost from the *Erebus* and *Terror*: extra winter boots, perhaps, but why sea boots, ankle boots and shoes? Why silk handkerchiefs, towels, sponges, nails, saws, files, large spoons, forks and teaspoons engraved with the crests of the officers? Yet the only food was a little tea and about forty pounds of chocolate. McClintock estimated that the boat and the sledge on which it had been hauled together weighed about 1400 pounds. The boat was pointing to the northeast, back in the direction of the ships. The men hauling it must originally have been headed toward the southwest, but they had probably decided to return to the *Erebus* and *Terror* to get more food. The two in the boat were in all likelihood too weak to continue and had been left by their companions with a little food, until the larger group should return with additional supplies. Altogether, it was a tragic find for men who had learned how to travel—and live—in the north.

Farther on McClintock found a note from Hobson explaining that he had discovered a second cairn. As before, great quantities of nonessentials lay scattered about. The list of articles raises an unavoidable question: who in his right mind would have set out across the barren lands a thousand miles to the nearest Hudson's Bay post carrying four heavy cooking stoves, pickaxes, shovels, four feet of iron lightning rod, long pieces of hollow brass curtain rods and much more?

McClintock, Hobson and Young, with their small parties, had shown a fierce determination to succeed and though they had endured great hardships in their travels, their efforts had been brilliantly rewarded. Besides determining the fate of the expedition, they had mapped almost 1000 miles of previously unknown coastline. By the end of June the three parties were back on board the *Fox* waiting for a chance to sail. As soon as ice conditions permitted, a quick retreat had to be made to avoid a third winter in the ice. The *Fox* reached London on September 21, 1859 and McClintock immediately wrote to Lady Franklin:

Hoping to find you in Town I did not write any letters for you and now have only time to say that we have returned all well. I am sure you entertained no high hopes of survivors being found and, this understood, you will I think receive our news as good news. Brief records have been found, but they tell us the Expedition wintered at Beechey Island after ascending Wellington Channel to Lat. 77°N, that they were beset in September, 1846 off the North West Coast of King William Island.

Sir John Franklin died on 11th June, 1847. The ships were abandoned nearly in the same place on 22nd April, 1848. The survivors, under Crozier and FitzJames, numbered in all 105; they proceeded with boats on sledges to the Great Fish River. One of their boats was found by us, untouched by the Eskimos, and many relics brought from her, as also obtained from the natives of Boothia and east shore of King William Island. We found them most friendly. The west shore of the island is not inhabited.

I carefully explored Montreal Island* and its vicinity without success, beyond a few scraps of copper and iron, and on my return came up the west shore of King William Island, along the line of retreat of the lost crews.

The whole of the shores which remained unexplored or unknown were discovered and searched by our three parties—Hobson, Young and myself, with men and dogs. It is almost certain that the Erebus and Terror passed down Peel Strait [Sound], but no records have anywhere been found, except one at Port [Point] Victory. . . and another a few miles further southward along the coast.

P.S. I cannot help remarking to you what instantly occurred to me on reading the records, that Sir John was not harassed either by want of success or forebodings of evil. It was the summer of 1847 that proved fatal to the hopes of the Expedition.

An editorial in *The Times* echoed the sentiment expressed by Mc-Clintock in his postscript to Lady Franklin: "The great navigator died in no sudden shock or great disaster. He was crushed by no iceberg. He did not starve miserably on some wandering ice floe nor did he drift away in storm or ice haze. No. He died surrounded by messmates and friends and in the discharge of his duty."

The success of his expedition brought McClintock honour and fame.

*Any survivors could have been expected to cross the tiny island en route to Back's River.

The Queen knighted him and the Admiralty gave him promotion. His fellow officers and men also received widespread expressions of gratitude and admiration. Henry Grinnell heard McClintock's news in New York. His letter to Lady Franklin reflects the world-wide emotion aroused by Franklin's disappearance and the universal respect that existed for his indomitable widow:

My dear Lady,

The information, which reached us on the 8th instant of the return to England of Captain McClintock, and of the consummation of his object, has caused intense interest and excitement in this country, perhaps quite as much as in old England; it is the general subject of conversation, the political affairs of Europe and this country are insignificant in comparison. I can truly say I thank the Great Disposer of events for the result attained by your expedition under the command of that most able and excellent officer, McClintock. He has acquired a just fame for himself, which the pages of history will never allow to be obliterated.

For yourself, it is better I should say nothing, for I have not the command of words to define the estimate I entertain of your character. I am not alone in this; the whole community are with me. . . .

I suppose now there can be no question as to your husband's Expedition being the first to ascertain the water communication between the Atlantic and Pacific, north of the American Continent, or otherwise the North-West Passage.

Again with my kind regards . . . believe me to remain,

Your friend
[Signed]

Lady Franklin had completed her work at last. A statement she had made earlier in a letter to the Prime Minister was now confirmed: "By attaining the northern coasts of America which have been surveyed already, it is clear that they solved the problem which was the object of their labour. In the beautiful words of Sir John Richardson, 'They forged the last link of the North West Passage with their lives'."

Statues of Franklin were erected in Tasmania and in Spilsby, Lincolnshire, where he was born. Another was placed in Waterloo Place, London, close to the one erected later to Captain Scott of Antarctic fame. The end of the story came sixteen years after McClintock's return from the Arctic, when a memorial to Franklin was dedicated in Westminster Abbey. The epitaph was written by Franklin's nephew Alfred, Lord Tennyson:

> *Not here: the white North hath thy bones, and thou*
> *Heroic Sailor Soul,*
> *Art passing on thy happier voyage now*
> *Toward no earthly pole.*

APPENDIX

Some evaluations of Franklin's achievements
Scientific achievements of Franklin's expeditions
Expeditions sent in search of Sir John Franklin

In his three expeditions to the Canadian Arctic Franklin left a record of achievement as explorer and geographer unequalled in his age. When he began, the northern shoreline of this continent was unknown from Repulse Bay almost as far west as Bering Strait, except for the two points where the Coppermine and Mackenzie rivers enter the Arctic sea. His first expedition put 550 miles of that shoreline accurately on the map, and his second added a further 1200 miles with equal accuracy. The final expedition ended in disaster but not before Franklin's men had completed the discovery of a northwest passage, while the ships and men sent in search of them completed the mapping of the Arctic coast and adjacent islands.

The cost in lives and suffering was high, but in undertaking their mission Franklin and his men began with no precedents, no maps and no means of communication other than canoes. Hearne and Mackenzie had travelled light and fast on their historic journeys, in contrast to Franklin's large and cumbersome expeditions, but they left few accurate geographical and scientific records to guide or inform those who followed them.

Franklin's leadership in the preparation and execution of the second expedition was masterly. Few of the mistakes that plagued the first venture were repeated. And he had a degree of cooperation from the united fur companies that had been sadly lacking earlier. Fog robbed him of his intended rendezvous with the *Blossom*, but in excellence of planning and overall results this was the pinnacle of his career.

If the white man discovered a coastline, the natives discovered a white man whom they learned to trust and love. Franklin's great humanity marked his relationship with Akaitcho, and his patience and flexibility contrasted sharply with the rigid life of discipline that he had known in the navy from the age of fourteen. As he came to know them, he scorned the word "savage" as a description of the native people, and they responded in full measure to his approach. The Eskimo Augustus became devoted to Franklin and his fellow officers. Indeed, it was his eagerness to join George Back when he returned to the north in 1833 that caused Augustus to lose his way, and his life. The language of Franklin's faith in God may strike modern readers as excessively pious, but the strength his faith gave him in times of danger and hardship was always undeniable, and was sometimes of crucial importance. Sir Edward Parry, a fellow Arctic explorer, saw in him "the superiority of moral and religious strength over the purely physical strength of the body." Franklin has been criticized for keeping himself and his officers aloof from the daily backbreaking tasks of northern travel and for failing to realize that he might have saved his men from scurvy and even from death if he had copied the natives and concentrated on hunting for fresh meat. These criticisms have some validity, but we cannot judge Franklin by today's standards any more than we would expect a contemporary government to send naval officers to map the Arctic coast in birch-bark canoes. The men involved in these expeditions were products of their age and their environment. Besides, the officers had been instructed by the Admiralty to perform a specialized task, and the mass of scientific data collected by them (not to mention the still larger amount that was lost) is a product of their disciplined commitment.

Many books have been written about the disappearance of the final Franklin expedition and about the thirty-two expeditions that were sent in search of it. We know from the document left by Crozier, Franklin's successor in command, that important geographical discoveries were made the first year. When Franklin died, scurvy must already have been making its deadly inroads among the men, but the possibility of disaster cannot have seemed to him more than a cloud that would disperse once the ships were freed from the ice. When it became clear that this would not happen, Crozier made a desperate attempt to lead his weakened men across the wastes southward. Whatever his reasons, he was fatally wrong to load them with all kinds of heavy and unnecessary articles.

The officers on board the *Erebus* and *Terror* had the latest instruments and were stationed near the north Magnetic Pole for over eighteen months. The scientific data and the specimens collected during that time may well have been as valuable as the geographical discoveries. All this was lost. It was poor compensation, though a fact, that the rescue expeditions added more to the knowledge of Arctic geography than

Franklin and his men could have achieved had they returned in triumph.

But Franklin cannot be judged by his last expedition alone. He "popularized" the Arctic for his generation, as the astronauts are popularizing the moon for ours. The nature and shape of the vast Arctic region, though not its wealth, became known to the world. Now that our generation is beginning to exploit this wealth (with comparative ease, thanks to the limitless technical resources now available), there is value in knowing about the men who discovered that frozen world for us, with almost no resources except for the strength of their bodies and their wills.

PAUL NANTON

In his book *Unsolved Mysteries of the Arctic*, published in 1938, the explorer Vilhjalmur Stefansson criticized Franklin's failure to learn how to live off the land by hunting for fresh meat:

> Because we are looking for clues to how the Franklin men of the third expedition starved and died, we pay little attention to the dramatic narrative of the retreat toward Fort Enterprise [on the first expedition] but study the causes which made the drama tragic.
>
> In the early stage of the journey the "hunters" were successful in getting caribou. The point which signifies is that the hunters were none of them Englishmen, not the lieutenant or two midshipmen from the Navy nor the surgeon—not even the sailor, Hepburn, though he is spoken of as a good marksman. The hunters were Indians or "Canadians" who were hired to hunt.
>
> Why were the Englishmen, in self-help, a complete dead weight on the party? Was it beneath their dignity to co-operate in securing food? Was helping the workers, in their minds, detrimental to discipline? Whatever the reason, there is no sign either that they tried to assist in the hunting, or that they studied the methods of the hunt so as to be able to use them later.
>
> .   .   .   .   .
>
> The party had rather extraordinary luck in discovering the remains of caribou that had been killed and eaten by wolves. What the wolves had left was mainly skin and the bones. Now skin is as nourishing, weight for weight, as lean meat; but only if you eat it either raw or prepared in one of the ways which we know as ordinary cooking. What the Franklin party did was to scorch the leather till it was at least partly converted to the equivalent of charcoal. They ate the skin after burning some or all of the nourishment out of it. . . .
>
> If they had pounded the bones with stone hammers and boiled them, they would have had a rich, nourishing soup. . . . What the Franklin party actually did was to hold the bones in the fire until they were "friable," whereupon they ate them—which means that they let most or all the food value go up in smoke and flame. Then they ate the charcoal.
>
> .   .   .   .   .
>
> [on the third expedition] Ten men could have looked after each of the Franklin ships during every month of the winter, leaving a hundred free to

scatter in parties of five, ten, fifteen, or twenty various distances in all directions. These parties could have taken with them as much British food as they
wanted, for there was an abundance on the ships . . . and men do not have to
live exclusively on fresh meat in order to prevent scurvy. All they need is
such a percentage as we nowadays call average.

. . . . .

None of the things which the British expeditions of a hundred years ago
relied upon will prevent scurvy. They themselves proved that the lime juices
and lemon juices and the "antiscorbutics" which they carried would not do
it. They proved also that physical exercise, devotional exercises, fresh air,
dramatic clubs, schooling of the illiterate, games and buffoonery would not
do it.
. . . .

We concede again that Franklin had the excuses which many others have
used; that medical men told him nothing about meat being a preventive of
scurvy, and that they told him instead about lime juice and lemon juice as
preventives and curatives. But we return to our point that a man who makes
exploration a profession, as Franklin had done, has no business to sacrifice
his men to the dogmas of current therapeutics when he can divide the entire
literature of his own craft into two chains of events, the expeditions which
had a good deal of fresh food and little or no scurvy; and those which had
little or no fresh food and much scurvy.

. . . . .

Franklin died a year before the main tragedy, possibly of some ailment
connected with his advanced years. A few others may have died from illnesses
which come in all countries and on all diets. The rest died from scurvy brought
on by dependence upon ships' stores . . .

. . . .

That some of the one hundred and five men who struggled ashore on King
William Island were far gone with scurvy, we know from descriptions correct
for advanced cases of this disease which were given by the Eskimos later.
These descriptions are the more convincing in that the Eskimos themselves,
constant livers on fresh meat, never have scurvy and therefore could not
describe it correctly unless they had observed its symptoms among the white
men.
. . . .

Our summary will have to be, then, that the crews of the *Erebus* and the
Terror perished as victims of the manners, customs, social outlook and medical
views of their time.

Leslie H. Neatby gives an evaluation of Franklin's first expedition in his
book *In Quest of the North West Passage*, published in 1951:

Franklin's first journey is by itself enough to give him high rank among
the explorers of the nineteenth century. In a single summer he had laid down
nearly six hundred miles of a coast which had cost Hearne and Mackenzie
much labour even to approach, and had acquired a first-hand knowledge of
conditions which permitted the rest of the Arctic shoreline to be mapped with
comparative cheapness and ease. He had put a roof on the map of Canada,
and given a definite shape to the North American continent. Yet his very
eminence has exposed him to the harsh process of "debunking" to which
all Victorians are liable; his reputation has been wantonly attacked by the
modern explorer, Vilhjalmur Stefansson, whose character is far too great to

gain any additional lustre from so cheap and common a device. It is true that
the performance of his First Journey cannot of itself excuse the loss of life by
which it was achieved. On the other hand, a man who laboured so long and
so strenuously for the extension of knowledge is not to be hastily condemned
for miscarriage in an enterprise which was quite experimental, and where
chance and the unknown exerted an influence beyond his power to predict
or control.

Franklin was the agent of the British Government, lent to it by the
Admiralty, to map the Arctic coast from the mouth of the Coppermine to the
northern limit of Hudson Bay. He was to navigate the shores of an unknown
and ice-infested sea by canoe for hundreds of miles with no trained nautical
assistance other than that provided by two midshipmen (chosen in part for
their proficiency as artists) and a naval surgeon. For the furnishing of
"guides, interpreters, and game-killers", as well as for supplies and transport to
the jumping-off point he was to rely on the fur companies and their Indian
clients. To them is to be attributed the condition in which the expedition
reached the mouth of the Coppermine. Franklin's undivided responsibility
began on July the 20th, 1821. With fifteen days' rations in hand, and not
knowing that the resources of the country would prove inadequate, he could
have turned back from the coast only at the cost of professional ruin. It
would have implied a censure on those who had planned the expedition, and
would have wasted the money and effort that had been already expended. He
therefore pursued his explorations while food and weather permitted, executed his orders to the limit of his powers, and paid the penalty which savage
nature seldom fails to exact from the too optimistic pioneer.

Though Stefansson asserts, rightly, no doubt, that Franklin could have
lived off the land, one ventures to suppose that the art of survival in the
Canadian North is the gift not of nature, but of experience, and that it is no
reproach to a British naval officer to have starved in those regions, when
Wentzel's Indians, who had grown up on the fringe of the Barren Lands,
went for eleven days without game. He may be to some degree blameworthy
for having poor relations with the traders and insufficient control over the
voyageurs. But in the first instance it is abundantly clear that the faults were
not all on one side; in the second, an officer who, from the age of fourteen,
had been bound to his associates for eighteen years by the ties of naval
discipline, professional spirit, and, in some cases, personal regard, may be
pardoned for his clumsy handling of frightened, unwilling men, alien to him
in language and sympathies, and serving for wages only. The true quality of
the man appears in the resolution with which he kept his *voyageurs* on the
march, when they were ready to lie down and die in their tracks.

The disaster, then, was due to the tenor of Franklin's instructions, for
which he was not responsible, to the unseasonably, early descent of winter
on the Barren Lands, for which he was not responsible either, and to the
failure to deposit supplies at Enterprise, an omission due either to Wentzel's
neglect or to the shortage of ammunition consequent upon confusion in the
fur-trade. The issue of the expedition, in so far as it was in the power of the
leader to determine it, was a success; and if in his Narrative it is rather Back
and Richardson who command our admiration, that is to be attributed to the
author's modesty, and not to his deficiency in manliness or qualities of leadership and administration. He was no ordinary man who, without means of
coercion, kept a starving, mutinous, and demoralized crew together for six
weeks by sheer force of character. His odyssey of the North is an episode
worthy to rank with any in the pioneer history of Canada.

Franklin's second expedition is evaluated by G. F. Lamb in *Franklin Happy Voyager*, published in 1956, and also in Neatby's *In Quest of the North West Passage*:

G. F. Lamb:

The expedition has not been fully successful, in that the link up with Capt. Beechey had not been performed. Yet its achievements were solid, even notable. More than 1200 miles of hitherto unknown coastline had been discovered and exactly delineated. Scientific observations made by various members of the party were recognized as exceedingly valuable by scientific and geographical societies and by the Admiralty. . . . Although by far the least sensational of Franklin's explorations it was in many respects his finest, and the absence of striking incident, though disappointing to narrators, was regarded differently by his companions. . . . Only about 150 miles of coast remained to be traced between Point Turnagain and Icy Cape.

Leslie H. Neatby:

By their combined exertions the members of the expedition had added some 800 miles (measured by crow flight) to the known limits of the Polar Sea. The operation, carried out with smoothness in exact accordance to plan, and with no more hardship than was the common lot of the explorer in those days, is proof of how readily its leader could adjust himself to new conditions when once these conditions were known. Sir John Franklin was and remains the marine geographer par excellence of the North American continent. The sum total of his discoveries, extending roughly from 105' to 150' W. comprised half the Arctic coast of Canada and a considerable stretch of the Alaskan seaboard.

A. H. Beesly summed up the achievements of all three expeditions in his book *Sir John Franklin*, published in 1881:

The history of Franklin's explorations is a record, never of failure but never of complete success. In 1818-22 he achieved a sea journey of great scientific value under extraordinary difficulties and fought his way home by land through appalling privations. But he failed to complete the survey of the Arctic coastline eastward from the mouth of the Coppermine, as he had hoped to do. In 1825-27 he added greatly to the geographical knowledge west of the Mackenzie River, but failed to join up with the ship sent to meet him from the Behring Strait. In 1845 he went to find the North West Passage. He discovered a route but did not live to traverse it. Yet he won for himself a name that could not have been more assured of permanent lustre if he had explored the whole coastline of Arctic America to the east in 1821 and to the west in 1825 and had sailed from the Atlantic to the Pacific in 1845. His countrymen and the whole civilized world recognized that the great but incomplete achievements of the traveller were outshone by the heroic qualities of the man, and the wealth of their admiration completed his inheritance.

Lastly, the famous explorer Roald Amundsen in his book *The North West Passage*, published in 1908 says:

> Franklin and all his men laid down their lives in the fight for the North West Passage. Let us raise a monument to them, more enduring than stone; the recognition that they were the first discoverers of the Passage.

The Franklin expeditions aimed at scientific as well as geographical discovery, and the Appendices at the end of the two volumes which cover the first two expeditions contain a vast amount of data. There are detailed descriptions of the rock formations encountered, the trees, vegetation, soil, lakes and rivers. Even more detailed are the records of temperature changes, wind and weather, solar radiation, velocity of sound, variations of the compass and every appearance of the Aurora Borealis. An example of the officers' thoroughness is shown in the record of temperature variations, taken round the clock every three hours over a period of eight months. More scientific information is available from the second expedition, since much of what was collected during the first expedition had to be abandoned on the way back to Fort Enterprise in 1821.

In addition, Dr. Richardson published, between 1829 and 1837, four magnificently illustrated volumes entitled *Flora Boreali Americana*, or *The Zoology of the Northern Parts of British North America*. It was the first thorough study of the animals, birds, fish and insects of north-western Canada.

The thoroughness of Richardson's and Drummond's work in the field is indicated by the detailed description of the following animals given in Volume 1:

Hoary Bat, Say's Bat, American Marsh Shrew, Forster's Shrew Mouse, small Shrew-Mouse, Shrew-Mole, Long tailed Star-nose, American Black Bear, Polar or Sea Bear, Grisly Bear, Raccoon, American Badger, Wolverine, Common Weasel, Ermine or Stoat, Pine Marten, White Pekan, Hudson's Bay Skunk, Canadian Otter, Sea Otter, American Wolf, Prairie Wolf, Common Gray Wolf, White Wolf, Pied Wolf, Dusky Wolf, Black American Wolf, Domestic Dog, Eskimo Dog, Hare Indian Dog, North American Dog, Carrier Indian Dog, Arctic Fox, Sooty Fox, American Fox, American Cross Fox, Black or Silver Fox, Gray Fox,

Kit Fox, Canadian Lynx, Bay Lynx, Branded Lynx, American Beaver, Black Beaver, Spotted Beaver, White Beaver, Musquash, Black Musquash, Pied Musquash, White Musquash, Bank Meadow Mouse, Yellow Cheeked Meadow Mouse, Wilson's Meadow Mouse, Sharp-nosed Meadow Mouse, Northern Meadow Mouse, Tawney Lemming, Back's Lemming, Hudson's Bay Lemming, Greenland Lemming, Rocky Mountain Neotoma, Black Rat, Common Mouse, American Field Mouse, Labrador Jumping Mouse, Quebec Marmot, Whistler, Short-Tailed Marmot, Woodchuck, Wiston Wish, Parry's Marmot, American Souslik, Tawney Marmot, Franklin's Marmot, Beechey's Marmot, Douglas' Marmot, Say's Marmot, Leopard Marmot, the Hackie, Four-banded Pouched Squirrel, Chickaree, Columbian Pine Squirrel, Black Squirrel, Severn River Flying Squirrel, Rocky Mountain Flying Squirrel, Columbia Land Rat, Leadbeater's Sand Rat, Canada Pouched Rat, Mole shaped Sand Rat, Camas Rat, Sewell, Canadian Porcupine, American Hare, Little-chief Hare, Tailless Marmot, Horse, Moose-Deer, Caribou, Wapiti, Black-tailed Deer, Prong-Horned Antelope, Long-tailed Deer, Rocky Mountain Goat, Musk-Ox, American Bison.

The following were among the birds described in Volume 2, specimens of which were sent to the British Museum:

Goshawk, Red Tailed Falcon, Marsh Hawk, Hawk Owl, Raven, Hudson's Bay Magpie, Blue Jay, Canada Jay, Red Winged Oriole, Baltimore Oriole, Purple Grackle, Meadowlark, Red-breasted Thrush, Yellow-polled Warbler, Snow Bunting, Pine Grosbeak, Red-breasted Grosbeak, Cowpen bird, Golden-winged Woodpecker, Hairy Woodpecker, Yellow-bellied Woodpecker, Belted Kingfisher, Purple Martin, White-bellied Martin, Passenger Pidgeon, Ruffed Grouse, Sharp-tailed Grouse, White Grouse, Ptarmigan, Canada Grouse, Golden Plover, Noisy Plover, Large Ringed Plover, Grey Plover, Turnstone, Brown Crane, American Bittern, Red-backed Sandpiper, Little Sandpiper, Tell-tale Godwit, Red-breasted Snipe, Yellow-legged Godwit, American Godwit, Black-tailed Godwit, American Coot, Red Phalarope, American Phalarope, Red-necked Grebe, Pied-bill Grebe, Horned Grebe, Arctic Tern, Black Tern, Herring Gull, Kittiwaki Gull, Laughing Gull, Little Gull, 26 varieties of Swans, Geese and Duck, American Widgeon, Ruddy Duck, Blue Winged Teal, Red-breasted Merganser, Hooded Merganser, Great Northern Diver, Red Throated Diver.

Richardson's first volume contains a full description of 114 animals, with 28 full-page black and white engravings. Volume two describes 267 birds, with 49 superb full-page engravings in colour, and numerous black and white engravings illustrating portions of a head, claws or feathers. Volume three describes 140 different fish, with 33 pages given to the different varieties of salmon alone. Volume four gives a description of 1000 varieties of insects.

1847-1850 Sir John Richardson & Dr. Rae, travelling overland, covered Arctic coast from Mackenzie to Coppermine Rivers.

1848-1850 Capt. Henry Kellett, HMS *Herald*, from the west through Bering's Strait.

1848-1850 Robert Snedden in yacht *Nancy Dawson*, same route.

1848-1852 Capt. Thomas Moore, HMS *Plover*, same route.

1848-1849 Capt. Sir James Clark Ross, HMS *Enterprise*, to Lancaster Strait [Sound], accompanied by Capt. E. J. Bird, HMS *Investigator*.

1849-1850 Lieut. James Saunders, HMS *North Star*, to Wolstenholme Sound and Pond's Bay.

1849 Dr. Robert Goodsir in the whaler *Advice*, to Baffin's Bay.

1849 Capt. W. J. S. Pullen, HMS *Herald*, from the west through Bering's Strait to Mackenzie River.

1850-1851 Lieut. De Haven, U.S. Navy, in the *Advance*, accompanied by Lieut. S. P. Griffin, U.S. Navy, in the *Rescue*, to Lancaster Strait [Sound] and Wellington Channel. Outfitted by Henry Grinnell of New York.

1850-1851 Capt. Horatio Austin, HMS *Resolute*, accompanied by HMS *Assistance*, *Intrepid* and *Pioneer*. To Lancaster Strait [Sound] and Cornwallis Island.

1850-1851 Capt. William Penney in the *Lady Franklin*, under Admiralty orders, to Lancaster Strait [Sound] and Wellington Channel. Alexander Stewart in the *Sophia*, accompanying.

1850-1851   Rear Admiral Sir John Ross in yacht *Felix*, to Lancaster Sound. Outfitted by the Hudson's Bay Company.

1850   Capt. C. C. Forsyth in the *Prince Albert*, to Regent's Inlet. Sent by Lady Franklin.

1850-1854   Commander Robert McClure, HMS *Investigator*, from the west through Bering's Strait to Bank's Island and Lancaster Strait. Ship abandoned, crew walked over ice to Beechey Island, returned to England with another party. First men to make the North West Passage.

1850-1855   Capt. Richard Collinson, HMS *Enterprise*, from the west through Bering's Strait to Bank's Island and Cambridge Bay. Then turned back.

1851   Dr. John Rae of the Hudson's Bay Company, down Coppermine River, traced . . . Victoria Land, up Victoria Straits. Sent by the Admiralty.

1851-1852   Capt. William Kennedy in the *Prince Albert*, to Prince Regent Inlet, Bellot's Strait and Prince Edward Island. Sent by Lady Franklin.

1852   Dr. R. McCormick. Wellington Channel.

1852   Commander Inglefield in the *Isabel*. Sent by Lady Franklin.

1852-1854   Capt. Sir Edward Belcher, HMS *Assistance*, accompanied by HMS *Resolute*, *Intrepid*, *Pioneer* and *North Star*, to Wellington Channel. *Resolute*, *Intrepid* and *Pioneer* abandoned.

1853-1854   Capt. Trollope in the *Rattlesnake*, from west by Bering's Strait.

1853-1854   Capt. Kennedy in the *Isabel*. Same route. Sent by Lady Franklin.

1853   William Fawckner in the *Breadalbane Transport*, to Beechey Island. Ship crushed in ice and sank.

1853   Capt. E. A. Inglefield, HMS *Phoenix*, to Beechey Island.

1853   Lieut. Elliott in store ship *Diligence*.

1853   Dr. John Rae, by sledge to Wollaston Land, by boat to Victoria Strait. Sent by the Admiralty.

1854   Capt. E. A. Inglefield, HMS *Phoenix*, to Beechey Island.

1853-1854   Commander Jenkins in the *Talbot*, to Beechey Island.

1853-1854 Dr. John Rae, by boat to Repulse Bay and east side of King William's Island. Brought first news of loss of *Erebus* and *Terror* and their crews. Sent by Hudson's Bay Company.

1853-1854 Dr. E. K. Kane, U.S. Navy, in the *Advance*, to Smith's Sound, Humboldt Glacier and Grinnell Land.

1855   Chief Factor John Anderson of the Hudson's Bay Company, by canoe down Great Fish River to Montreal Island and Point Ogle. Found further relics of *Erebus* and *Terror*.

1857-1859 Capt. F. L. McClintock in the yacht *Fox*, to Peel Sound, Regent's Inlet, Bellot Strait, King William's Island, Montreal Island. Sent by Lady Franklin. Found conclusive intelligence of fate of *Erebus* and *Terror*.

From Sir John Richardson's book, *The Polar Regions* (Edinburgh: A. and C. Black, 1861).

BIBLIOGRAPHY

Bibliography

Amundsen, Roald.	*The North West Passage*. London: Archibald Constable, 1908.
Asher, G. M.	*Henry Hudson the Navigator*. London: Hakluyt Society, 1894.
Back, Sir George.	*Narrative of the Arctic Land Expedition*. London: John Murray, 1836. Edmonton: Hurtig, 1970.
Barrington, Daines.	*The Possibility of Approaching the North Pole*. London: C. Heydringer, 1775.
Barrow, Sir John.	*Voyages of Discovery and Research within the Arctic regions*. New York: Harper & Brothers, 1846.
Beechey, Captain F. W.	*Narrative of a Voyage to the Pacific and Beering's Strait*. London: R. Bentley, 1831.
Beechey, Captain F. W.	*A Voyage of discovery towards the North Pole*. London: R. Bentley, 1843.
Beesly, A. H.	*Sir John Franklin, a Narrative of his Life*. New York: G. M. Putman's Sons, 1881.
Belcher, Sir Edward.	*The Last of the Arctic Voyages*. London: Lovell Reeve, 1855.
Bellot, Joseph René.	*Memoirs and Journal of Lieut. Joseph René Bellot*. London: Hurst & Blackett, 1855.
Best, George.	*The Three Voyages of Martin Frobisher 1576-1578*. London: Hakluyt Society, 1857.
Bethune, W. C.	*Canada's eastern Arctic*. Ottawa: King's Printer, 1934.
Bethune, W. C.	*Canada's western northland*. Ottawa: King's Printer, 1937.
Brown, John.	*The North-west passage and the plans for the search for Sir John Franklin*. London: E. Stanford, 1858.
Brown, John.	*A Sequel to the North-west passage*. London: E. Stanford, 1860.
Browne, W. H. J.	*Ten coloured views taken during the Arctic expedition of H.M.S. Enterprise and Investigator*. London: Ackermann & Co., 1850.
Campbell, M. W.	*McGillivray, Lord of the North West*. Toronto: Clarke Irwin, 1962.
Collinson, Sir Richard.	*Journal of H.M.S. Enterprise on the expedition in search of Sir John Franklin's ships by Behring Strait. 1850-1851.* London: Samson Low, Maiston, Searle & Rivington. 1889.

Crouse, N. M.   *In Quest of the Western Ocean.* London: J. M. Dent & Sons, 1928.

Cyriax, Richard J.   *Sir John Franklin's last Arctic expedition.* London: Methune & Company, 1939.

Debenham, Frank.   *Discovery and Exploration. An Atlas-History of Man's Journeys into the Unknown.* London: Geographical Prospects Limited, 1960.

De la Roquette, M.   *Notice Biographique sur l'Amiral Sir John Franklin.* Paris: L. Martinet.

Dennett, J. F.   *The voyages and travels of Captains Ross, Parry, Franklin and Mr. Bolzoni.* London: William Wright, 1835.

Dobbs, Arthur.   *An Account of the Countries Adjoining to Hudson's Bay, in the Northwest Part of America.* London, 1744. New York: Johnson Reprint, 1937.

Dodge, E. S.   *Northwest by Sea.* New York: Oxford University Press, 1961.

Dunbar, Moira and Keith R. Greenaway.   *Arctic Canada from the Air.* Ottawa: Queen's Printer, 1956.

Ellis, Henry.   *Considerations of the Great Advantages that would Arise from the Discovery of the North West Passage.* London, 1750.

Fitzpatrick, K. E.   *Sir John Franklin in Tasmania.* Melbourne: Melbourne University Press, 1949.

Franklin, John.   *Narrative of a journey to the shores of the polar seas in the Years 1819-1822.* London: John Murray, 1823. Edmonton: Hurtig, 1969.

Franklin, John.   *Narrative of a second expedition to the shores of the polar sea in the Years 1825-1827.* London: John Murray, 1828.

Gell, E. M.   *Sir John Franklin's Bride.* London: John Murray, 1930.

Great Britain.   *British Parliamentary Papers on Arctic explorations, Nos. 45210-45250,* The "Arctic Blue Books," 1848-1858.

Greely, A. W.   *Handbook of polar discoveries.* Boston: Little Brown, 1906.

Hall, Charles F.   *Arctic researches and life among the Esquimaux.* New York: Harper & Brothers, 1865.

Harrison, John.   *A Complete Collection of Voyages and Travels.* [Henry Hudson, 1610]. London, 1705.

Hearne, Samuel.   *A Journey from Prince of Wales Fort in Hudson's Bay to the northern ocean, 1769-72.* Toronto: Champlain Society, 1911. Toronto: Macmillan Company of Canada, 1958.

Hyde, Alexander.   *The Frozen zone and its explorers.* Hartford, Connecticut: Columbian Book Company, 1874.

Inglefield, Sir Edward.   *A summer search for Sir John Franklin.* London: Thomas Harrison. 1853.

Kane, Elisha K.   *The Second Grinnell expedition in search of Sir John Franklin. 1853-1855.* Philadelphia: Childs & Peterson, 1856.

King, Richard.   *The Franklin Expedition from first to last.* London: John Churchill, 1855.

King, Richard.   *Narrative of a journey to the shores of the Arctic Ocean. 1833-1835.* London: Richard Bentley, 1836.

Lamb, G. F.   *Franklin, happy voyager.* London: Ernest Benn, 1956.

Leacock, Stephen.   *Adventures of the far North.* Toronto: Glasgow, Brook & Company, 1914.

Mackenzie, Alexander.   *Sir Alexander Mackenzie's Journal of a Voyage to the Pacific Ocean, 1789.* London: R. Nobe, 1801. University of Oklahoma Press, 1966.

Markham, Sir A. H.   *Life of Sir John Franklin.* London: George Philip & Son, 1891.

Markham, Sir A. H.   *Voyages and Works of John Davis.* London: Hakluyt Society, 1880.

Markham, Sir Clements. *A Life of John Davis.* London, George Philip & Son, 1889.

Markham, Sir Clements. *The Voyages of William Baffin, 1612-1622.* London: Hakluyt Society, 1881.

McClintock, Sir F. L.   *A Narrative of the discovery of the fate of Sir John Franklin and his Companions.* London: John Murray, 1859.

McClintock, Sir F. L.   *The voyage of the 'Fox' into the Arctic Seas.* London: John Murray, 1860.

McClure, Sir Robert.   *Discovery of the North West Passage.* London: Longman, Brown, Green & Longman's, 1856.

McIlwraith, John.   *Life of Sir John Richardson.* London: Longman's Green, 1868.

Mowat, Farley.   *Canada North.* Toronto: McClelland & Stewart, 1967.

Mowat, Farley.   *Ordeal by Ice.* Toronto: McClelland & Stewart, 1960.

Neatby, Leslie H.   *In Quest of the North West Passage.* Toronto: Longman's Green & Co., 1958.

Osborn, Sherard.   *The Career, Last Voyage and Fate of Sir John Franklin.* Edinburgh: William Blackwood & Sons, 1865.

Osborn, Sherard.   *Stray Leaves from an Arctic journal.* London: Longman, Brown, Green and Longman's, 1852.

Parry, Ann.   *Parry of the Arctic.* London: Chatto & Windus, 1963.

Rae, John.   *Dr. John Rae's Report to the Admiralty, 1854.*

Rawnsley, William Franklin. *Life, Diaries and Correspondence of Jane, Lady Franklin.* London: Erskine Macdonald, 1923.

Rich, E. E.   *The Fur Trade and the North West to 1857.* Toronto: McClelland & Stewart, 1967.

Rich, E. E., ed.   *John Rae's Correspondence with the Hudson's Bay Company on Arctic Exploration.* London: Hudson's Bay Record Society, 1953.

Rich, E. E.   *The History of the Hudson's Bay Company. 1670-1870.* London: Hudson's Bay Record Society, 1958.

Richardson, Sir John.   *Arctic searching expedition.* London: Longman, Brown, Green & Longman's, 1851.

Richardson, Sir John.   *The Polar Regions.* Edinburgh: Adam & Charles Black, 1861.

Richardson, Sir John.   *Fauna-Boreali-Americana or the Zoology of the Northern Parts of British North America.* 4 vols. London: John Murray, 1829, 1831. 1836. 1837.

Ross, Sir John.   *Narrative of a Second voyage in search of a North-west passage*. London: A. W. Webster, 1835.

Ross, Sir John.   *Rear Admiral Sir John Franklin*. London: Longman's Green Brown & Longman, 1855.

Ross, Sir John.   *A voyage of discovery for the Purpose of exploring Baffin's Bay*. London: Longman, Hurst, Rees, Arme & Brown, 1819.

Scoresby, William.   *The Franklin Expedition*. London: Longman, Brown, Green & Longman's, 1850.

Simmonds, P. L.   *Sir John Franklin and the Arctic regions*. Buffalo: George H. Derby & Co., 1852.

Smith, I. N.   *The Unbelievable Land*. Ottawa: Queen's Printer, 1964.

Stefansson,   *Unsolved Mysteries of the Arctic*. New York: Macmillan &
  Vilhjalmur.   Company, 1939.

Story, Norah.   *The Oxford Companion to Canadian History & Literature*. Toronto: Oxford University Press, 1967.

Thompson, Donald.   *Men and Meridians. The History of Surveying and Mapping in Canada*. Ottawa: Queen's Printer, 1966.

Traill, H. D.   *Life of Sir John Franklin*. London: John Murray, 1896.

Wade, M. S.   *Mackenzie of Canada*. Edinburgh: William Blackwood & Sons, 1927.

Warbenton, John, ed.   *The Western Interior of Canada. A Record of Geographical Discovery. 1612-1917*. Toronto: McClelland & Stewart, 1964.

Woodward, F. W.   *Portrait of Jane. A Life of Lady Franklin*. London: Hodder & Stoughton, 1951.

Wright, Noel.   *Quest for Franklin*. London: Heinemann, 1959.

                         Dictionary of National Biography. Oxford, 1964.

                         The Knights of the Frozen Sea. London: Seeley, Jackson & Holliday, 1867.

                         ARTICLES
Gibson, William.   "Sir John Franklin's Last Voyage" in *The Beaver*. June 1937.

INDEX

Index